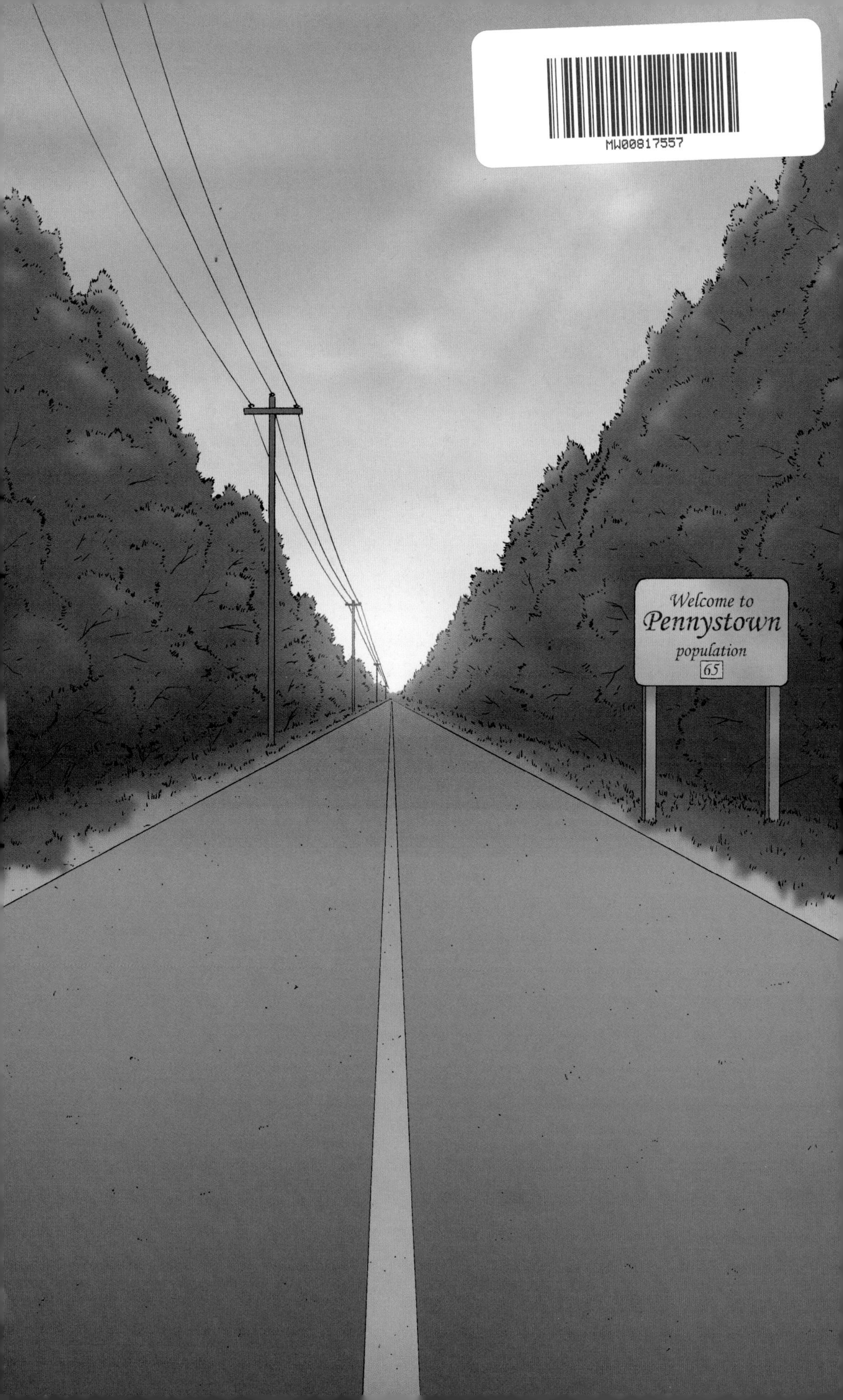
Welcome to
Pennystown
population
65

GIRLS™

Volume 1
CONCEPTION

Special Thanks to

Edward Lopategui
Maria Castro
Rommel Calderon
and Grifty McGrift

Image Comics, Inc.

www.ImageComics.com

www.LunaBrothers.com

GIRLS, VOL. 1: CONCEPTION. 2005. Published by Image Comics, Inc., Office of publication: 1942 University Avenue, Suite 305, Berkeley, California 94704. Copyright © 2005 The Luna Brothers. Originally published in single magazine form as GIRLS #1-6. All rights reserved. GIRLS™ (including all prominent characters featured in this issue), its logo and all character likenesses are trademarks of The Luna Brothers, unless otherwise noted. Image Comics® is a trademark of Image Comics, Inc. All rights reserved. No part of this publication may be reproduced or transmitted, in any form or by any means (except for short excerpts for review purposes) without the express written permission of Image Comics, Inc. All names, characters, events and locales in this publication are entirely fictional. Any resemblance to actual persons (living or dead), events or places, without satiric intent, is coincidental. PRINTED IN CANADA

Joshua Luna
Plot, Script, Layouts, Letters

Jonathan Luna
Plot, Art, Colors, Letters

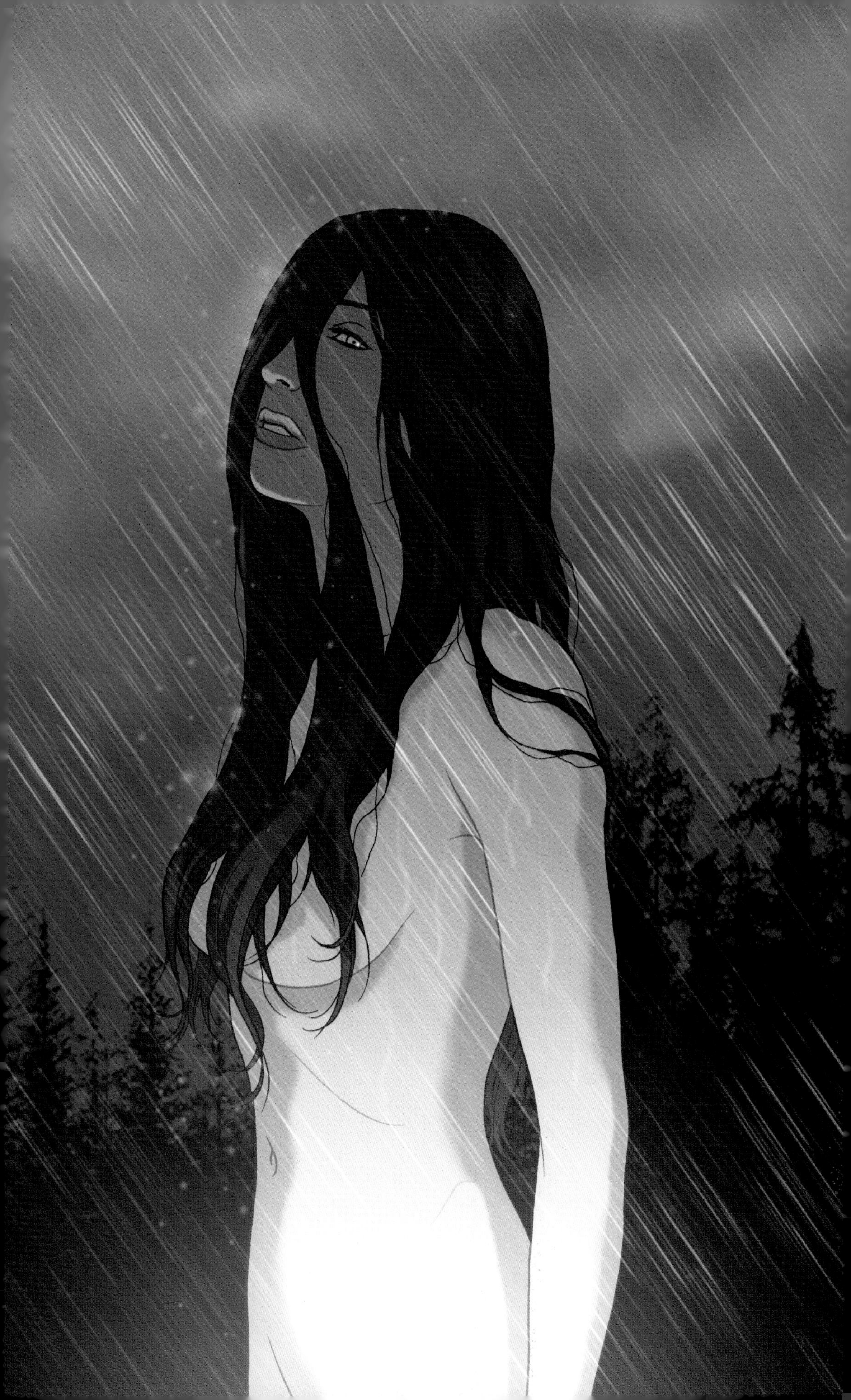

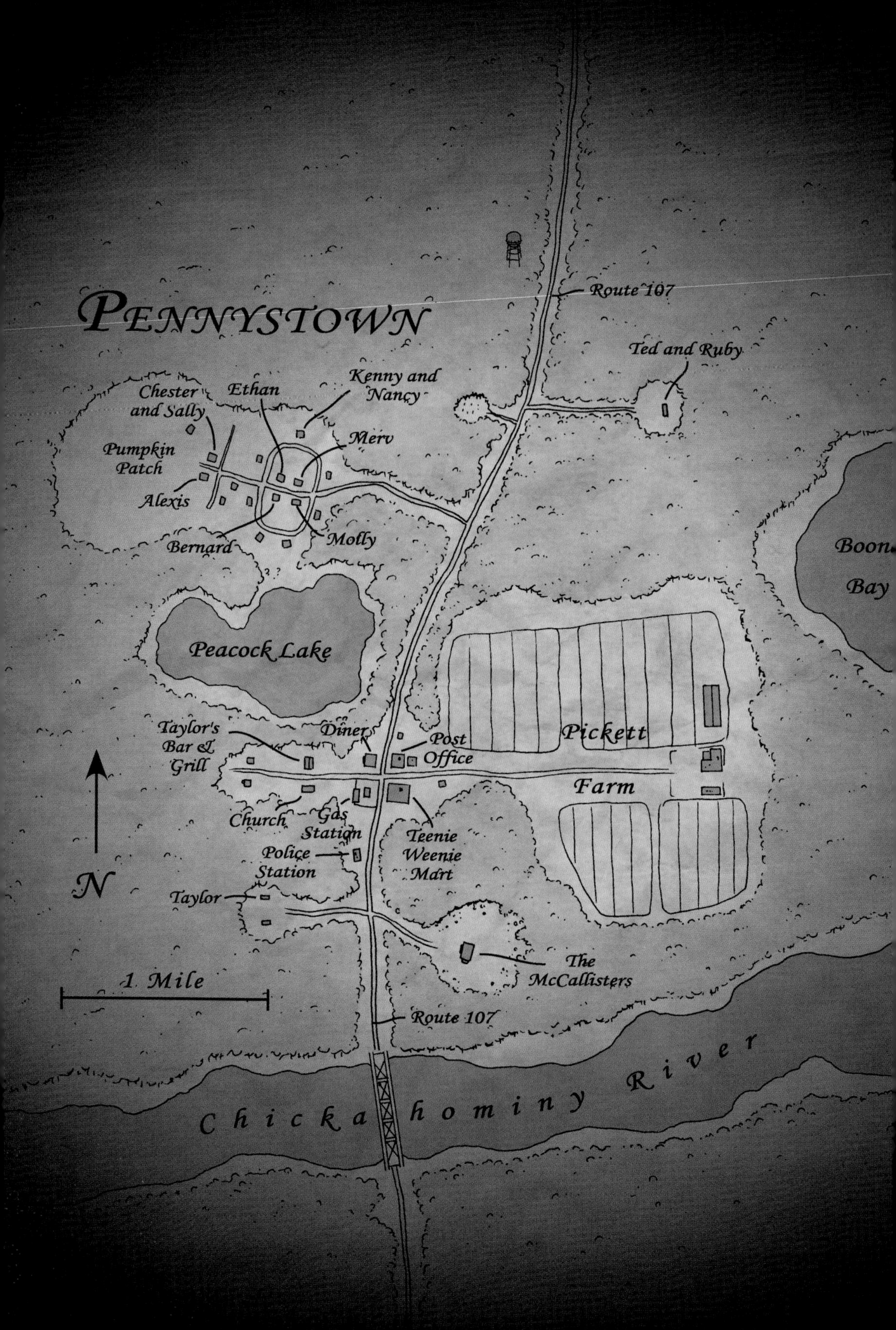
Pennystown
Route 107
Ted and Ruby
Kenny and Nancy
Chester and Sally
Ethan
Merv
Pumpkin Patch
Alexis
Bernard
Molly
Boon Bay
Peacock Lake
Taylor's Bar & Grill
Diner
Post Office
Pickett Farm
Church
Gas Station
Teenie Weenie Mart
Police Station
Taylor
N
1 Mile
The McCallisters
Route 107
Chickahominy River

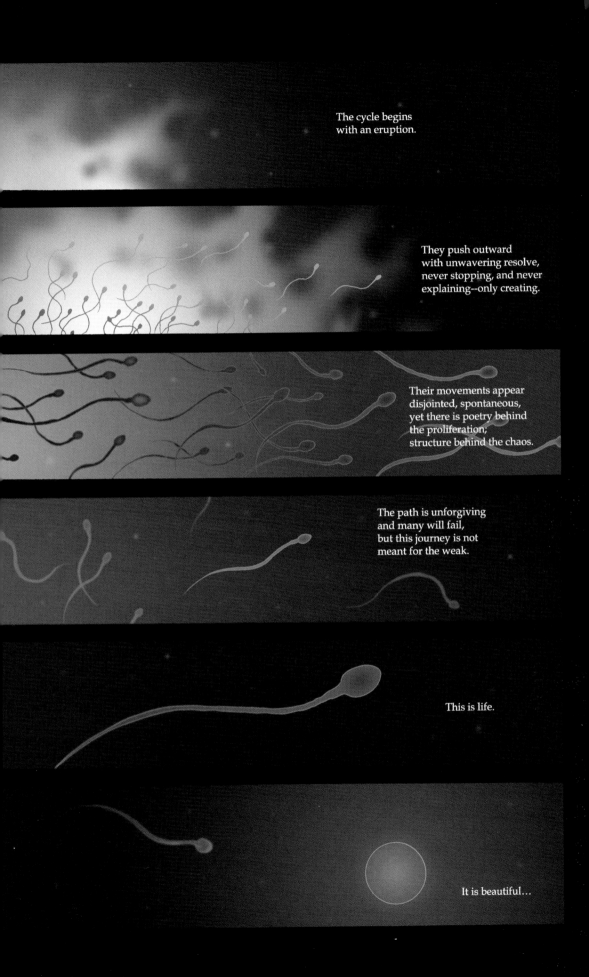

The cycle begins
with an eruption.

They push outward
with unwavering resolve,
never stopping, and never
explaining--only creating.

Their movements appear
disjointed, spontaneous,
yet there is poetry behind
the proliferation;
structure behind the chaos.

The path is unforgiving
and many will fail,
but this journey is not
meant for the weak.

This is life.

It is beautiful...

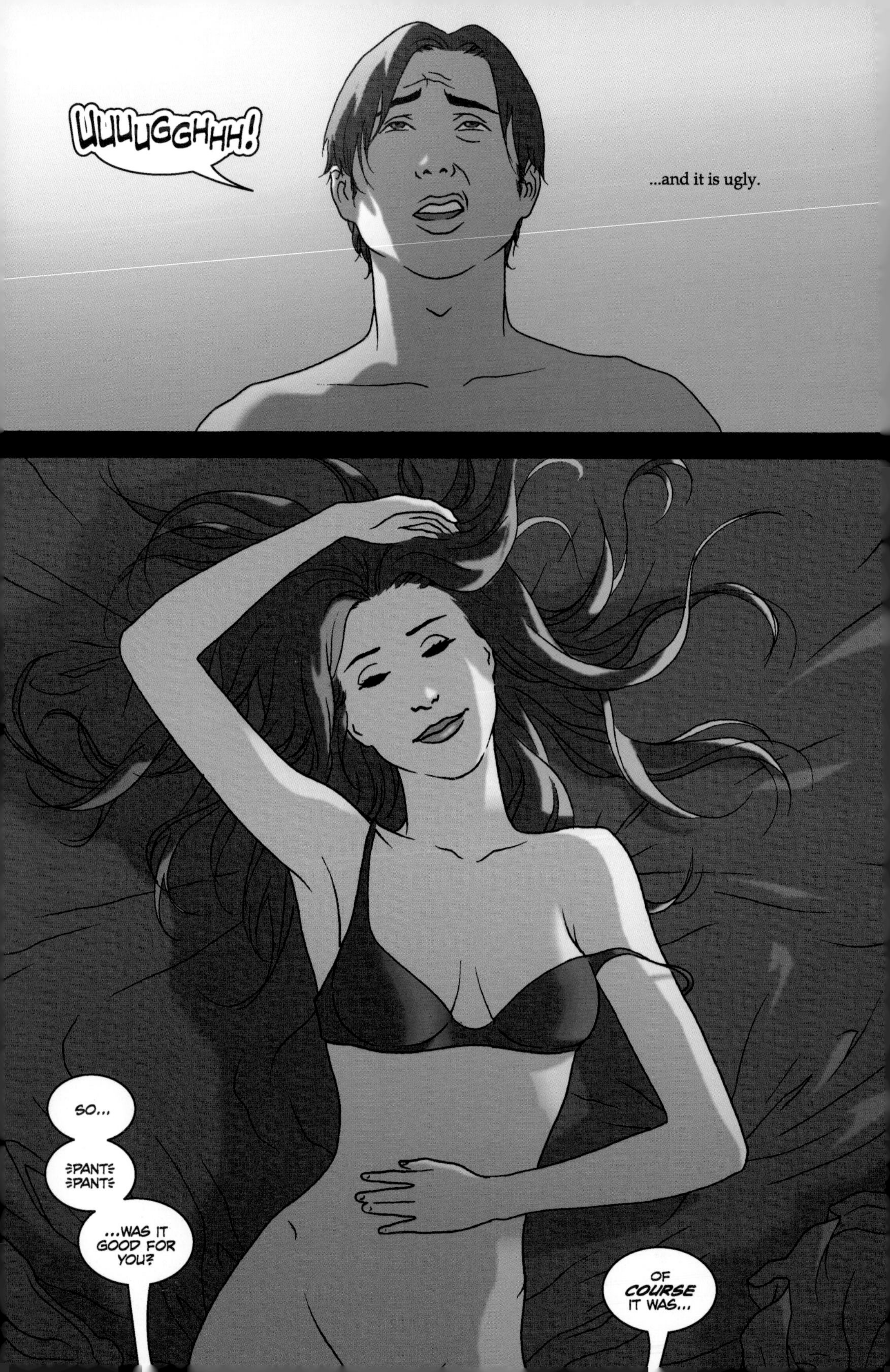
UUUUGGHHH!
...and it is ugly.
SO...
PANT PANT
...WAS IT GOOD FOR YOU?
OF *COURSE* IT WAS...

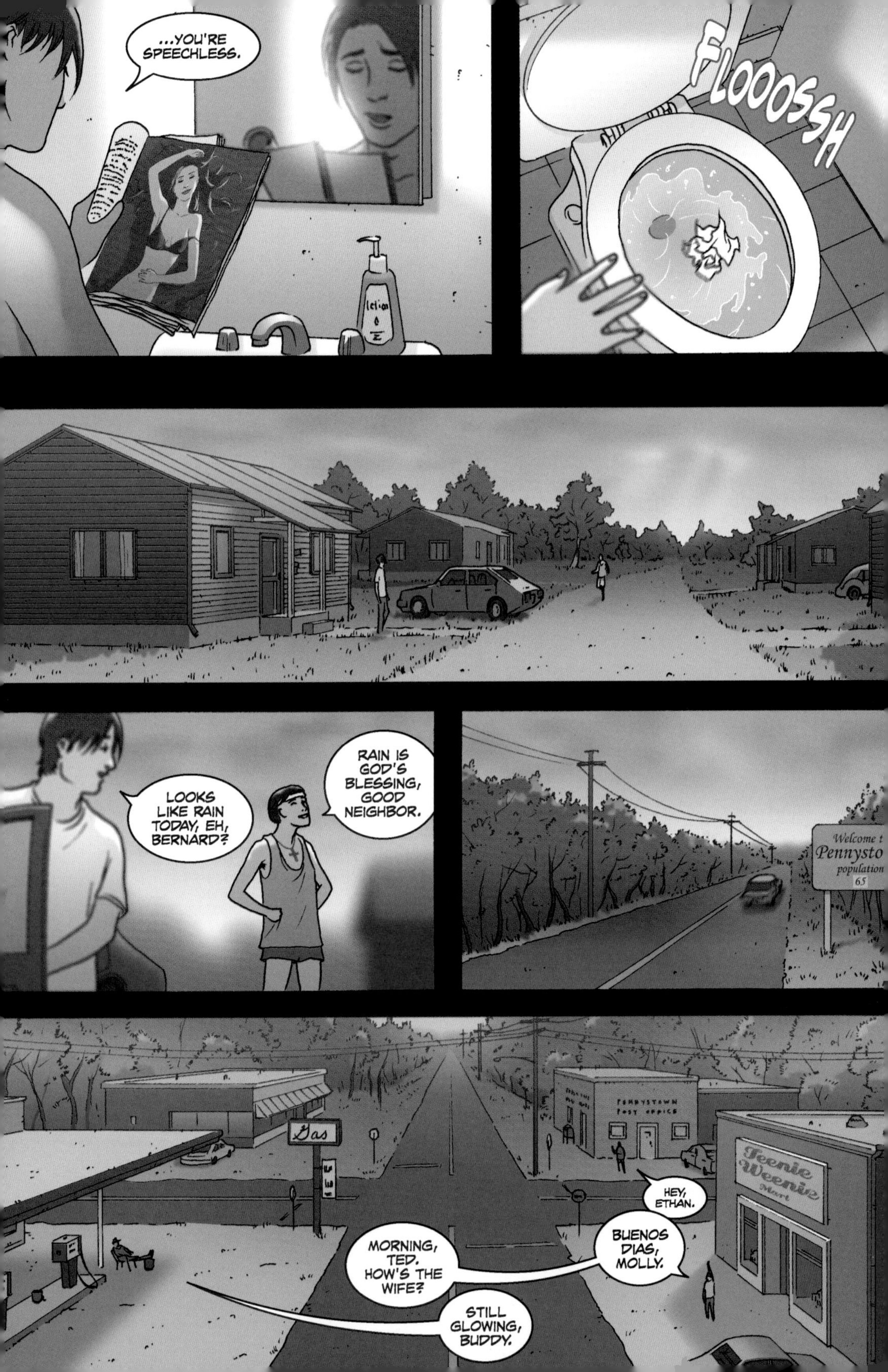
...YOU'RE SPEECHLESS.
Lotion
FLOOOSSH
LOOKS LIKE RAIN TODAY, EH, BERNARD?
RAIN IS GOD'S BLESSING, GOOD NEIGHBOR.
Welcome t
Pennysto
population
65
Gas
PENNYSTOWN POST OFFICE
Teenie Weenie Mart
HEY, ETHAN.
BUENOS DIAS, MOLLY.
MORNING, TED. HOW'S THE WIFE?
STILL GLOWING, BUDDY.

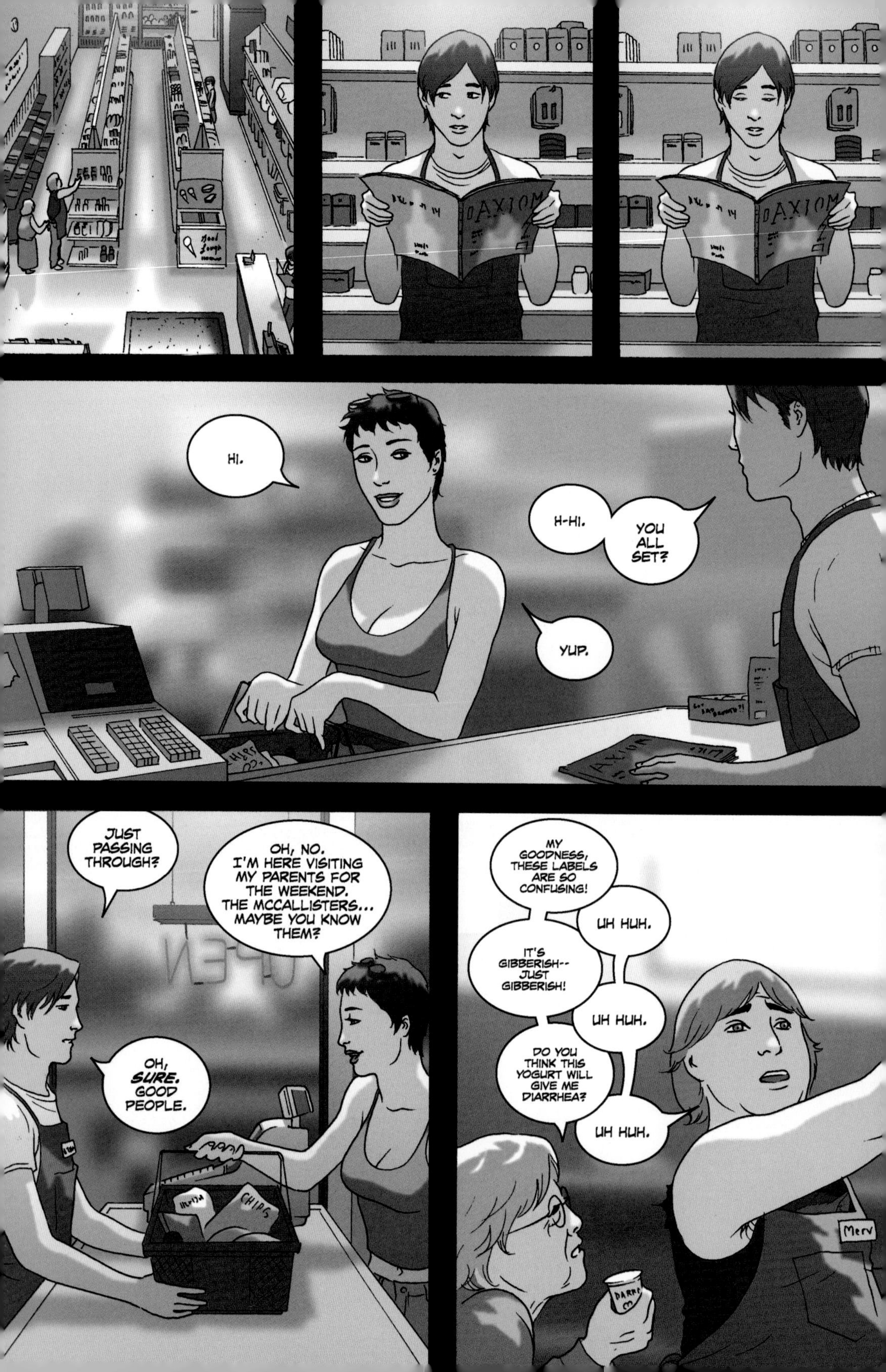
DAXIOM
HI.
H-HI.
YOU ALL SET?
YUP.
JUST PASSING THROUGH?
OH, NO. I'M HERE VISITING MY PARENTS FOR THE WEEKEND. THE MCCALLISTERS... MAYBE YOU KNOW THEM?
OH, *SURE.* GOOD PEOPLE.
CHIPS
MY GOODNESS, THESE LABELS ARE SO CONFUSING!
UH HUH.
IT'S GIBBERISH-- JUST GIBBERISH!
UH HUH.
DO YOU THINK THIS YOGURT WILL GIVE ME DIARRHEA?
UH HUH.
Merv

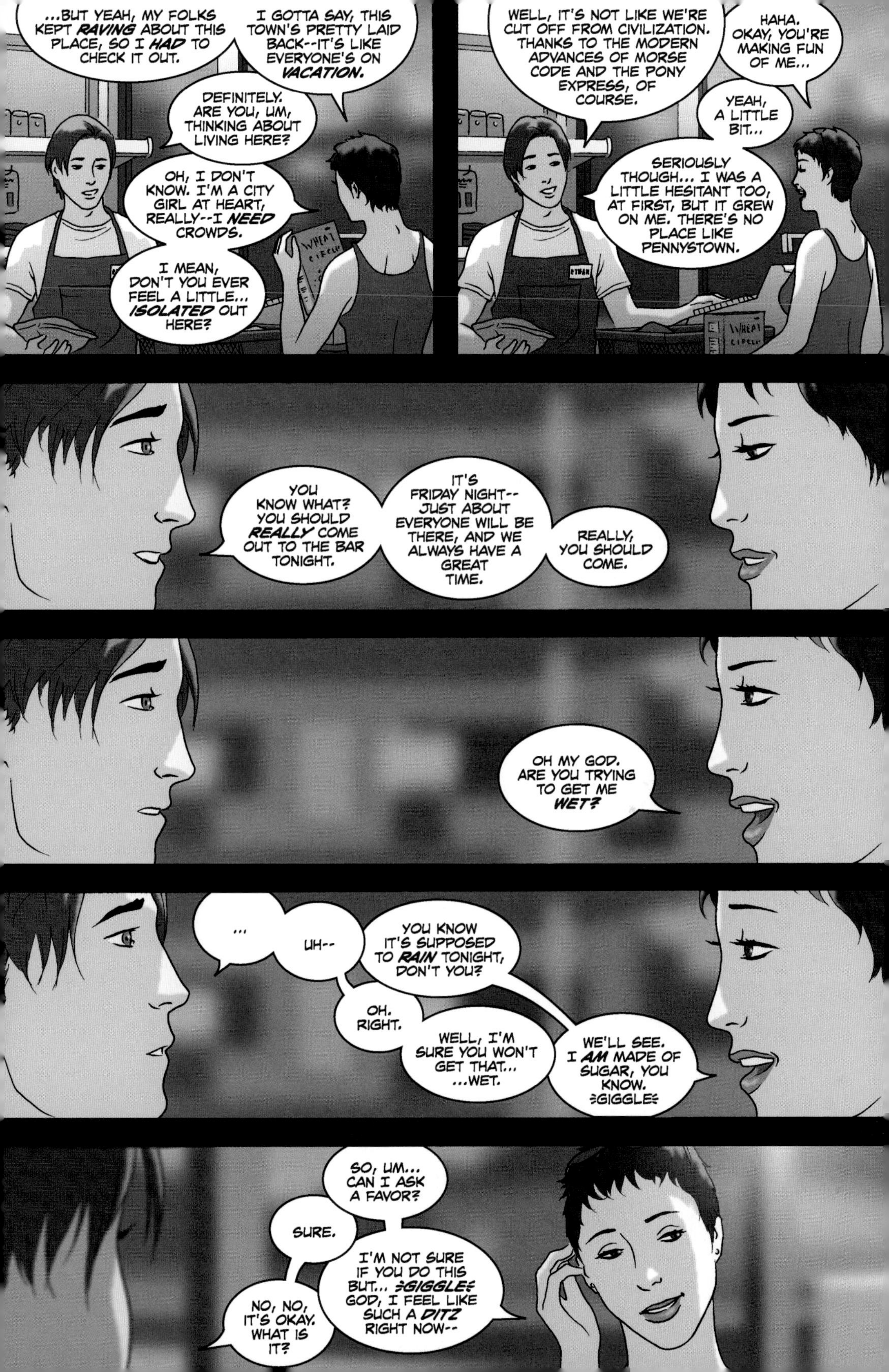
...BUT YEAH, MY FOLKS KEPT RAVING ABOUT THIS PLACE, SO I HAD TO CHECK IT OUT.
I GOTTA SAY, THIS TOWN'S PRETTY LAID BACK--IT'S LIKE EVERYONE'S ON VACATION.
DEFINITELY. ARE YOU, UM, THINKING ABOUT LIVING HERE?
OH, I DON'T KNOW. I'M A CITY GIRL AT HEART, REALLY--I NEED CROWDS.
I MEAN, DON'T YOU EVER FEEL A LITTLE... ISOLATED OUT HERE?
WHEAT
WELL, IT'S NOT LIKE WE'RE CUT OFF FROM CIVILIZATION. THANKS TO THE MODERN ADVANCES OF MORSE CODE AND THE PONY EXPRESS, OF COURSE.
HAHA. OKAY, YOU'RE MAKING FUN OF ME...
YEAH, A LITTLE BIT...
SERIOUSLY THOUGH... I WAS A LITTLE HESITANT TOO, AT FIRST, BUT IT GREW ON ME. THERE'S NO PLACE LIKE PENNYSTOWN.
ETHAN
WHEAT
YOU KNOW WHAT? YOU SHOULD REALLY COME OUT TO THE BAR TONIGHT.
IT'S FRIDAY NIGHT--JUST ABOUT EVERYONE WILL BE THERE, AND WE ALWAYS HAVE A GREAT TIME.
REALLY, YOU SHOULD COME.
OH MY GOD. ARE YOU TRYING TO GET ME WET?
...
UH--
YOU KNOW IT'S SUPPOSED TO RAIN TONIGHT, DON'T YOU?
OH. RIGHT.
WELL, I'M SURE YOU WON'T GET THAT... ...WET.
WE'LL SEE. I AM MADE OF SUGAR, YOU KNOW. ≶GIGGLE≶
SO, UM... CAN I ASK A FAVOR?
SURE.
I'M NOT SURE IF YOU DO THIS BUT... ≶GIGGLE≶ GOD, I FEEL LIKE SUCH A DITZ RIGHT NOW--
NO, NO, IT'S OKAY. WHAT IS IT?

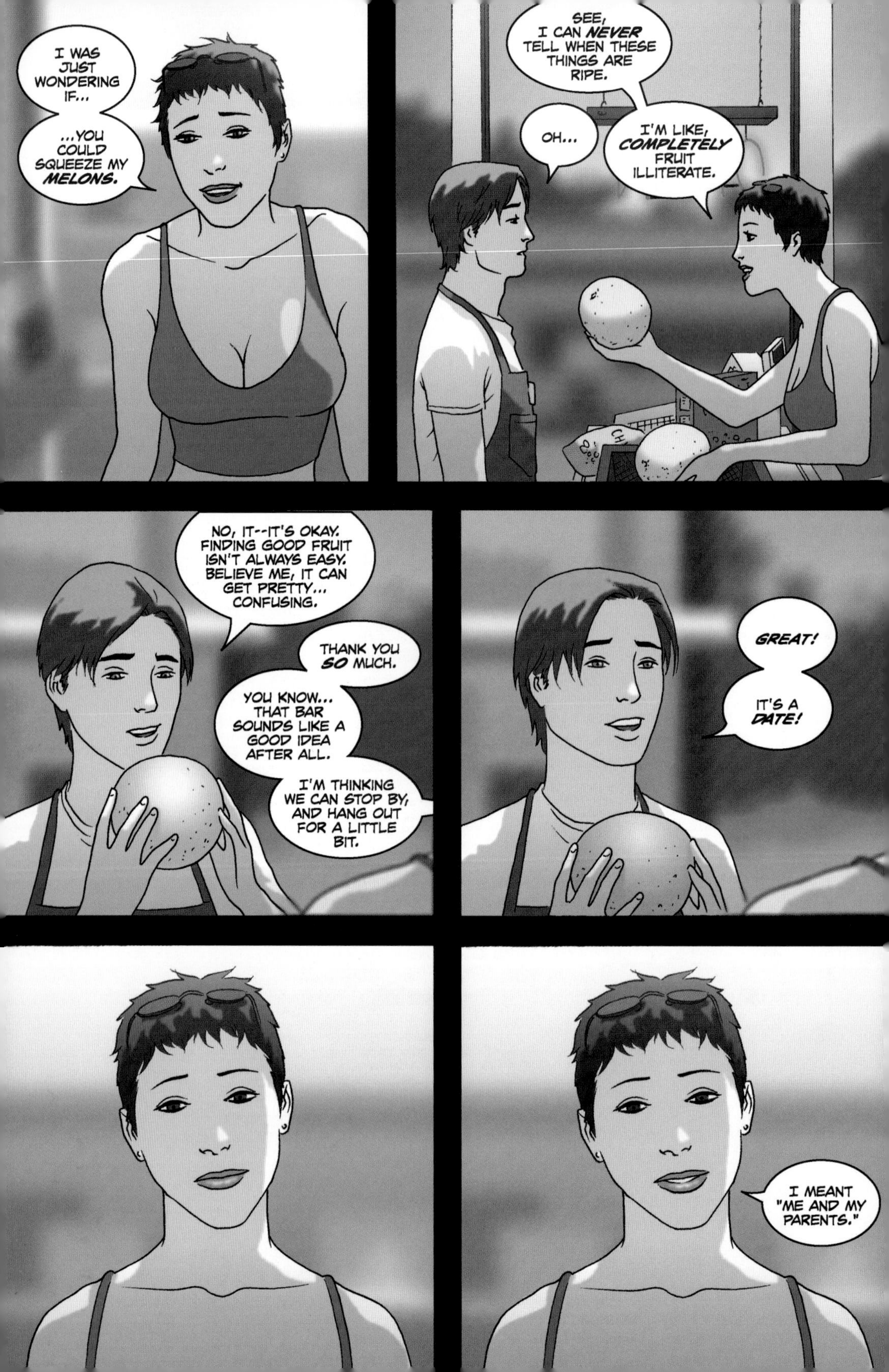
I WAS JUST WONDERING IF...
...YOU COULD SQUEEZE MY MELONS.
SEE, I CAN NEVER TELL WHEN THESE THINGS ARE RIPE.
OH...
I'M LIKE, COMPLETELY FRUIT ILLITERATE.
NO, IT--IT'S OKAY. FINDING GOOD FRUIT ISN'T ALWAYS EASY. BELIEVE ME, IT CAN GET PRETTY... CONFUSING.
THANK YOU SO MUCH.
YOU KNOW... THAT BAR SOUNDS LIKE A GOOD IDEA AFTER ALL.
I'M THINKING WE CAN STOP BY, AND HANG OUT FOR A LITTLE BIT.
GREAT!
IT'S A DATE!
I MEANT "ME AND MY PARENTS."

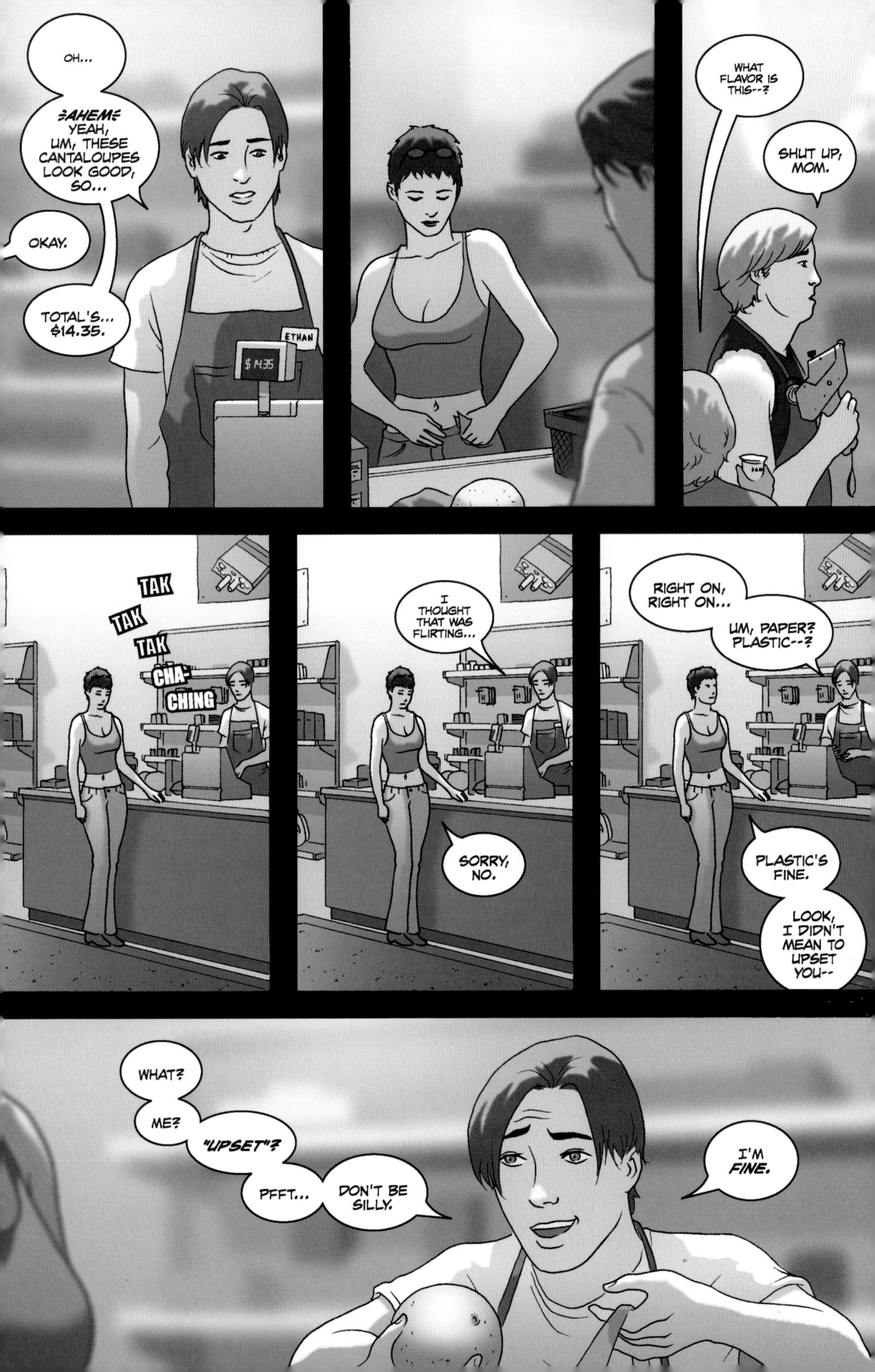
OH...
AHEM YEAH, UM, THESE CANTALOUPES LOOK GOOD, SO...
OKAY.
TOTAL'S... $14.35.
ETHAN
$ 14.35
WHAT FLAVOR IS THIS--?
SHUT UP, MOM.
TAK
TAK
TAK
CHA-CHING
I THOUGHT THAT WAS FLIRTING...
SORRY, NO.
RIGHT ON, RIGHT ON...
UM, PAPER? PLASTIC--?
PLASTIC'S FINE.
LOOK, I DIDN'T MEAN TO UPSET YOU--
WHAT?
ME?
"UPSET"?
PFFT...
DON'T BE SILLY.
I'M FINE.

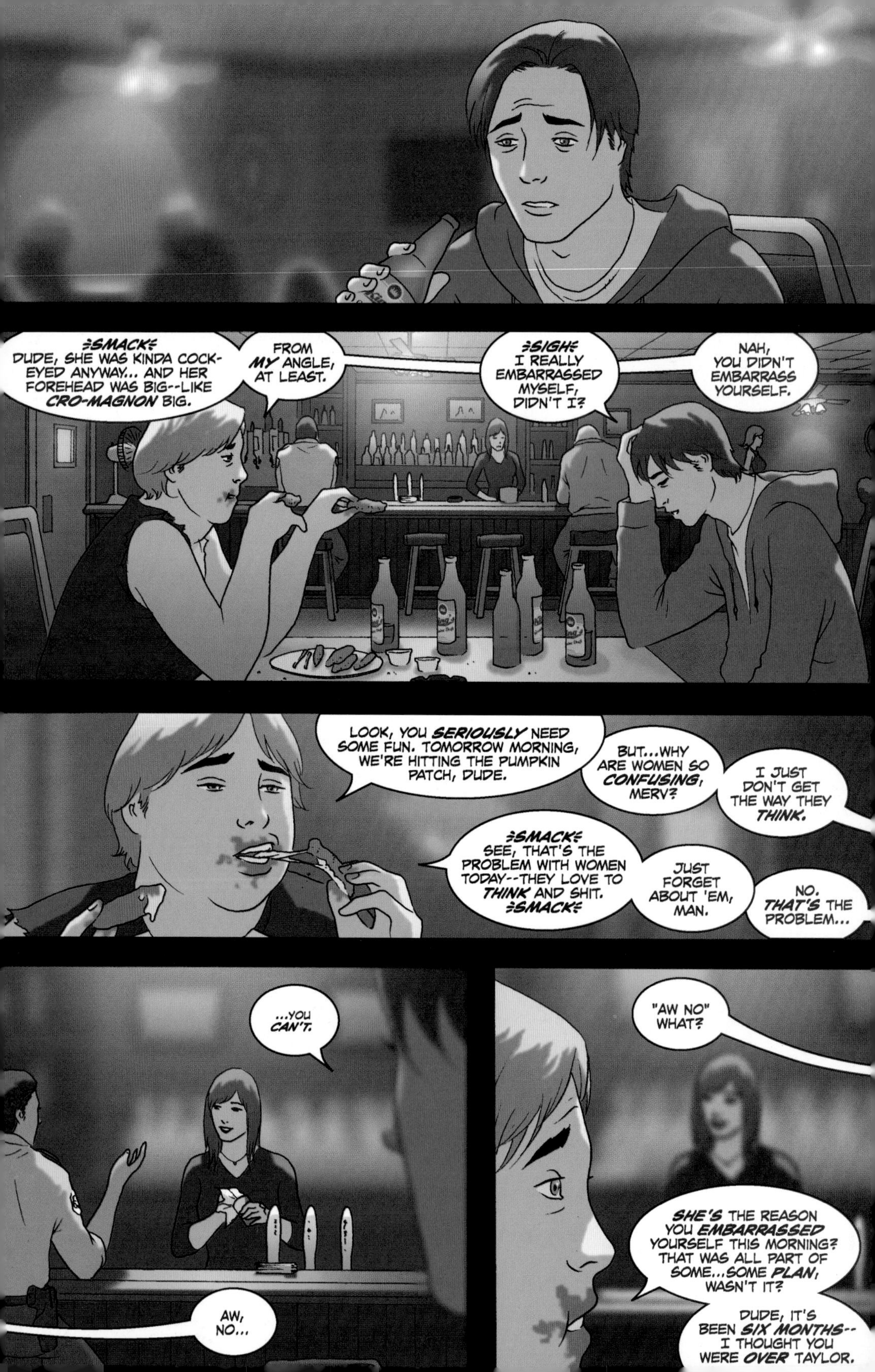

SMACK
DUDE, SHE WAS KINDA COCK-EYED ANYWAY... AND HER FOREHEAD WAS BIG--LIKE CRO-MAGNON BIG.
FROM MY ANGLE, AT LEAST.
SIGH
I REALLY EMBARRASSED MYSELF, DIDN'T I?
NAH, YOU DIDN'T EMBARRASS YOURSELF.
LOOK, YOU SERIOUSLY NEED SOME FUN. TOMORROW MORNING, WE'RE HITTING THE PUMPKIN PATCH, DUDE.
BUT...WHY ARE WOMEN SO CONFUSING, MERV?
I JUST DON'T GET THE WAY THEY THINK.
SMACK
SEE, THAT'S THE PROBLEM WITH WOMEN TODAY--THEY LOVE TO THINK AND SHIT.
SMACK
JUST FORGET ABOUT 'EM, MAN.
NO. THAT'S THE PROBLEM...
...YOU CAN'T.
AW, NO...
"AW NO" WHAT?
SHE'S THE REASON YOU EMBARRASSED YOURSELF THIS MORNING? THAT WAS ALL PART OF SOME...SOME PLAN, WASN'T IT?
DUDE, IT'S BEEN SIX MONTHS--I THOUGHT YOU WERE OVER TAYLOR.

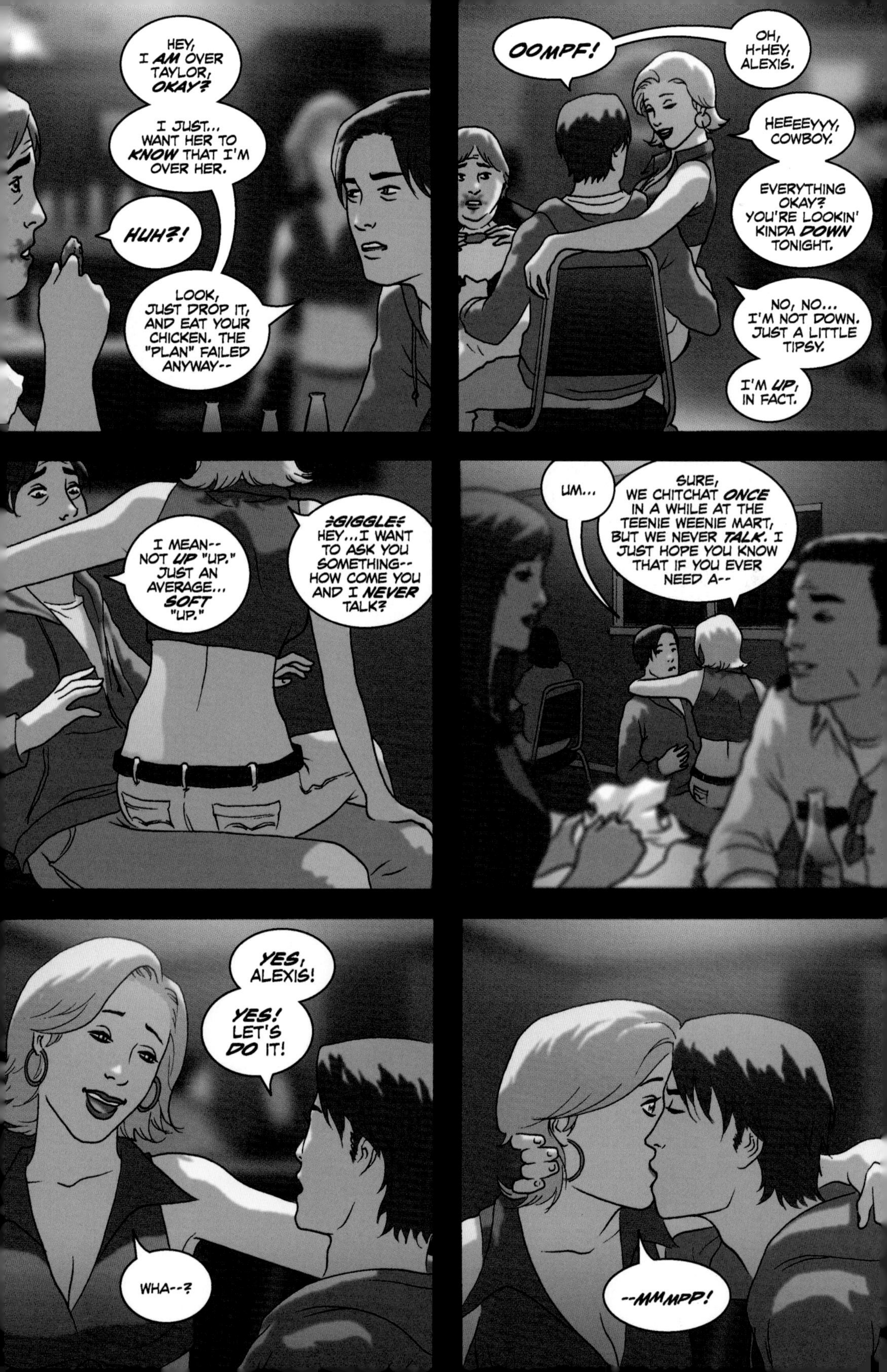
HEY, I AM OVER TAYLOR, OKAY?
I JUST... WANT HER TO KNOW THAT I'M OVER HER.
HUH?!
LOOK, JUST DROP IT, AND EAT YOUR CHICKEN. THE "PLAN" FAILED ANYWAY--
OOMPF!
OH, H-HEY, ALEXIS.
HEEEEYYY, COWBOY.
EVERYTHING OKAY? YOU'RE LOOKIN' KINDA DOWN TONIGHT.
NO, NO... I'M NOT DOWN. JUST A LITTLE TIPSY.
I'M UP, IN FACT.
I MEAN-- NOT UP "UP." JUST AN AVERAGE... SOFT "UP."
GIGGLE HEY... I WANT TO ASK YOU SOMETHING-- HOW COME YOU AND I NEVER TALK?
UM...
SURE, WE CHITCHAT ONCE IN A WHILE AT THE TEENIE WEENIE MART, BUT WE NEVER TALK. I JUST HOPE YOU KNOW THAT IF YOU EVER NEED A--
YES, ALEXIS!
YES! LET'S DO IT!
WHA--?
--MMMPP!

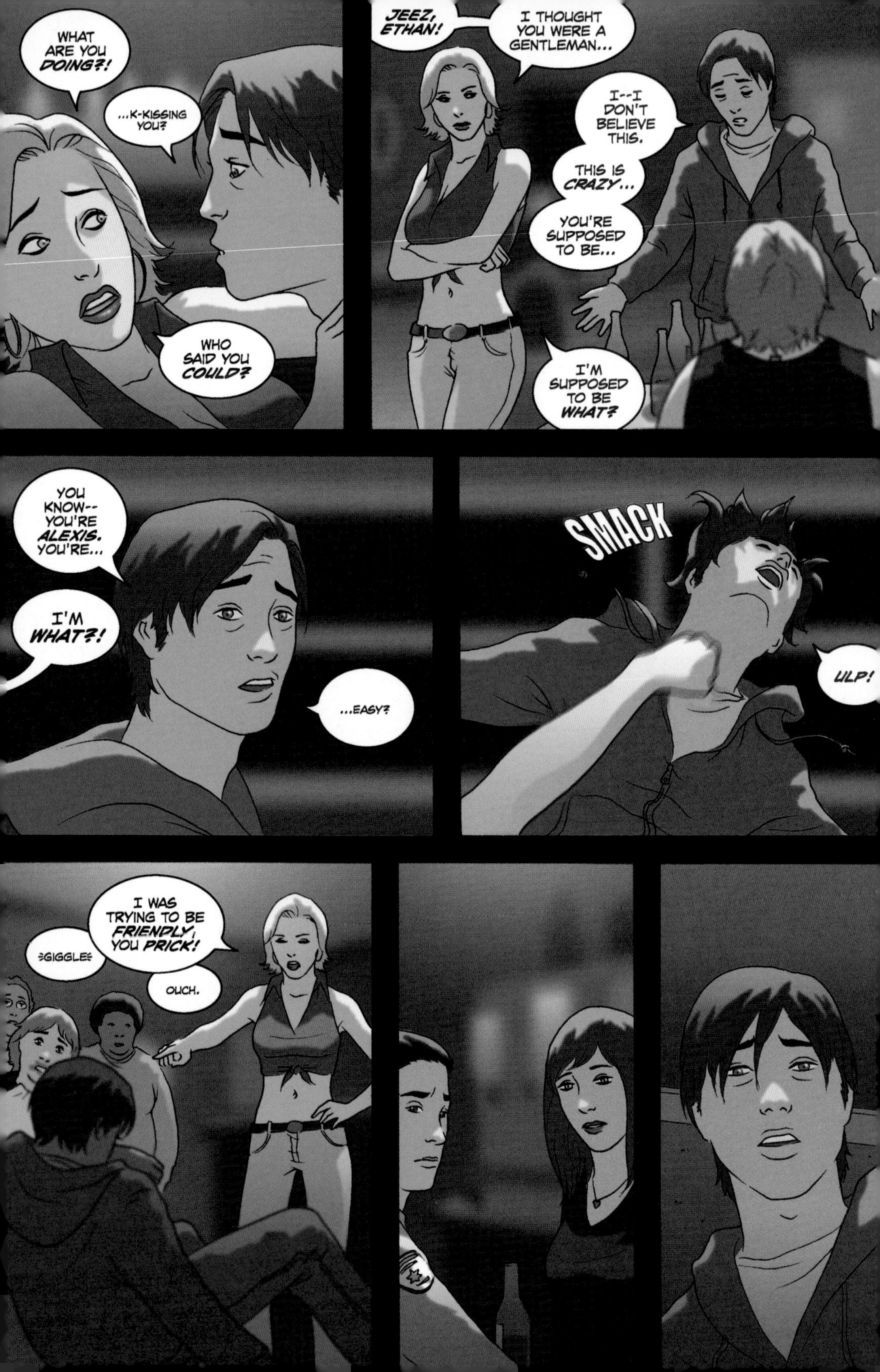
WHAT ARE YOU DOING?!
...K-KISSING YOU?
WHO SAID YOU COULD?
JEEZ, ETHAN!
I THOUGHT YOU WERE A GENTLEMAN...
I--I DON'T BELIEVE THIS.
THIS IS CRAZY...
YOU'RE SUPPOSED TO BE...
I'M SUPPOSED TO BE WHAT?
YOU KNOW-- YOU'RE ALEXIS. YOU'RE...
I'M WHAT?!
...EASY?
SMACK
ULP!
I WAS TRYING TO BE FRIENDLY, YOU PRICK!
=GIGGLE=
OUCH.

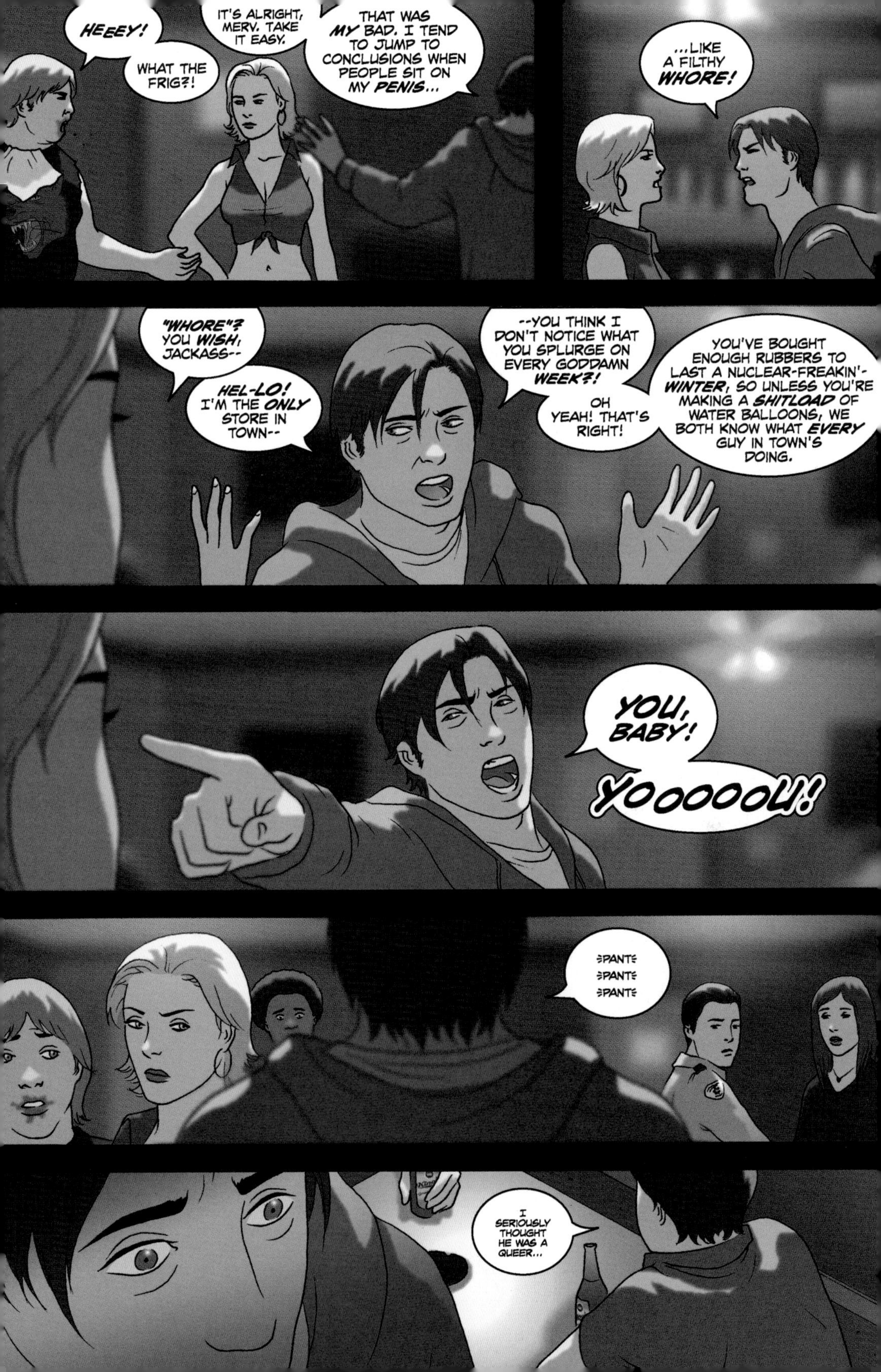
HEEEY!
WHAT THE FRIG?!
IT'S ALRIGHT, MERV. TAKE IT EASY.
THAT WAS MY BAD. I TEND TO JUMP TO CONCLUSIONS WHEN PEOPLE SIT ON MY PENIS...
...LIKE A FILTHY WHORE!
"WHORE"? YOU WISH, JACKASS--
HEL-LO! I'M THE ONLY STORE IN TOWN--
--YOU THINK I DON'T NOTICE WHAT YOU SPLURGE ON EVERY GODDAMN WEEK?!
OH YEAH! THAT'S RIGHT!
YOU'VE BOUGHT ENOUGH RUBBERS TO LAST A NUCLEAR-FREAKIN'-WINTER, SO UNLESS YOU'RE MAKING A SHITLOAD OF WATER BALLOONS, WE BOTH KNOW WHAT EVERY GUY IN TOWN'S DOING.
YOU, BABY!
YOOOOOU!
PANT
PANT
PANT
I SERIOUSLY THOUGHT HE WAS A QUEER...

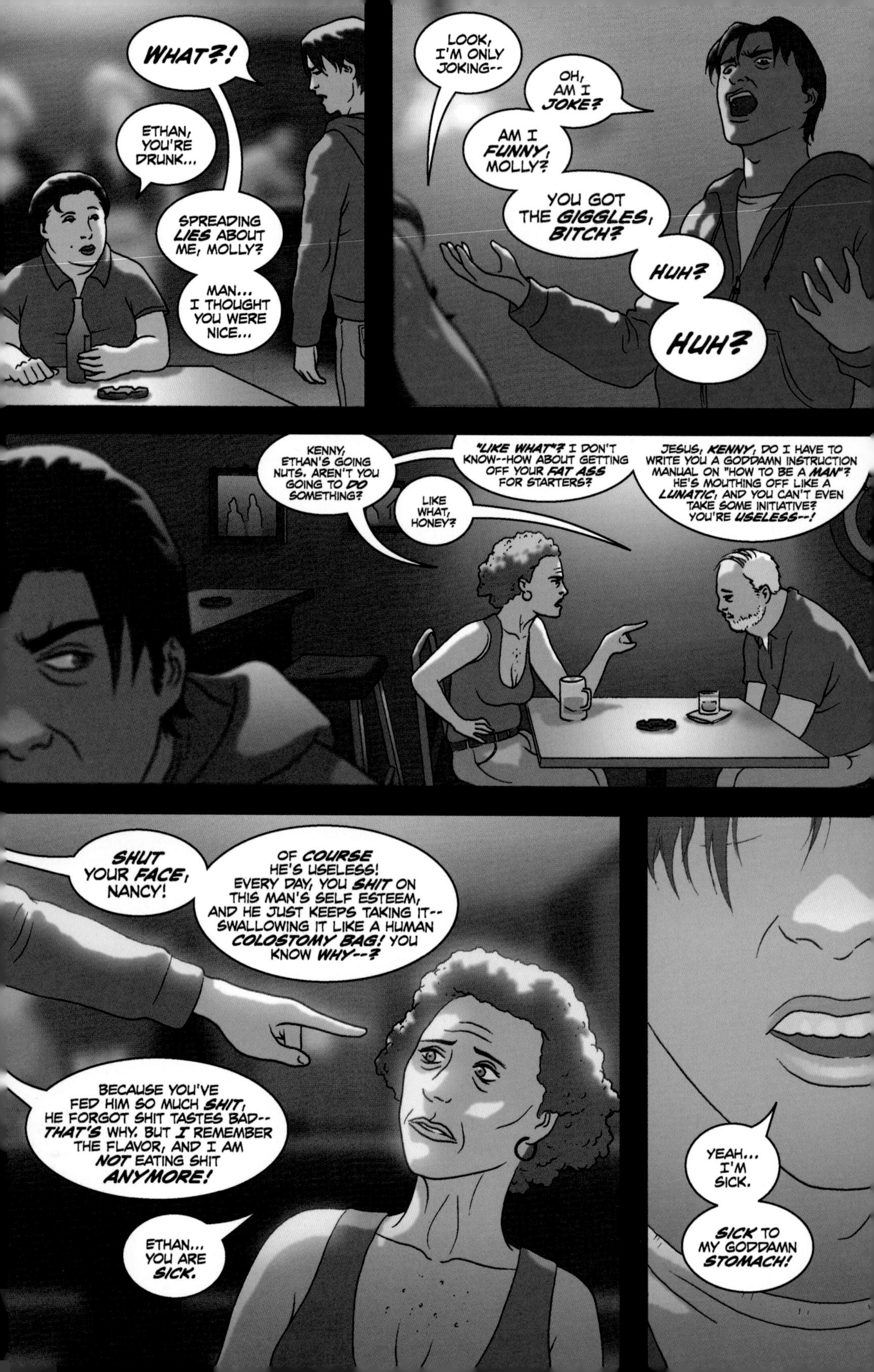
WHAT?!
ETHAN, YOU'RE DRUNK...
SPREADING LIES ABOUT ME, MOLLY?
MAN... I THOUGHT YOU WERE NICE...
LOOK, I'M ONLY JOKING--
OH, AM I JOKE?
AM I FUNNY, MOLLY?
YOU GOT THE GIGGLES, BITCH?
HUH?
HUH?
KENNY, ETHAN'S GOING NUTS. AREN'T YOU GOING TO DO SOMETHING?
LIKE WHAT, HONEY?
"LIKE WHAT"? I DON'T KNOW--HOW ABOUT GETTING OFF YOUR FAT ASS FOR STARTERS?
JESUS, KENNY, DO I HAVE TO WRITE YOU A GODDAMN INSTRUCTION MANUAL ON "HOW TO BE A MAN"? HE'S MOUTHING OFF LIKE A LUNATIC, AND YOU CAN'T EVEN TAKE SOME INITIATIVE? YOU'RE USELESS--!
SHUT YOUR FACE, NANCY!
OF COURSE HE'S USELESS! EVERY DAY, YOU SHIT ON THIS MAN'S SELF ESTEEM, AND HE JUST KEEPS TAKING IT-- SWALLOWING IT LIKE A HUMAN COLOSTOMY BAG! YOU KNOW WHY--?
BECAUSE YOU'VE FED HIM SO MUCH SHIT, HE FORGOT SHIT TASTES BAD-- THAT'S WHY. BUT I REMEMBER THE FLAVOR, AND I AM NOT EATING SHIT ANYMORE!
ETHAN... YOU ARE SICK.
YEAH... I'M SICK.
SICK TO MY GODDAMN STOMACH!

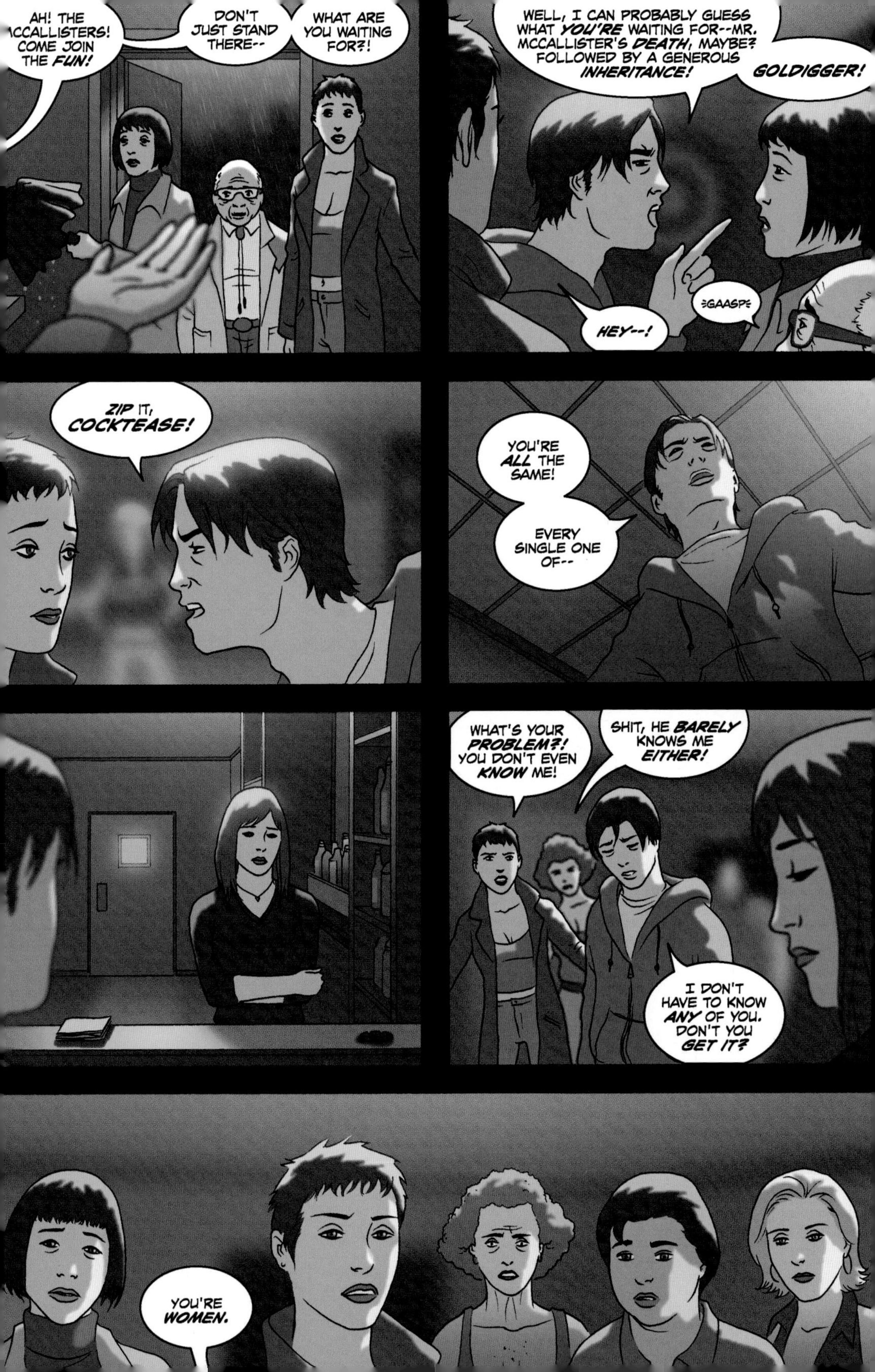
AH! THE MCCALLISTERS! COME JOIN THE FUN!
DON'T JUST STAND THERE--
WHAT ARE YOU WAITING FOR?!
WELL, I CAN PROBABLY GUESS WHAT YOU'RE WAITING FOR--MR. MCCALLISTER'S DEATH, MAYBE? FOLLOWED BY A GENEROUS INHERITANCE!
GOLDIGGER!
HEY--!
GAASP
ZIP IT, COCKTEASE!
YOU'RE ALL THE SAME!
EVERY SINGLE ONE OF--
WHAT'S YOUR PROBLEM?! YOU DON'T EVEN KNOW ME!
SHIT, HE BARELY KNOWS ME EITHER!
I DON'T HAVE TO KNOW ANY OF YOU. DON'T YOU GET IT?
YOU'RE WOMEN.

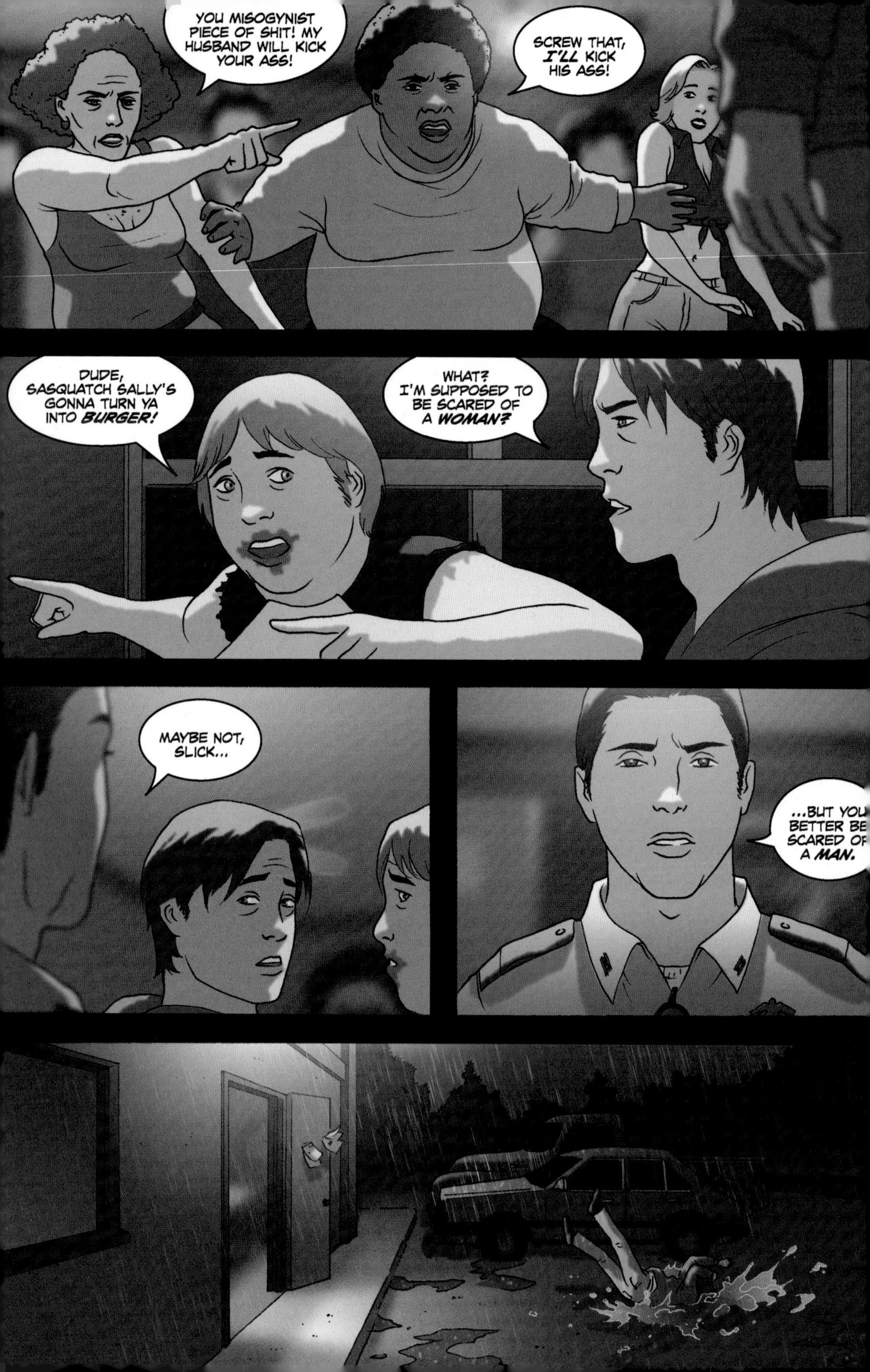
YOU MISOGYNIST PIECE OF SHIT! MY HUSBAND WILL KICK YOUR ASS!
SCREW THAT, I'LL KICK HIS ASS!
DUDE, SASQUATCH SALLY'S GONNA TURN YA INTO BURGER!
WHAT? I'M SUPPOSED TO BE SCARED OF A WOMAN?
MAYBE NOT, SLICK...
...BUT YOU BETTER BE SCARED OF A MAN.

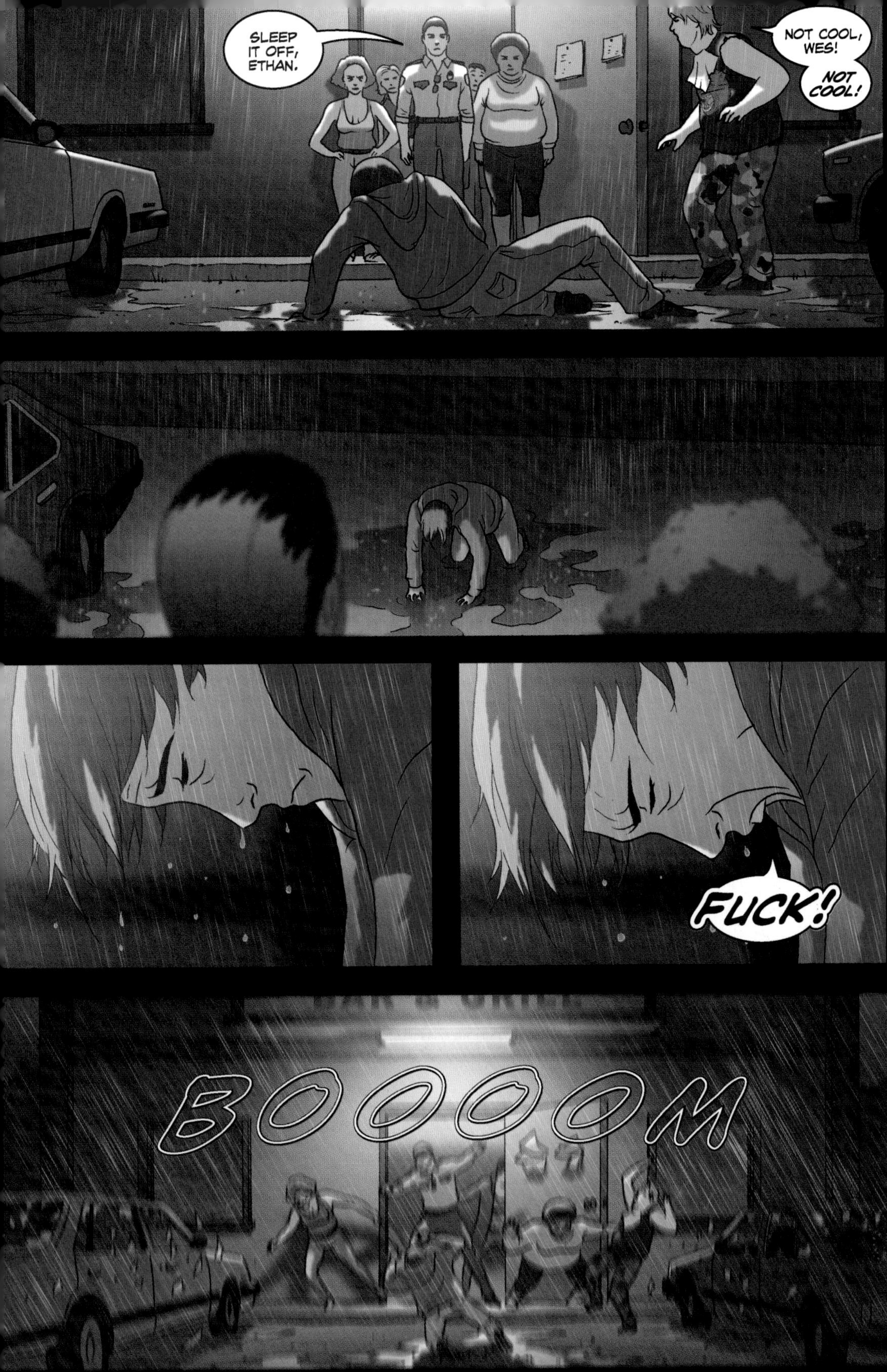
SLEEP IT OFF, ETHAN.
NOT COOL, WES!
NOT COOL!
FUCK!
BOOOOM

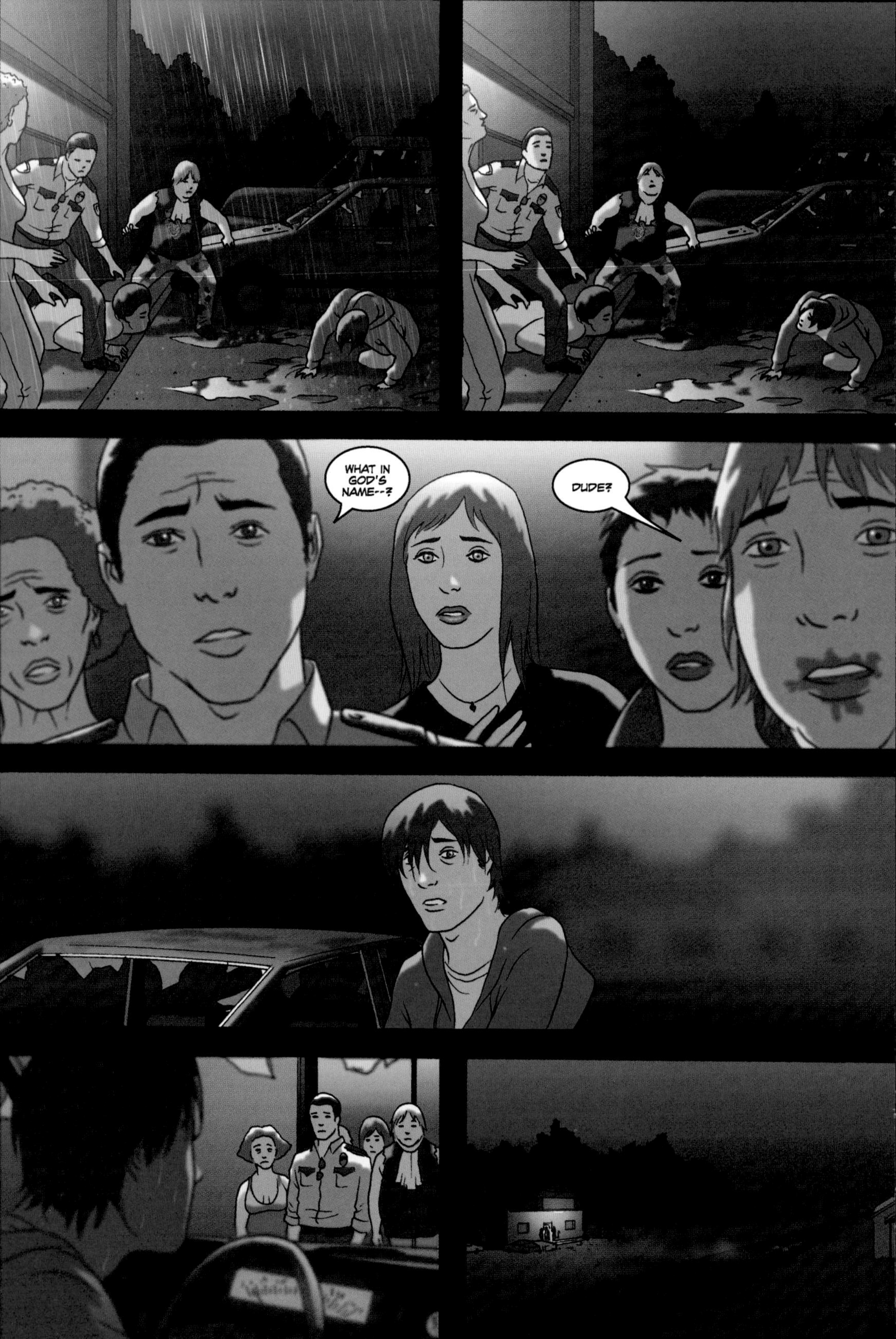
WHAT IN GOD'S NAME--?
DUDE?

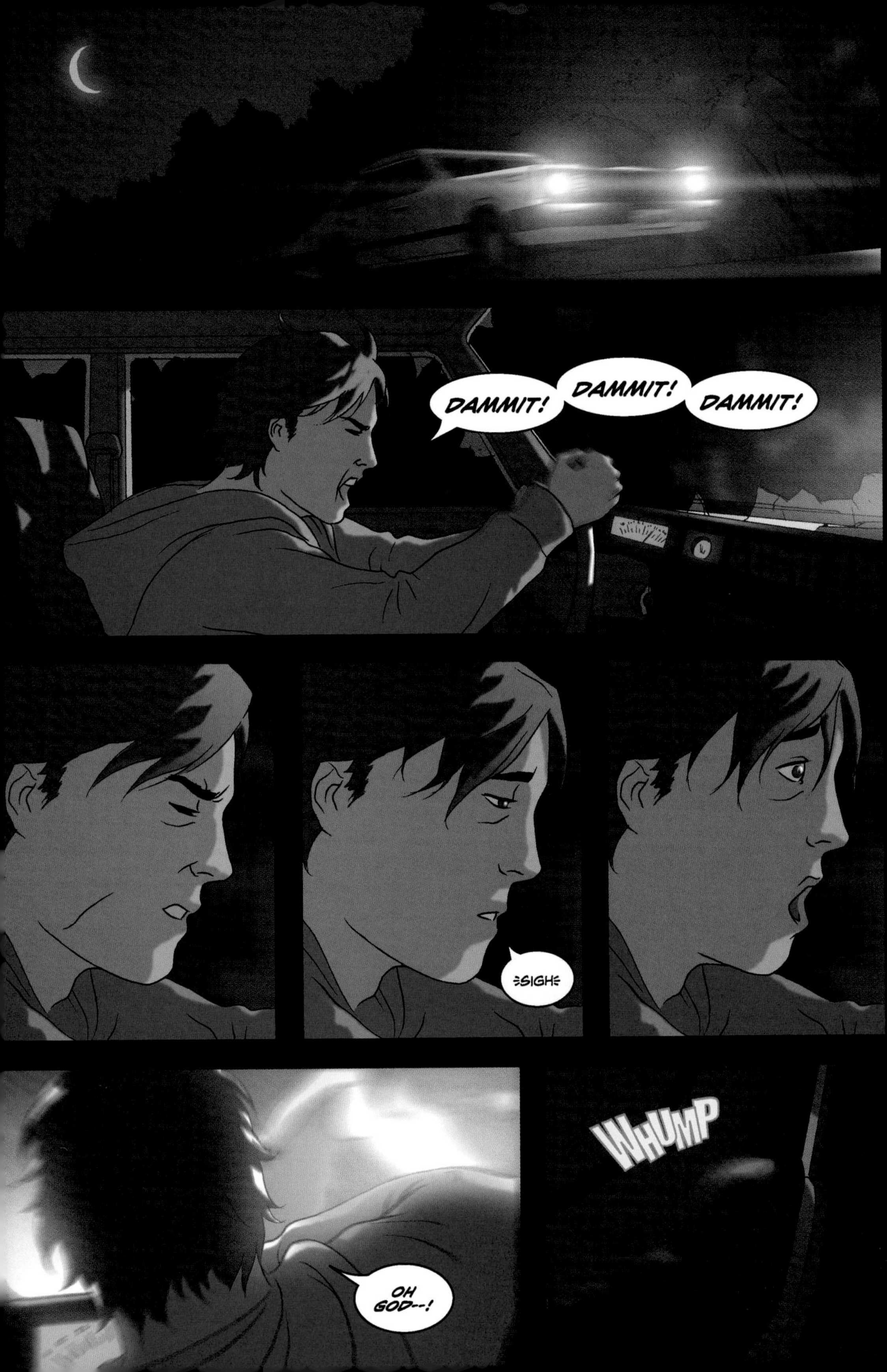
DAMMIT!
DAMMIT!
DAMMIT!
≡SIGH≡
WHUMP
OH GOD--!

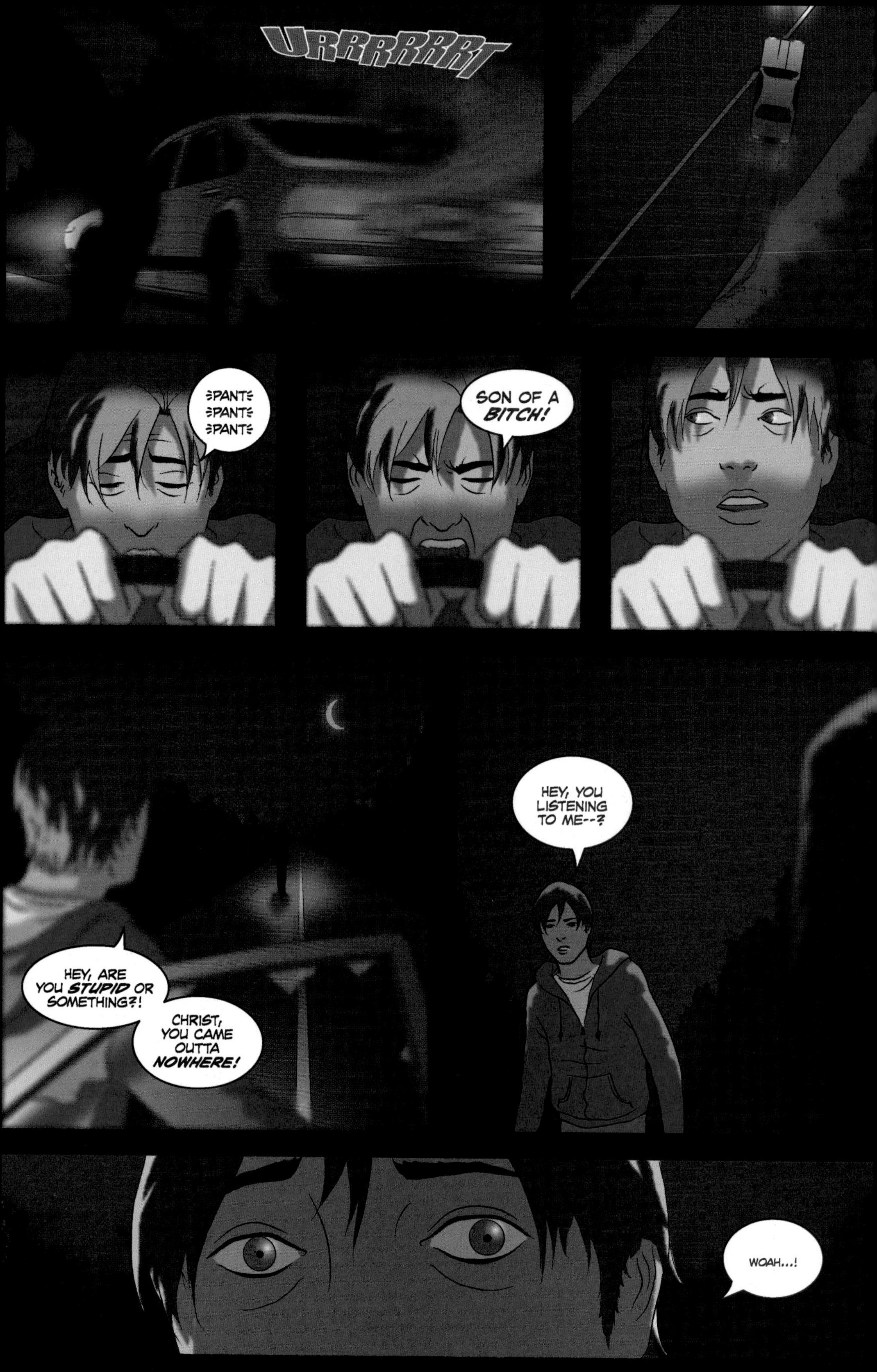
URRRRRRT
=PANT=
=PANT=
=PANT=
SON OF A BITCH!
HEY, ARE YOU STUPID OR SOMETHING?!
CHRIST, YOU CAME OUTTA NOWHERE!
HEY, YOU LISTENING TO ME--?
WOAH...!

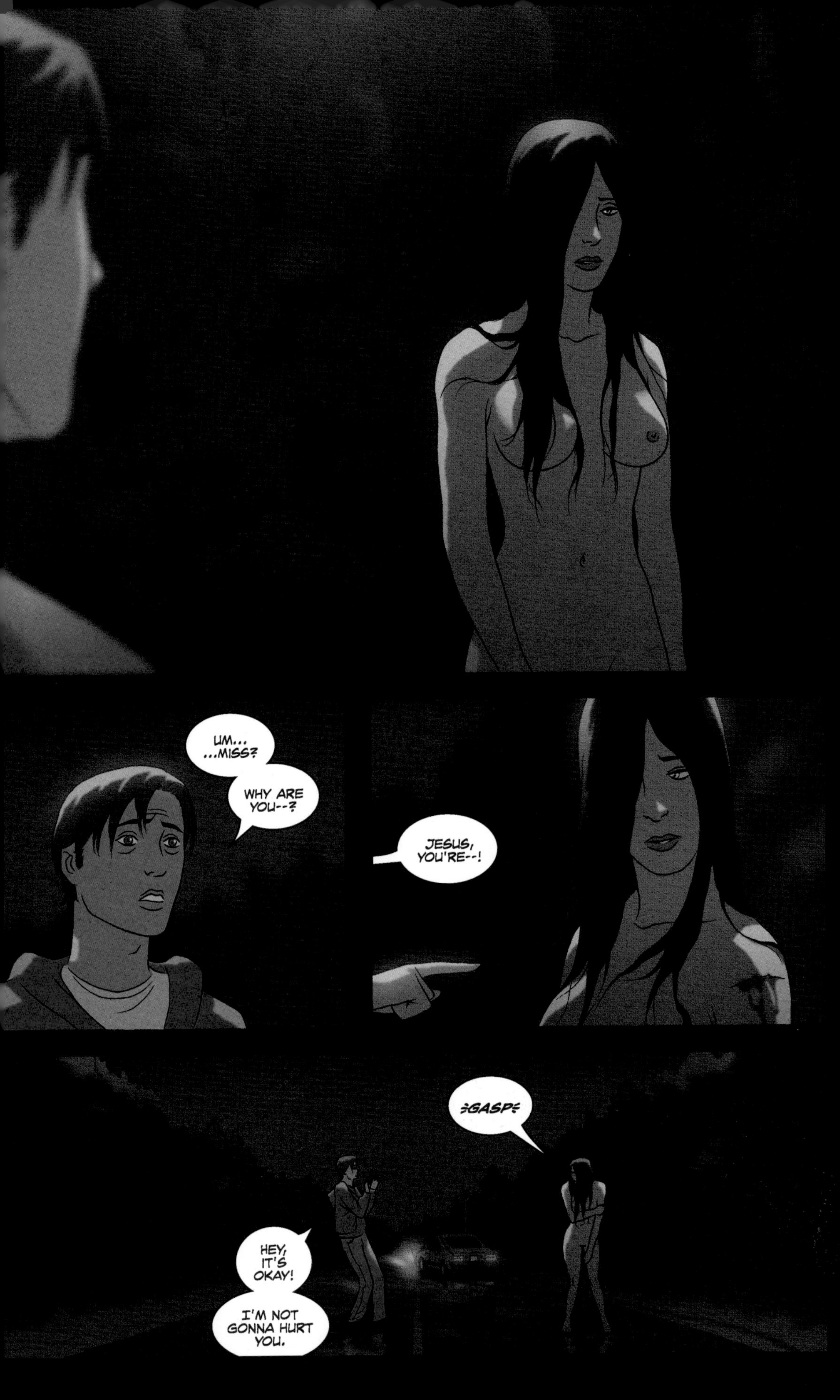
UM...
...MISS?
WHY ARE YOU--?
JESUS, YOU'RE--!
GASP
HEY, IT'S OKAY!
I'M NOT GONNA HURT YOU.

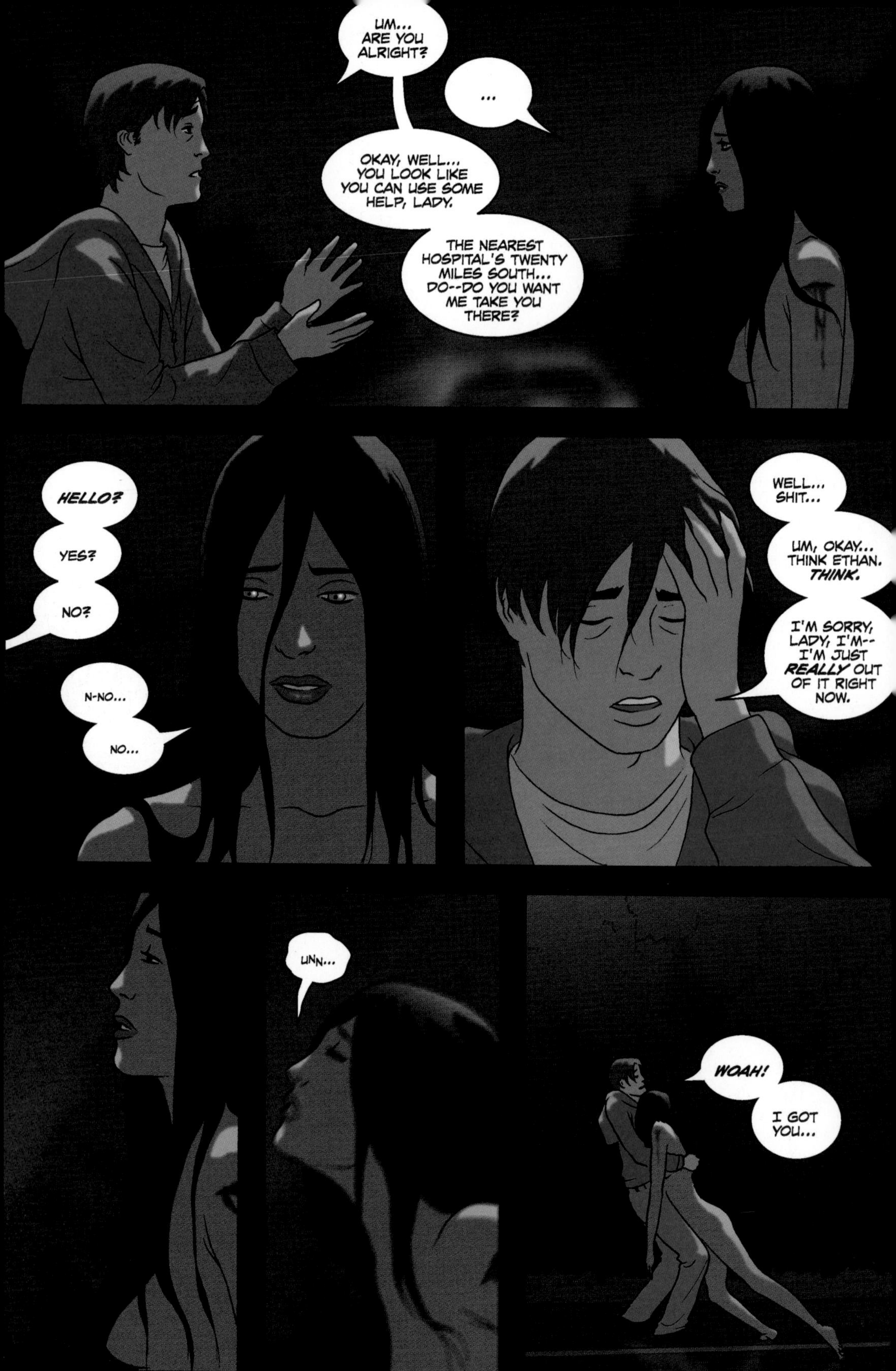
UM... ARE YOU ALRIGHT?
...
OKAY, WELL... YOU LOOK LIKE YOU CAN USE SOME HELP, LADY.
THE NEAREST HOSPITAL'S TWENTY MILES SOUTH... DO--DO YOU WANT ME TAKE YOU THERE?
HELLO?
YES?
NO?
N-NO...
NO...
WELL... SHIT...
UM, OKAY... THINK ETHAN. THINK.
I'M SORRY, LADY, I'M-- I'M JUST REALLY OUT OF IT RIGHT NOW.
UNN...
WOAH!
I GOT YOU...

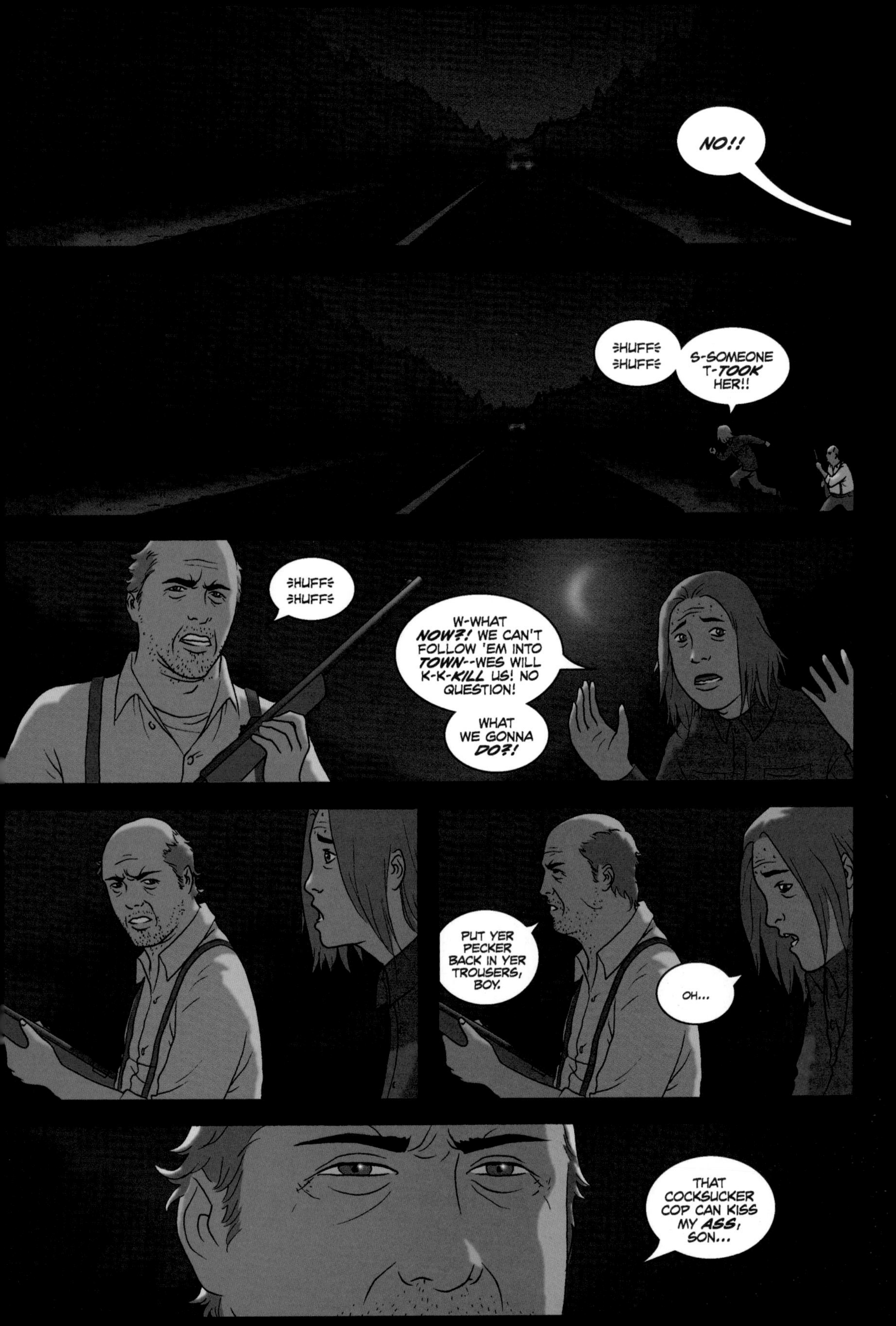
NO!!
≈HUFF≈ ≈HUFF≈
S-SOMEONE T-TOOK HER!!
≈HUFF≈ ≈HUFF≈
W-WHAT NOW?! WE CAN'T FOLLOW 'EM INTO TOWN--WES WILL K-K-KILL US! NO QUESTION!
WHAT WE GONNA DO?!
PUT YER PECKER BACK IN YER TROUSERS, BOY.
OH...
THAT COCKSUCKER COP CAN KISS MY ASS, SON...

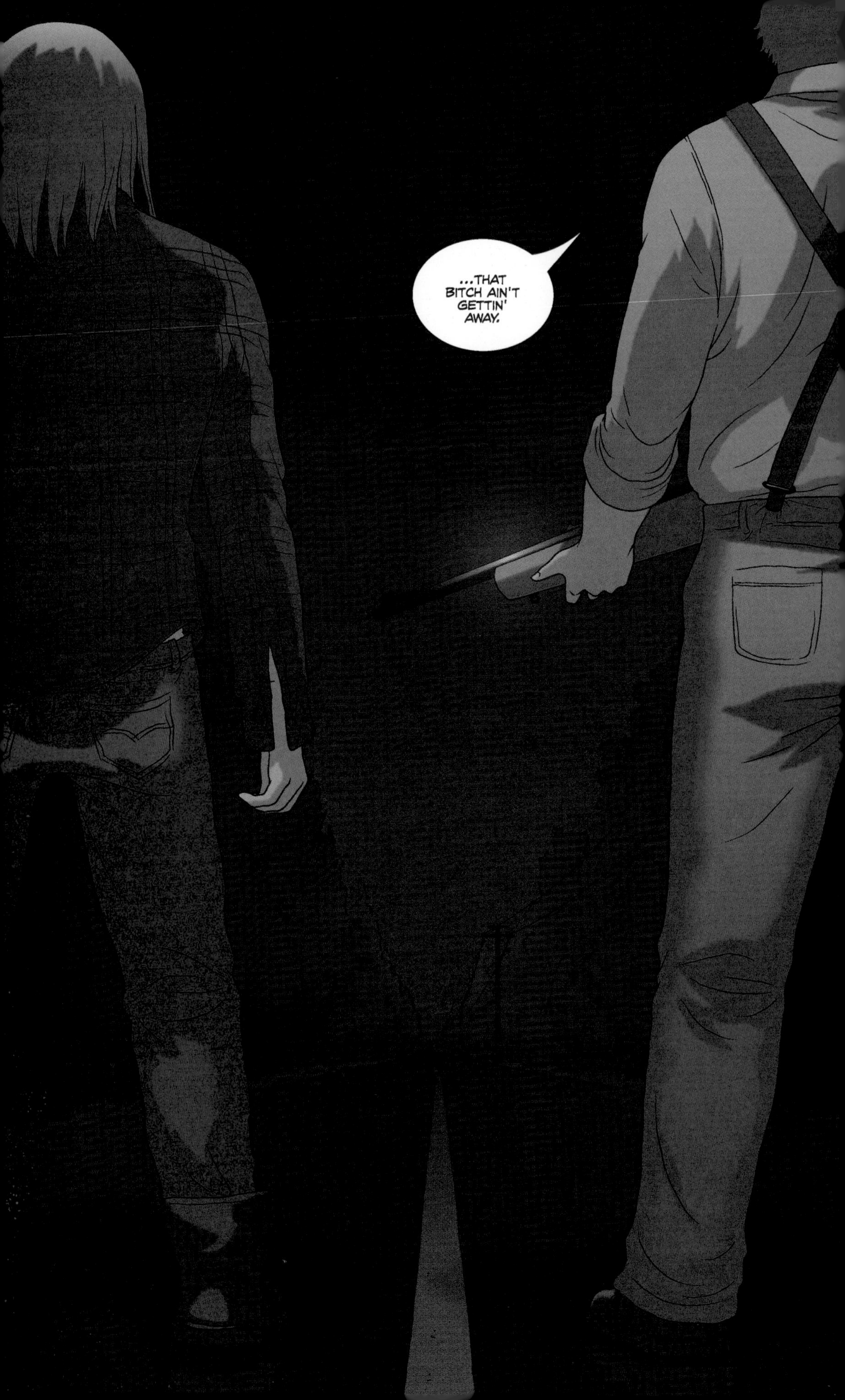
...THAT BITCH AIN'T GETTIN' AWAY.

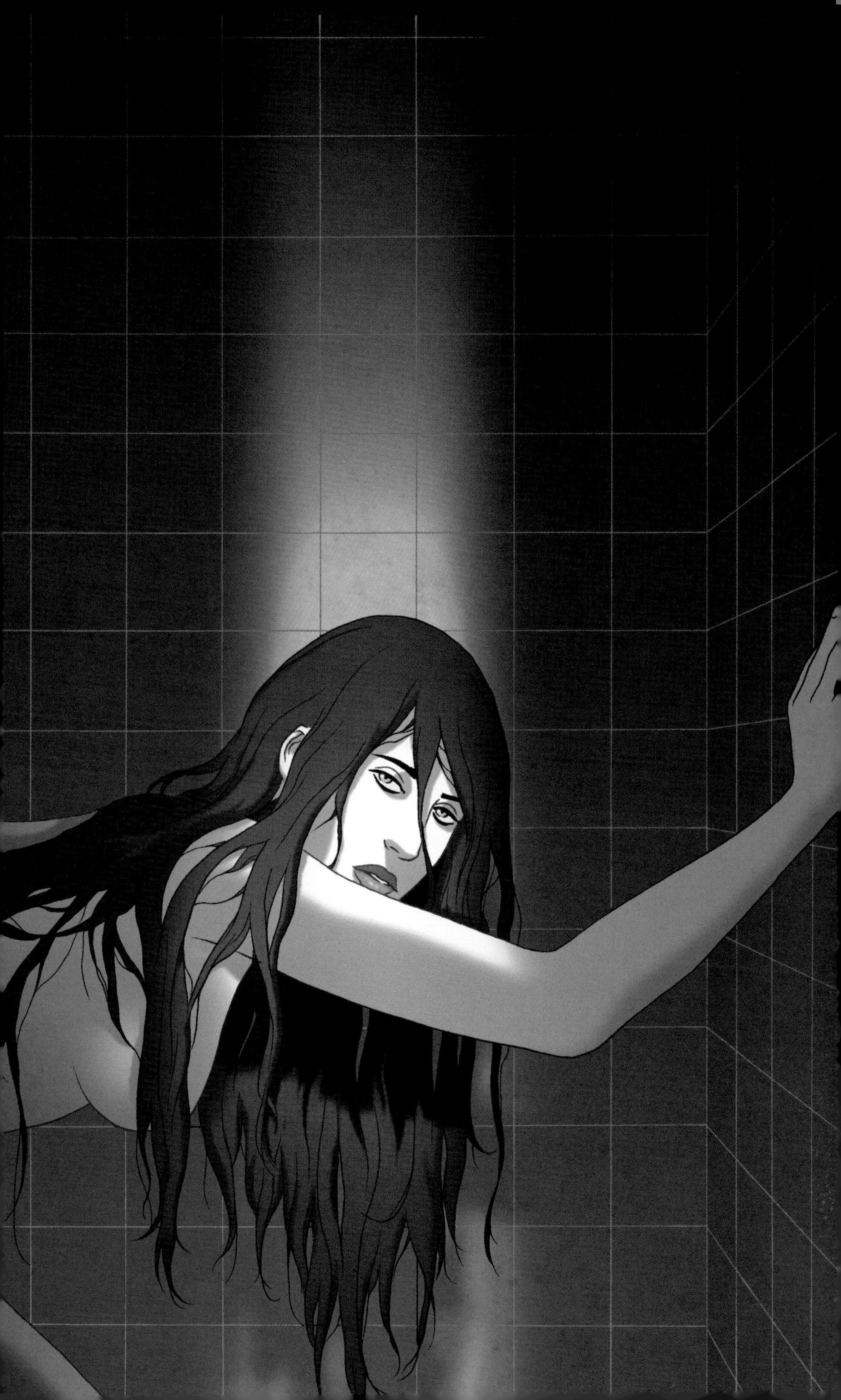

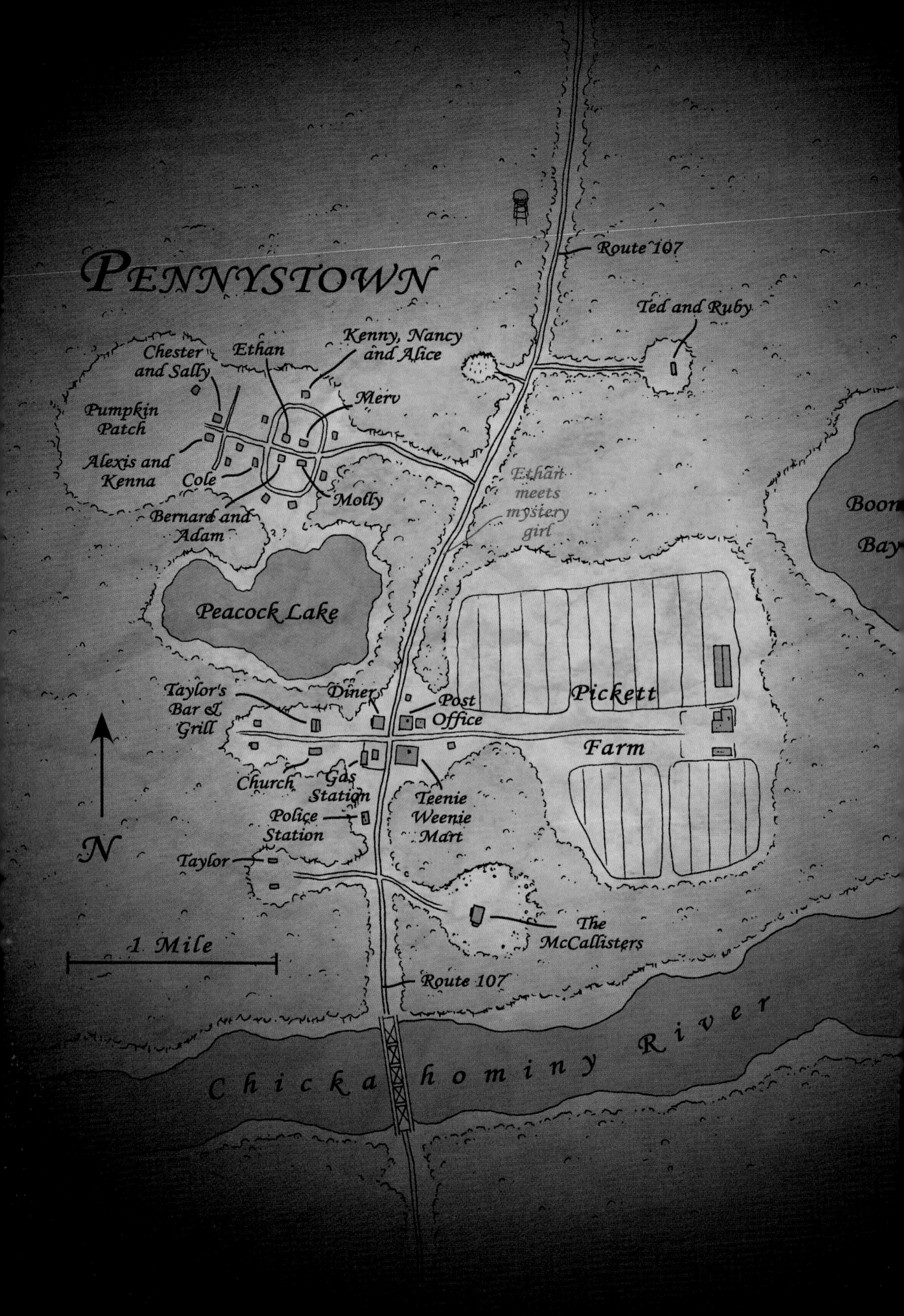
Pennystown
Route 107
Ted and Ruby
Chester and Sally
Ethan
Kenny, Nancy and Alice
Merv
Pumpkin Patch
Alexis and Kenna
Cole
Molly
Bernard and Adam
Ethan meets mystery girl
Boon Bay
Peacock Lake
Taylor's Bar & Grill
Diner
Post Office
Pickett Farm
Church
Gas Station
Teenie Weenie Mart
Police Station
Taylor
N
The McCallisters
1 Mile
Route 107
Chickahominy River

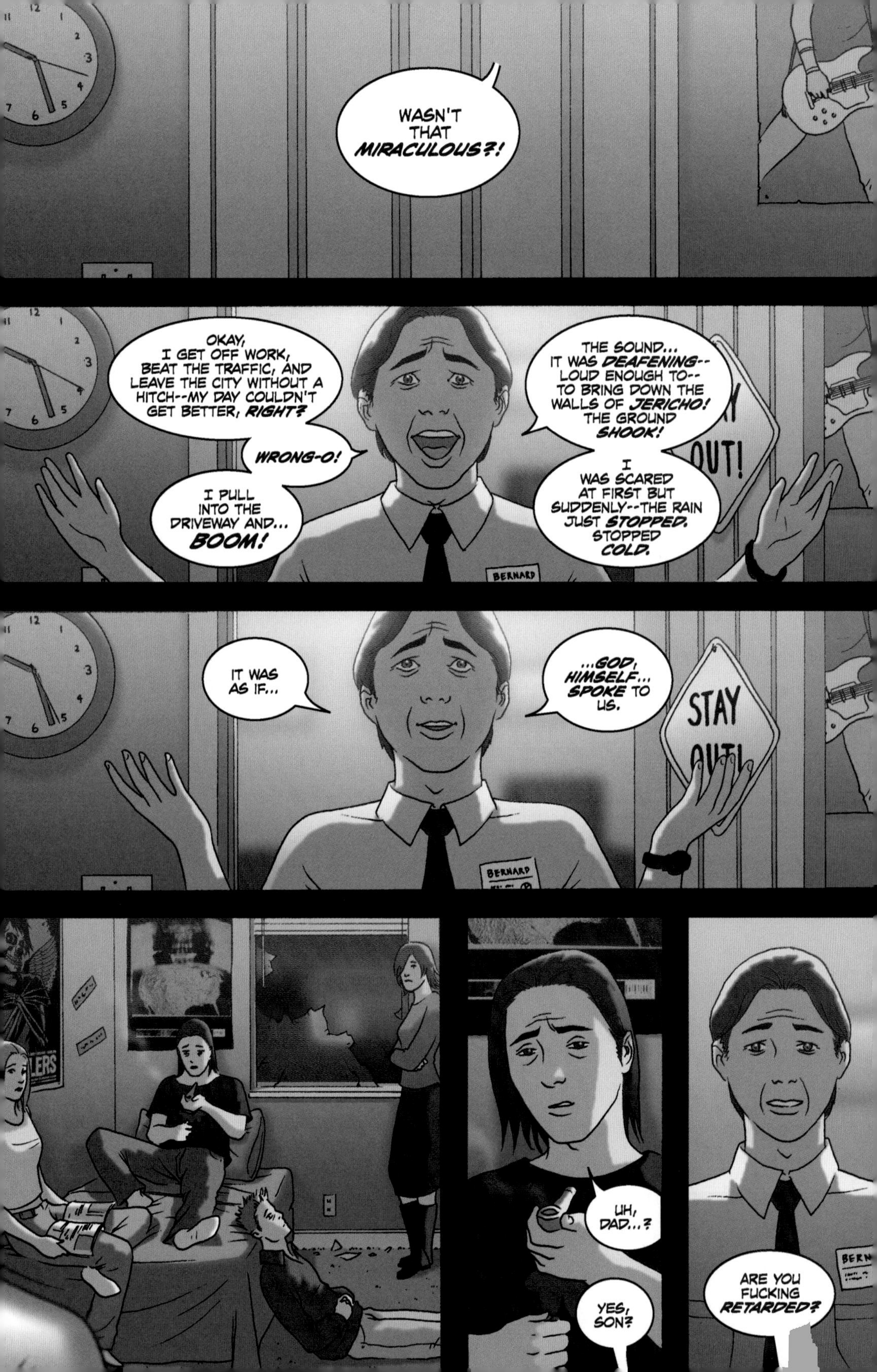
WASN'T THAT MIRACULOUS?!
OKAY, I GET OFF WORK, BEAT THE TRAFFIC, AND LEAVE THE CITY WITHOUT A HITCH--MY DAY COULDN'T GET BETTER, RIGHT?
WRONG-O!
I PULL INTO THE DRIVEWAY AND... BOOM!
THE SOUND... IT WAS DEAFENING--LOUD ENOUGH TO--TO BRING DOWN THE WALLS OF JERICHO! THE GROUND SHOOK!
I WAS SCARED AT FIRST BUT SUDDENLY--THE RAIN JUST STOPPED. STOPPED COLD.
BERNARD
IT WAS AS IF...
...GOD, HIMSELF... SPOKE TO US.
STAY OUT!
BERNARD
UH, DAD...?
YES, SON?
ARE YOU FUCKING RETARDED?

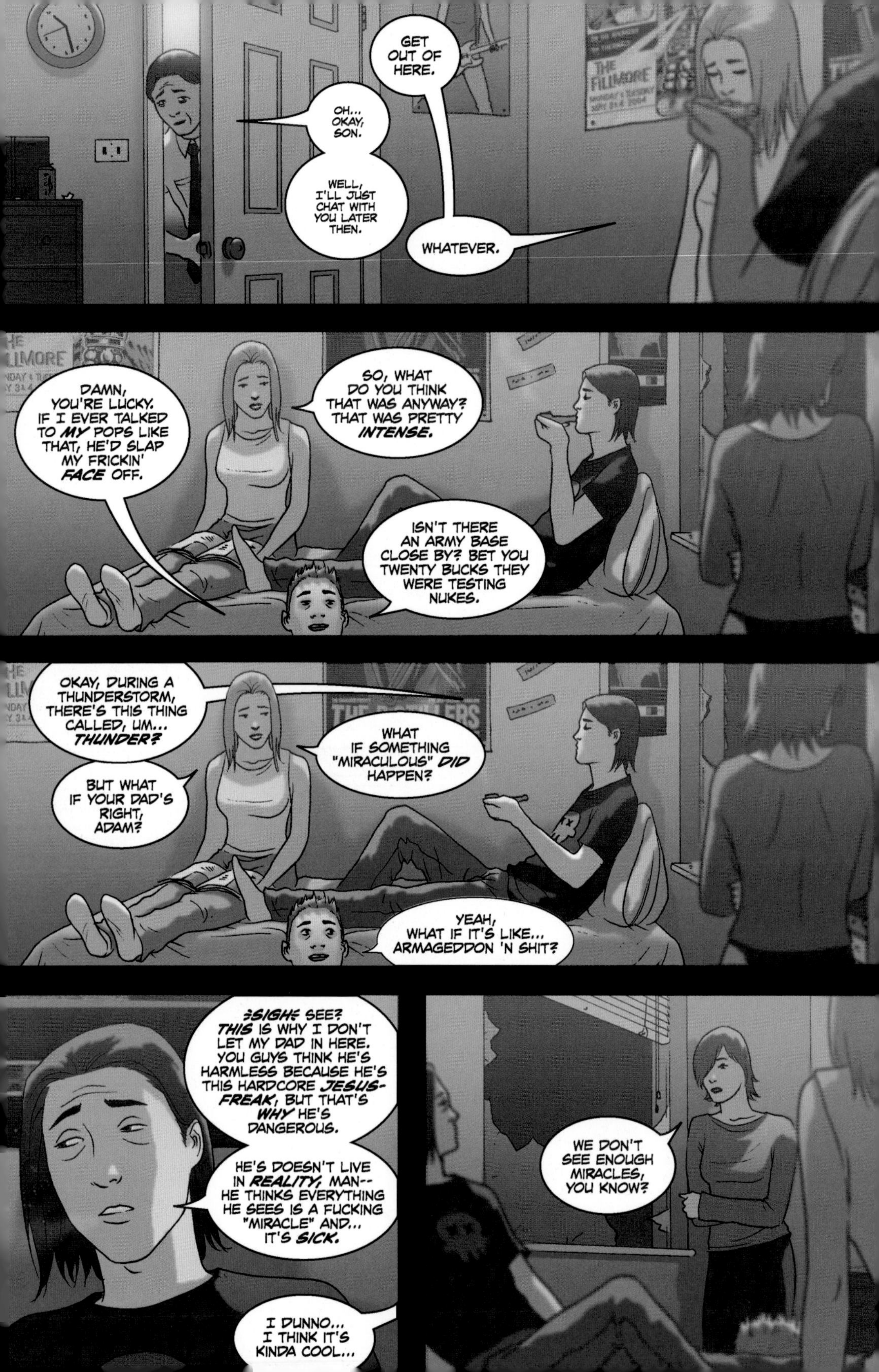
GET OUT OF HERE.
OH... OKAY, SON.
WELL, I'LL JUST CHAT WITH YOU LATER THEN.
WHATEVER.
THE FILLMORE
DAMN, YOU'RE LUCKY. IF I EVER TALKED TO MY POPS LIKE THAT, HE'D SLAP MY FRICKIN' FACE OFF.
SO, WHAT DO YOU THINK THAT WAS ANYWAY? THAT WAS PRETTY INTENSE.
ISN'T THERE AN ARMY BASE CLOSE BY? BET YOU TWENTY BUCKS THEY WERE TESTING NUKES.
OKAY, DURING A THUNDERSTORM, THERE'S THIS THING CALLED, UM... THUNDER?
WHAT IF SOMETHING "MIRACULOUS" DID HAPPEN?
BUT WHAT IF YOUR DAD'S RIGHT, ADAM?
YEAH, WHAT IF IT'S LIKE... ARMAGEDDON 'N SHIT?
:SIGH: SEE? THIS IS WHY I DON'T LET MY DAD IN HERE. YOU GUYS THINK HE'S HARMLESS BECAUSE HE'S THIS HARDCORE JESUS-FREAK, BUT THAT'S WHY HE'S DANGEROUS.
HE'S DOESN'T LIVE IN REALITY, MAN-- HE THINKS EVERYTHING HE SEES IS A FUCKING "MIRACLE" AND... IT'S SICK.
I DUNNO... I THINK IT'S KINDA COOL...
WE DON'T SEE ENOUGH MIRACLES, YOU KNOW?

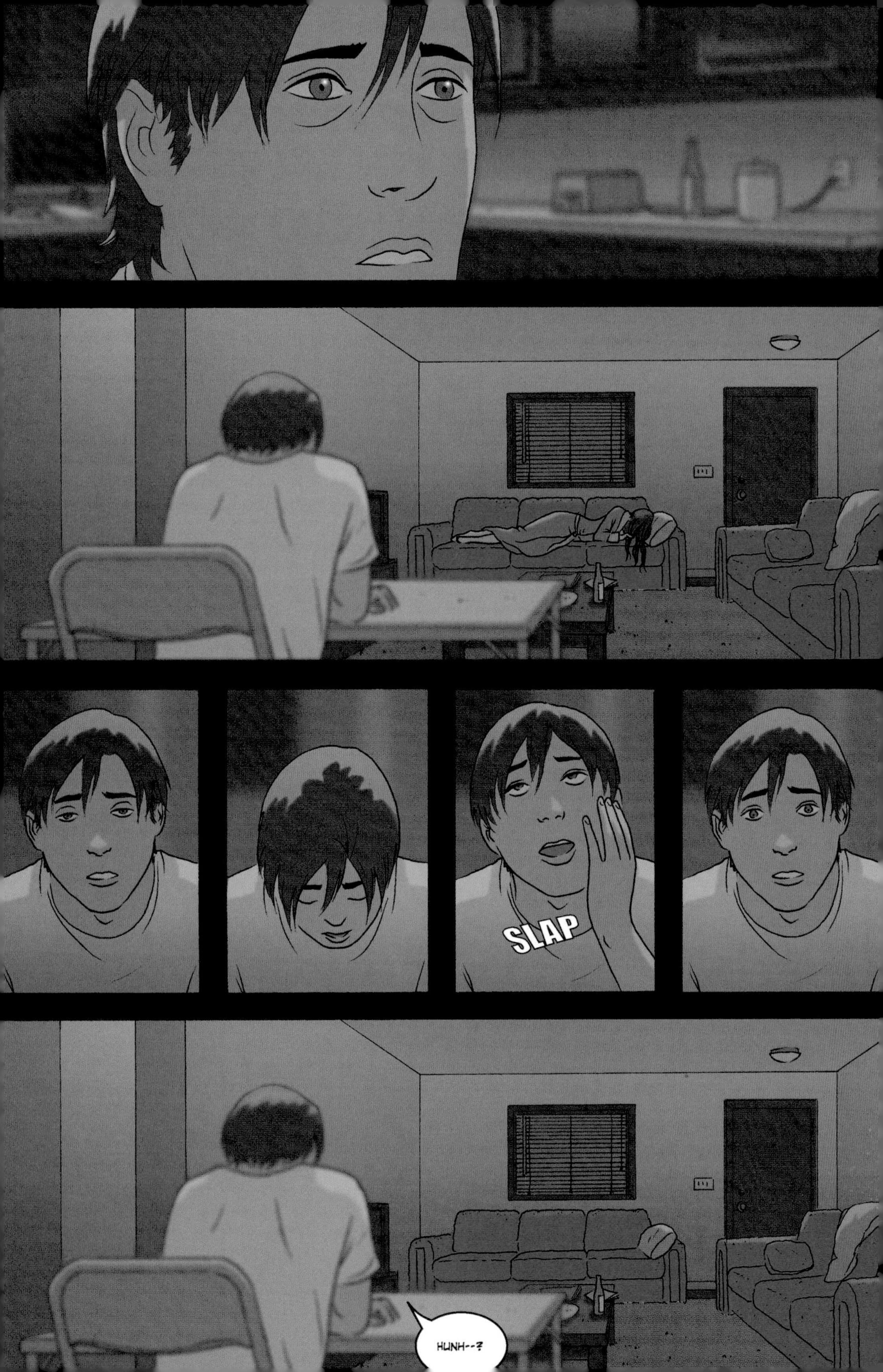
SLAP
HUNH--?

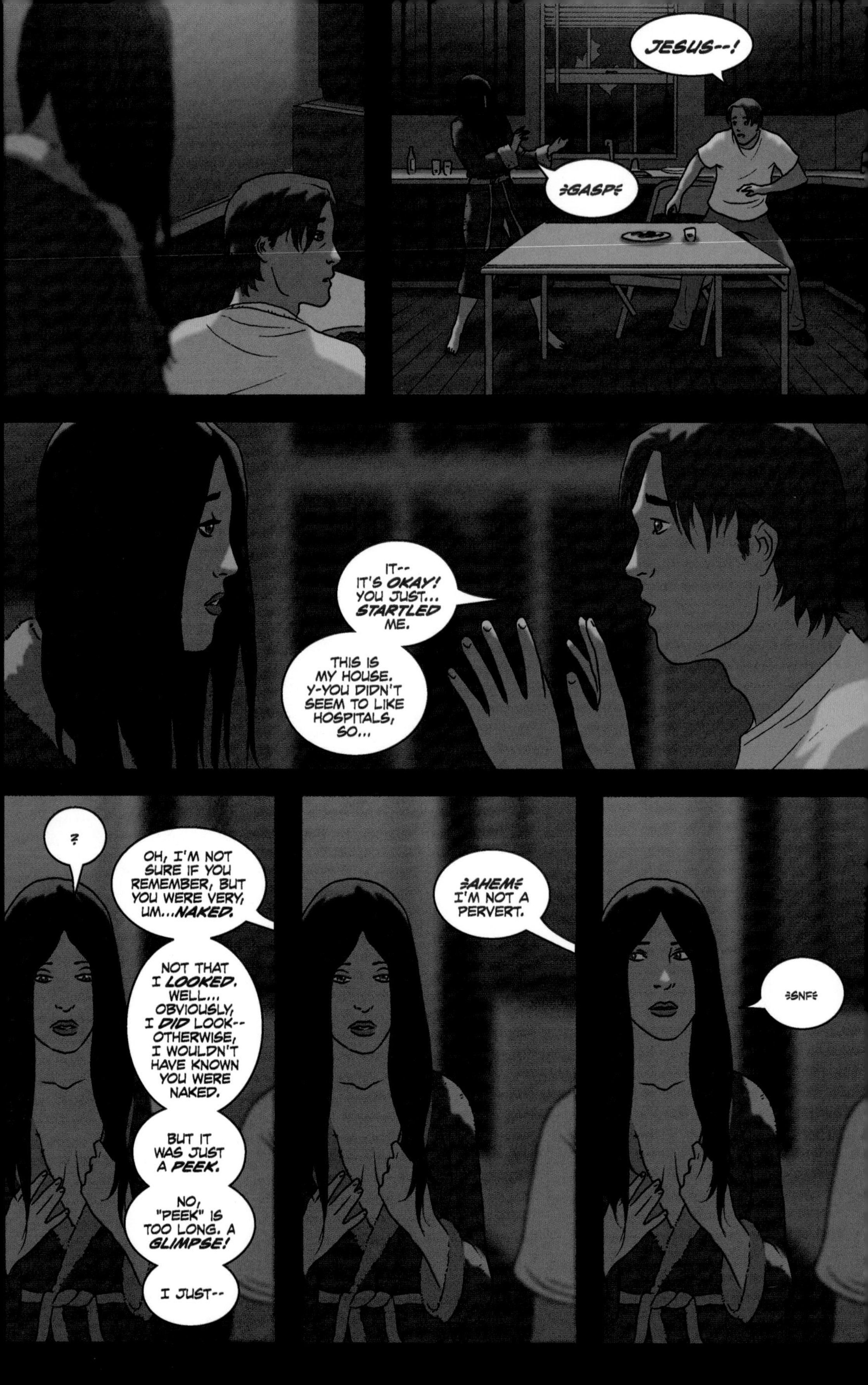
JESUS--!
GASP
IT-- IT'S OKAY! YOU JUST... STARTLED ME.
THIS IS MY HOUSE. Y-YOU DIDN'T SEEM TO LIKE HOSPITALS, SO...
?
OH, I'M NOT SURE IF YOU REMEMBER, BUT YOU WERE VERY, UM...NAKED.
NOT THAT I LOOKED. WELL... OBVIOUSLY, I DID LOOK-- OTHERWISE, I WOULDN'T HAVE KNOWN YOU WERE NAKED.
BUT IT WAS JUST A PEEK.
NO, "PEEK" IS TOO LONG. A GLIMPSE!
I JUST--
AHEM
I'M NOT A PERVERT.
SNF

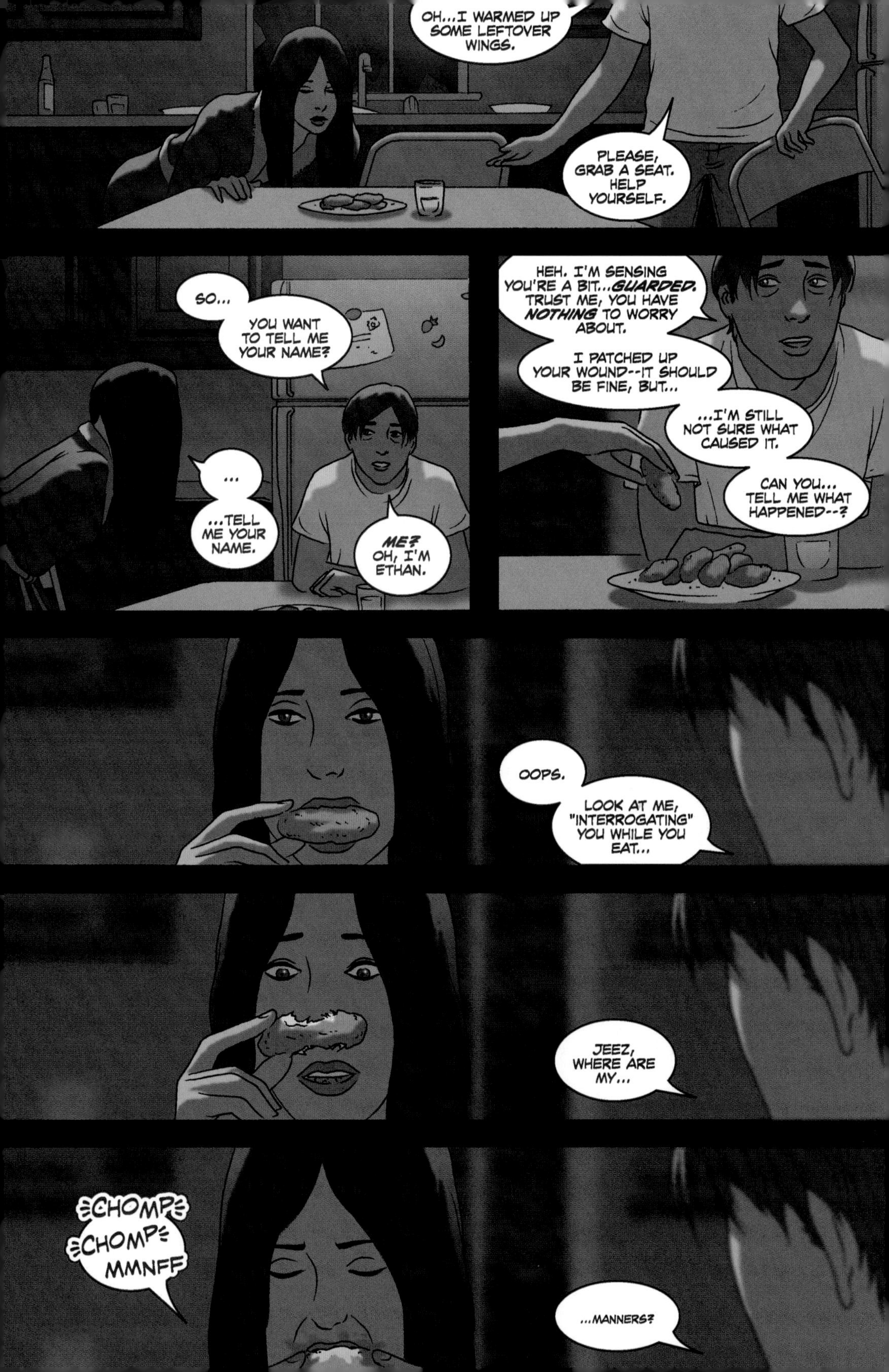
OH...I WARMED UP SOME LEFTOVER WINGS.
PLEASE, GRAB A SEAT. HELP YOURSELF.
SO...
YOU WANT TO TELL ME YOUR NAME?
...
...TELL ME YOUR NAME.
ME? OH, I'M ETHAN.
HEH. I'M SENSING YOU'RE A BIT...GUARDED. TRUST ME, YOU HAVE NOTHING TO WORRY ABOUT.
I PATCHED UP YOUR WOUND--IT SHOULD BE FINE, BUT...
...I'M STILL NOT SURE WHAT CAUSED IT.
CAN YOU... TELL ME WHAT HAPPENED--?
OOPS.
LOOK AT ME, "INTERROGATING" YOU WHILE YOU EAT...
JEEZ, WHERE ARE MY...
CHOMP CHOMP MMNFF
...MANNERS?

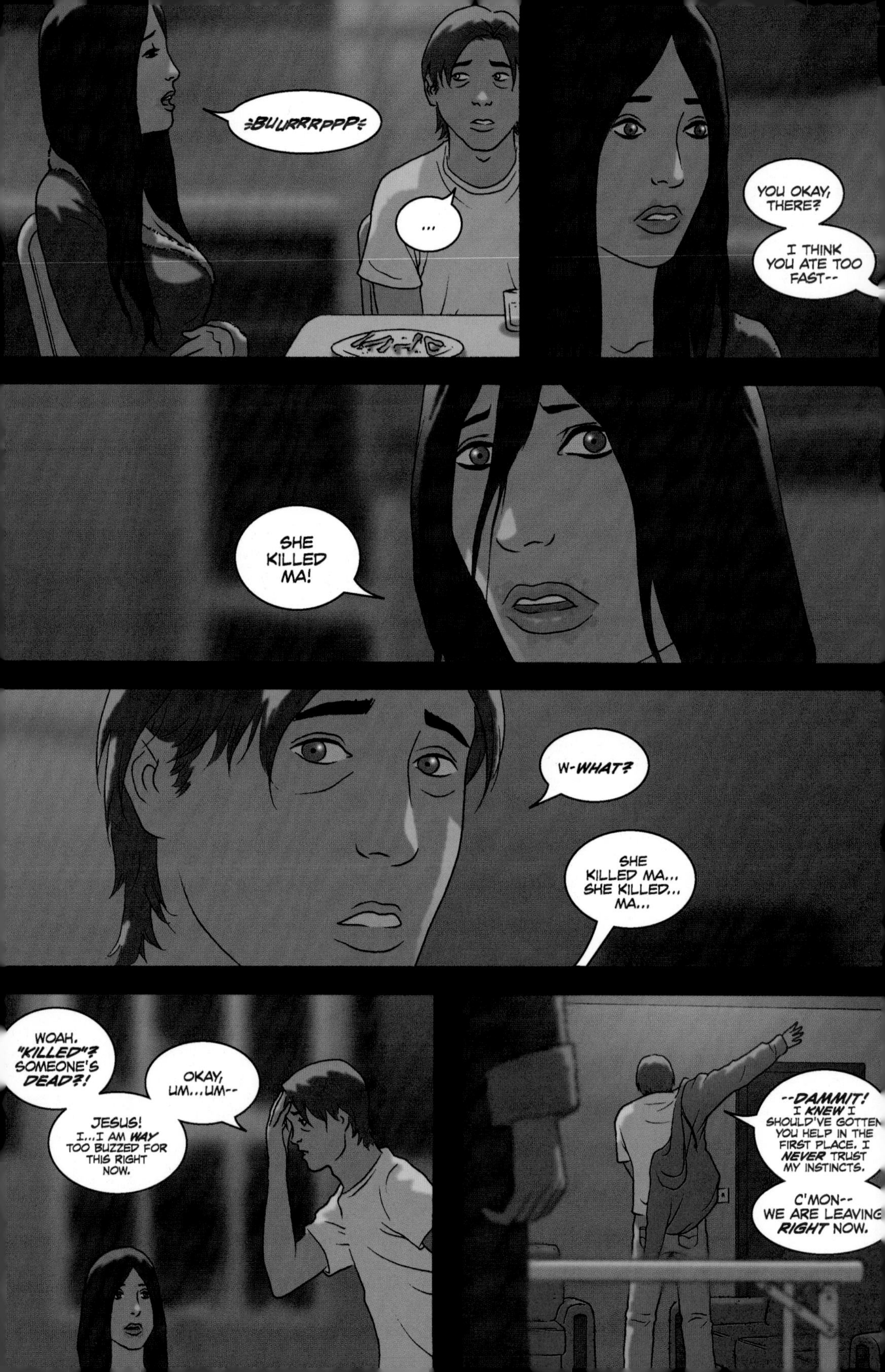
BUURRRPPP
...
YOU OKAY, THERE?
I THINK YOU ATE TOO FAST--
SHE KILLED MA!
W-WHAT?
SHE KILLED MA... SHE KILLED... MA...
WOAH. "KILLED"? SOMEONE'S DEAD?!
OKAY, UM...UM--
JESUS! I...I AM WAY TOO BUZZED FOR THIS RIGHT NOW.
--DAMMIT! I KNEW I SHOULD'VE GOTTEN YOU HELP IN THE FIRST PLACE. I NEVER TRUST MY INSTINCTS.
C'MON-- WE ARE LEAVING RIGHT NOW.

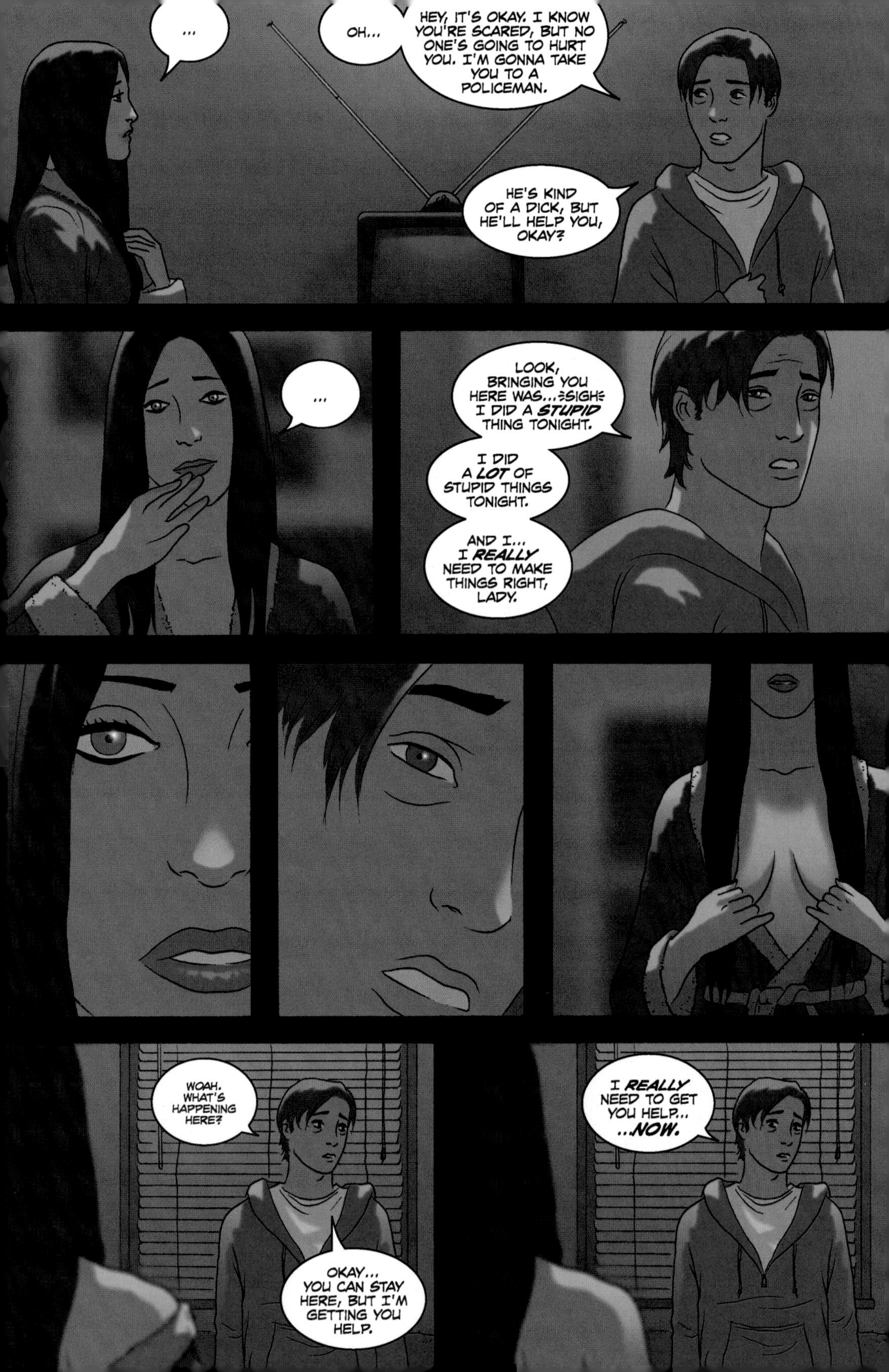
...
OH...
HEY, IT'S OKAY. I KNOW YOU'RE SCARED, BUT NO ONE'S GOING TO HURT YOU. I'M GONNA TAKE YOU TO A POLICEMAN.
HE'S KIND OF A DICK, BUT HE'LL HELP YOU, OKAY?
...
LOOK, BRINGING YOU HERE WAS... ≈SIGH≈ I DID A STUPID THING TONIGHT.
I DID A LOT OF STUPID THINGS TONIGHT.
AND I... I REALLY NEED TO MAKE THINGS RIGHT, LADY.
WOAH. WHAT'S HAPPENING HERE?
OKAY... YOU CAN STAY HERE, BUT I'M GETTING YOU HELP.
I REALLY NEED TO GET YOU HELP... ...NOW.

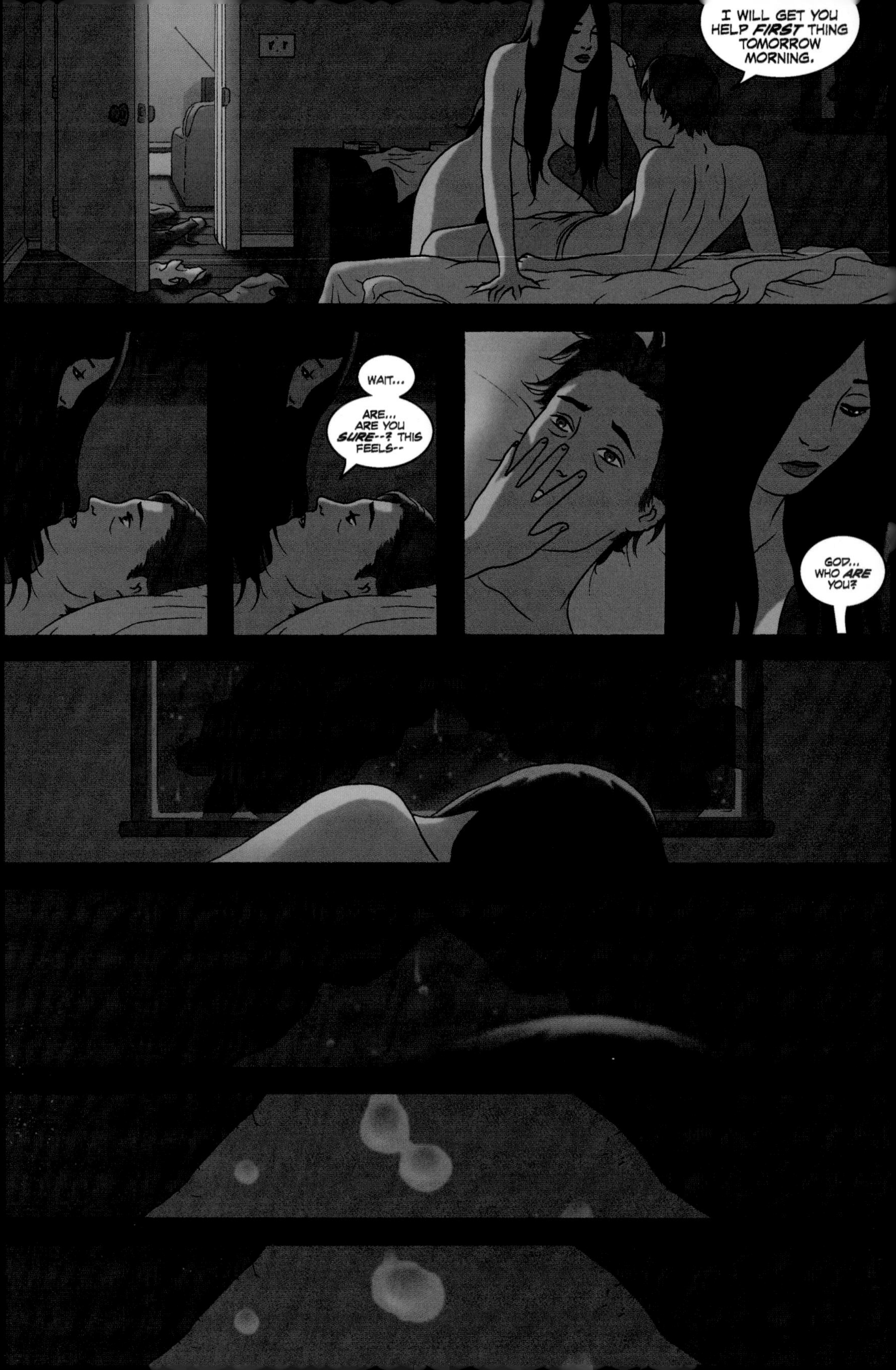
I WILL GET YOU HELP FIRST THING TOMORROW MORNING.
WAIT...
ARE... ARE YOU SURE--? THIS FEELS--
GOD... WHO ARE YOU?

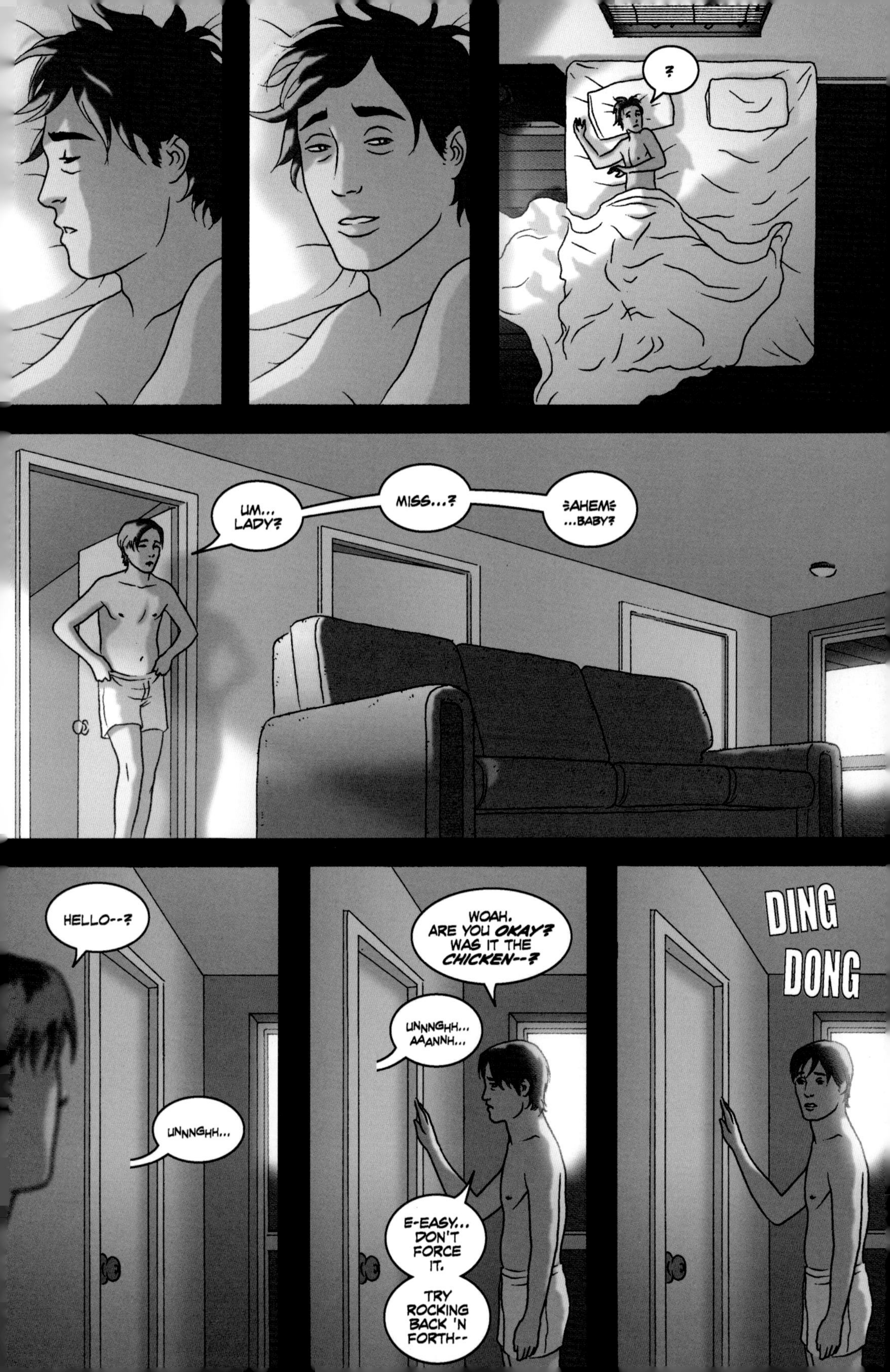
?
UM... LADY?
MISS...?
AHEM ...BABY?
HELLO--?
UNNNGHH...
WOAH. ARE YOU OKAY? WAS IT THE CHICKEN--?
UNNNGHH... AAANNH...
E-EASY... DON'T FORCE IT.
TRY ROCKING BACK 'N FORTH--
DING DONG

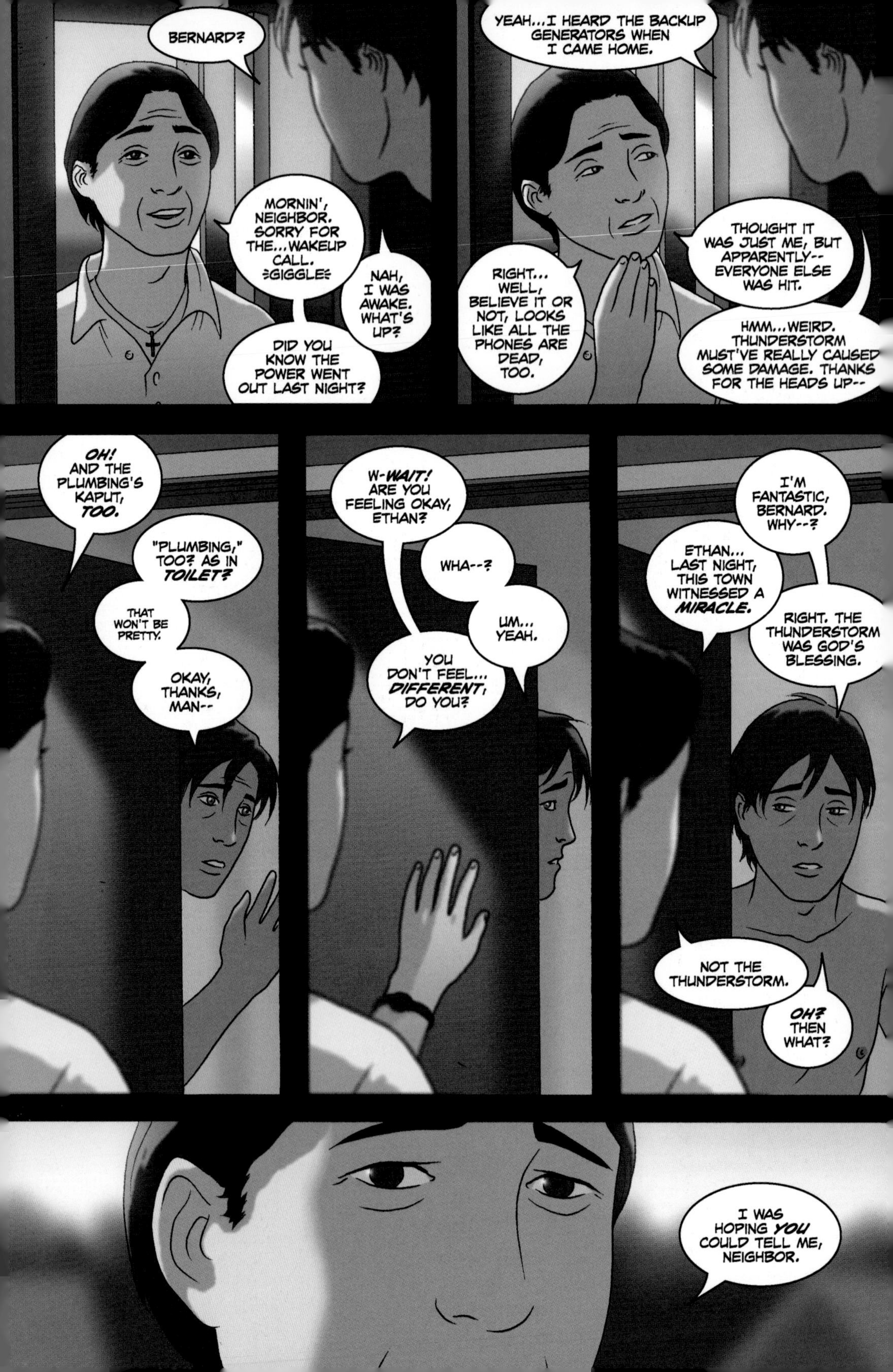
BERNARD?
MORNIN', NEIGHBOR. SORRY FOR THE...WAKEUP CALL. ≥GIGGLE≤
NAH, I WAS AWAKE. WHAT'S UP?
DID YOU KNOW THE POWER WENT OUT LAST NIGHT?
YEAH...I HEARD THE BACKUP GENERATORS WHEN I CAME HOME.
RIGHT... WELL, BELIEVE IT OR NOT, LOOKS LIKE ALL THE PHONES ARE DEAD, TOO.
THOUGHT IT WAS JUST ME, BUT APPARENTLY-- EVERYONE ELSE WAS HIT.
HMM...WEIRD. THUNDERSTORM MUST'VE REALLY CAUSED SOME DAMAGE. THANKS FOR THE HEADS UP--
OH! AND THE PLUMBING'S KAPUT, TOO.
"PLUMBING," TOO? AS IN TOILET?
THAT WON'T BE PRETTY.
OKAY, THANKS, MAN--
W-WAIT! ARE YOU FEELING OKAY, ETHAN?
WHA--?
UM... YEAH.
YOU DON'T FEEL... DIFFERENT, DO YOU?
I'M FANTASTIC, BERNARD. WHY--?
ETHAN... LAST NIGHT, THIS TOWN WITNESSED A MIRACLE.
RIGHT. THE THUNDERSTORM WAS GOD'S BLESSING.
NOT THE THUNDERSTORM.
OH? THEN WHAT?
I WAS HOPING YOU COULD TELL ME, NEIGHBOR.

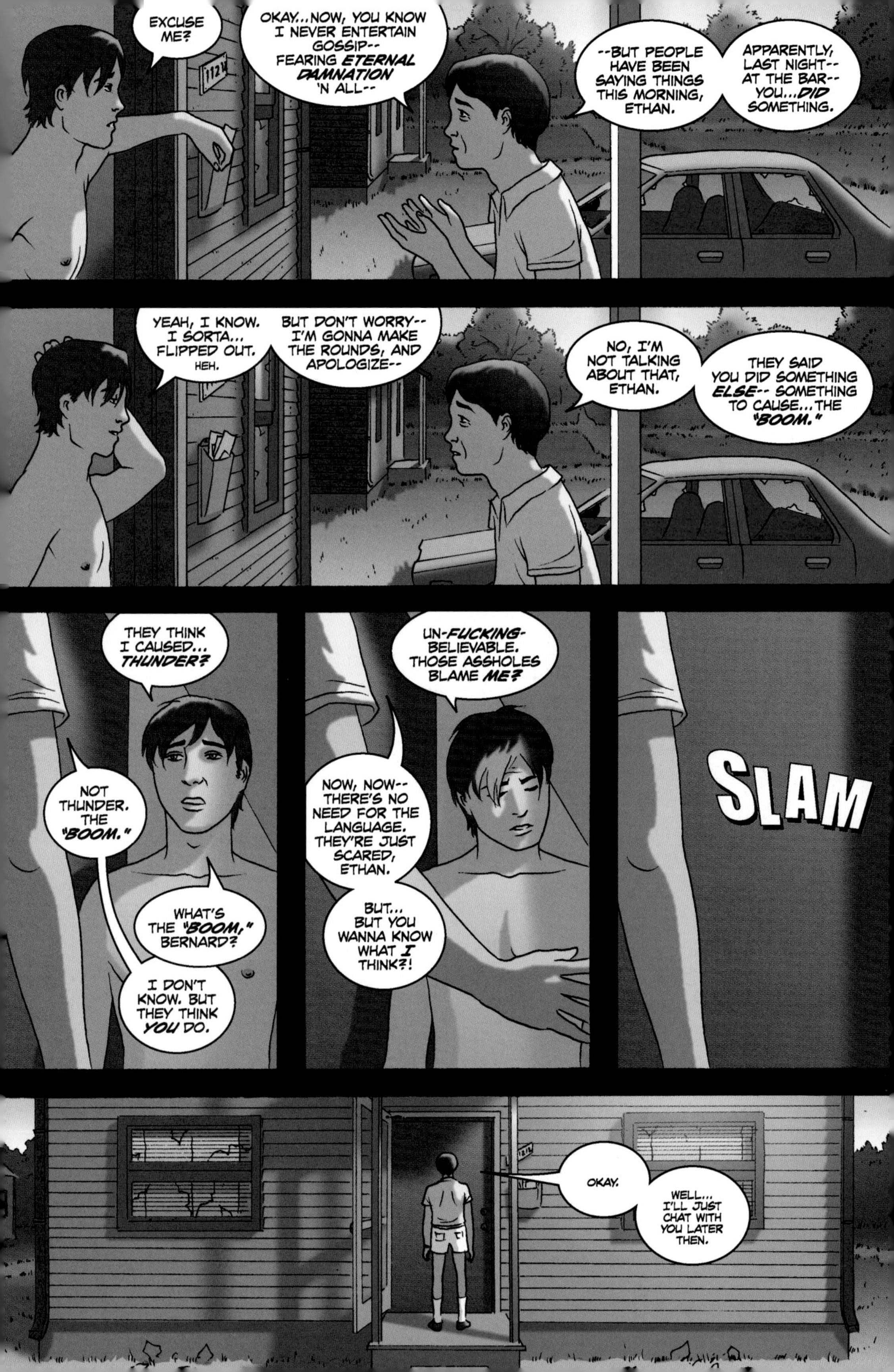
EXCUSE ME?
OKAY...NOW, YOU KNOW I NEVER ENTERTAIN GOSSIP-- FEARING ETERNAL DAMNATION 'N ALL--
--BUT PEOPLE HAVE BEEN SAYING THINGS THIS MORNING, ETHAN.
APPARENTLY, LAST NIGHT-- AT THE BAR-- YOU...DID SOMETHING.
YEAH, I KNOW. I SORTA... FLIPPED OUT. HEH.
BUT DON'T WORRY-- I'M GONNA MAKE THE ROUNDS, AND APOLOGIZE--
NO, I'M NOT TALKING ABOUT THAT, ETHAN.
THEY SAID YOU DID SOMETHING ELSE-- SOMETHING TO CAUSE...THE "BOOM."
THEY THINK I CAUSED... THUNDER?
NOT THUNDER. THE "BOOM."
WHAT'S THE "BOOM," BERNARD?
I DON'T KNOW. BUT THEY THINK YOU DO.
UN-FUCKING-BELIEVABLE. THOSE ASSHOLES BLAME ME?
NOW, NOW-- THERE'S NO NEED FOR THE LANGUAGE. THEY'RE JUST SCARED, ETHAN.
BUT... BUT YOU WANNA KNOW WHAT I THINK?!
SLAM
OKAY.
WELL... I'LL JUST CHAT WITH YOU LATER THEN.

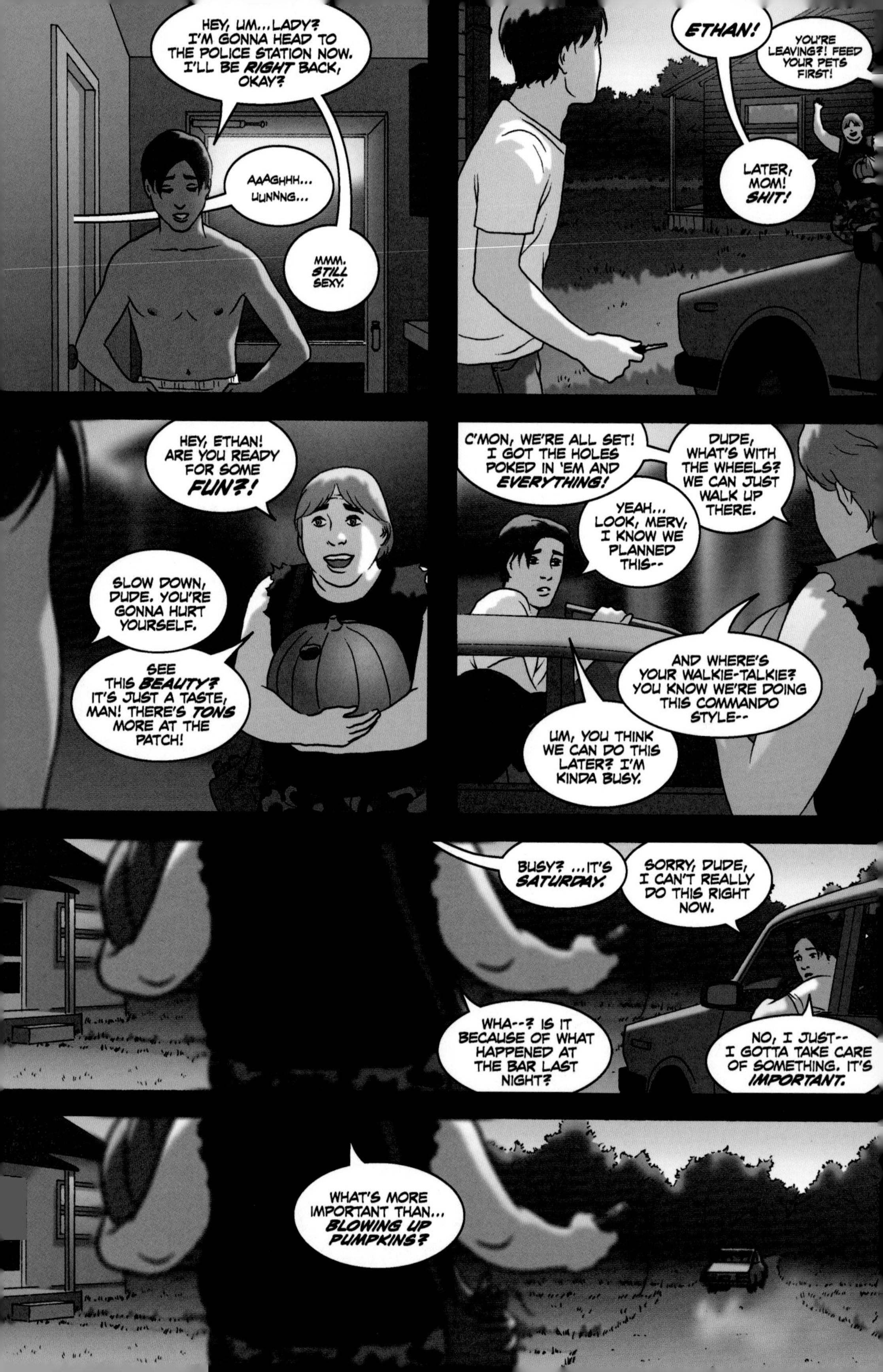
HEY, UM...LADY? I'M GONNA HEAD TO THE POLICE STATION NOW. I'LL BE RIGHT BACK, OKAY?
AAAGHHH... UUNNNG...
MMM. STILL SEXY.
ETHAN!
YOU'RE LEAVING?! FEED YOUR PETS FIRST!
LATER, MOM! SHIT!
HEY, ETHAN! ARE YOU READY FOR SOME FUN?!
SLOW DOWN, DUDE. YOU'RE GONNA HURT YOURSELF.
SEE THIS BEAUTY? IT'S JUST A TASTE, MAN! THERE'S TONS MORE AT THE PATCH!
C'MON, WE'RE ALL SET! I GOT THE HOLES POKED IN 'EM AND EVERYTHING!
DUDE, WHAT'S WITH THE WHEELS? WE CAN JUST WALK UP THERE.
YEAH... LOOK, MERV, I KNOW WE PLANNED THIS--
AND WHERE'S YOUR WALKIE-TALKIE? YOU KNOW WE'RE DOING THIS COMMANDO STYLE--
UM, YOU THINK WE CAN DO THIS LATER? I'M KINDA BUSY.
BUSY? ...IT'S SATURDAY.
SORRY, DUDE, I CAN'T REALLY DO THIS RIGHT NOW.
WHA--? IS IT BECAUSE OF WHAT HAPPENED AT THE BAR LAST NIGHT?
NO, I JUST-- I GOTTA TAKE CARE OF SOMETHING. IT'S IMPORTANT.
WHAT'S MORE IMPORTANT THAN... BLOWING UP PUMPKINS?

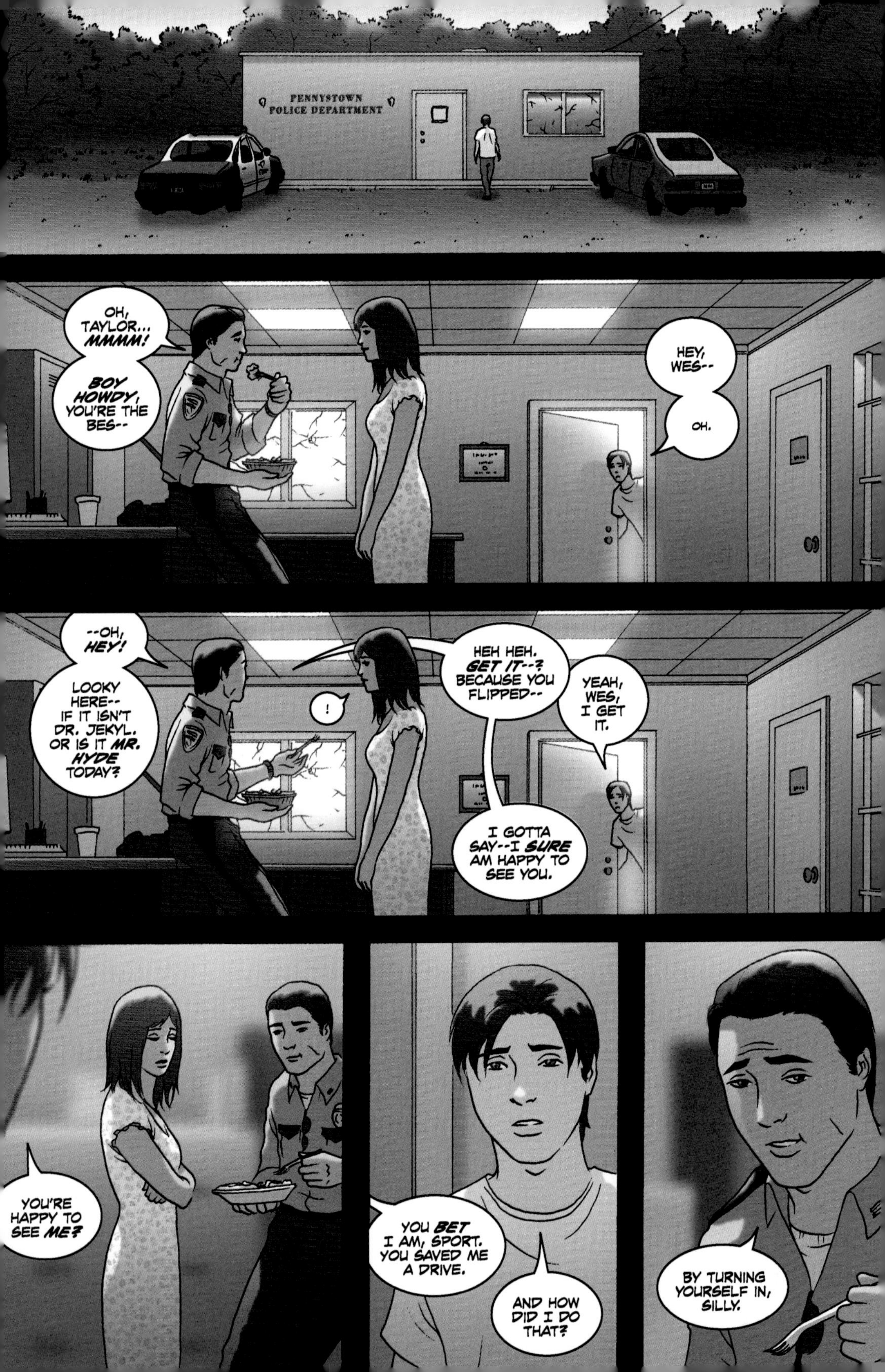
PENNYSTOWN POLICE DEPARTMENT
OH, TAYLOR... MMMM!
BOY HOWDY, YOU'RE THE BES--
HEY, WES--
OH.
--OH, HEY!
LOOKY HERE-- IF IT ISN'T DR. JEKYL. OR IS IT MR. HYDE TODAY?
!
HEH HEH. GET IT--? BECAUSE YOU FLIPPED--
YEAH, WES, I GET IT.
I GOTTA SAY--I SURE AM HAPPY TO SEE YOU.
YOU'RE HAPPY TO SEE ME?
YOU BET I AM, SPORT. YOU SAVED ME A DRIVE.
AND HOW DID I DO THAT?
BY TURNING YOURSELF IN, SILLY.

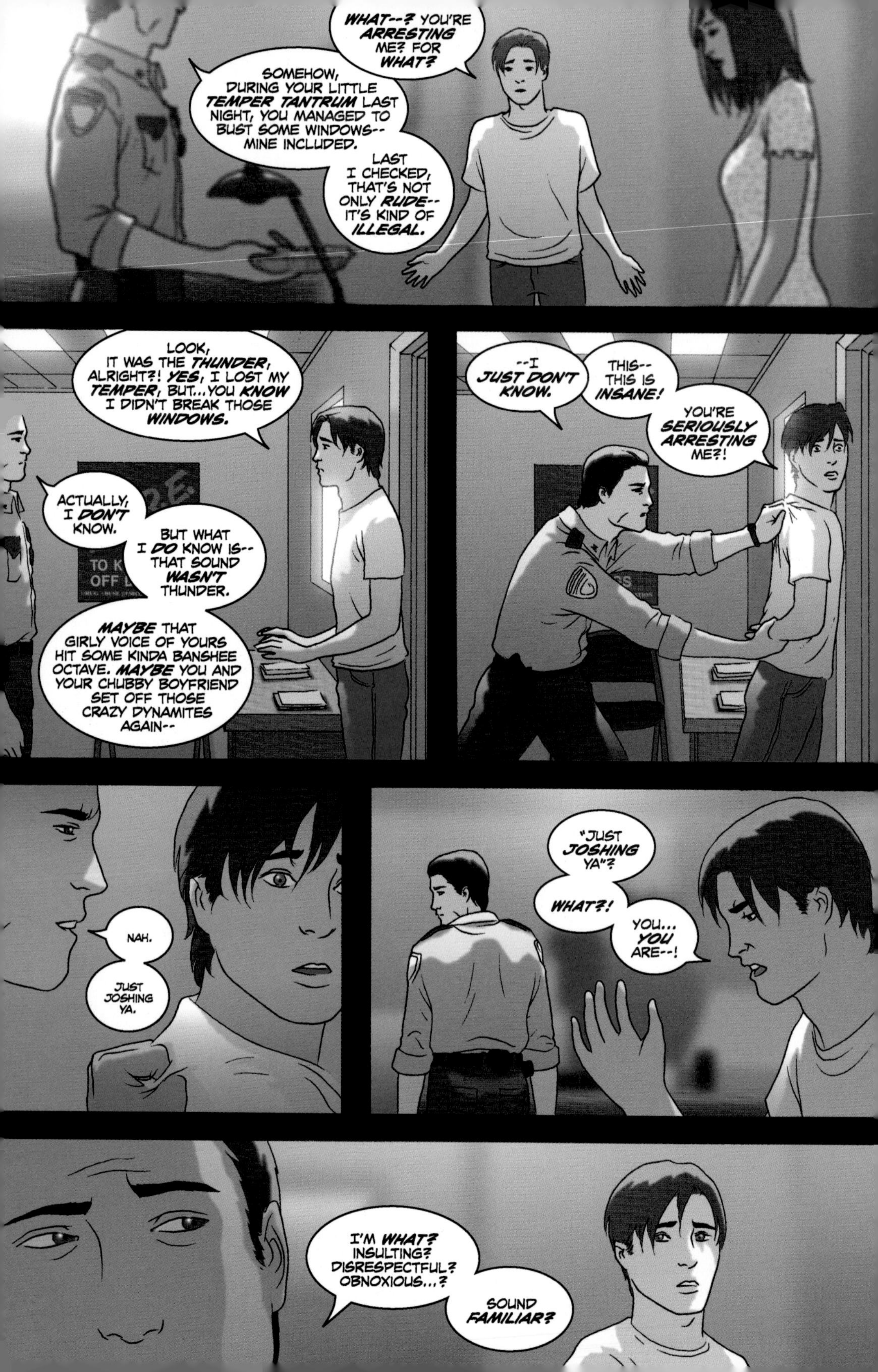
WHAT--? YOU'RE ARRESTING ME? FOR WHAT?
SOMEHOW, DURING YOUR LITTLE TEMPER TANTRUM LAST NIGHT, YOU MANAGED TO BUST SOME WINDOWS-- MINE INCLUDED.
LAST I CHECKED, THAT'S NOT ONLY RUDE-- IT'S KIND OF ILLEGAL.
LOOK, IT WAS THE THUNDER, ALRIGHT?! YES, I LOST MY TEMPER, BUT...YOU KNOW I DIDN'T BREAK THOSE WINDOWS.
ACTUALLY, I DON'T KNOW.
BUT WHAT I DO KNOW IS-- THAT SOUND WASN'T THUNDER.
MAYBE THAT GIRLY VOICE OF YOURS HIT SOME KINDA BANSHEE OCTAVE. MAYBE YOU AND YOUR CHUBBY BOYFRIEND SET OFF THOSE CRAZY DYNAMITES AGAIN--
--I JUST DON'T KNOW.
THIS-- THIS IS INSANE!
YOU'RE SERIOUSLY ARRESTING ME?!
NAH.
JUST JOSHING YA.
"JUST JOSHING YA"?
WHAT?!
YOU... YOU ARE--!
I'M WHAT? INSULTING? DISRESPECTFUL? OBNOXIOUS...?
SOUND FAMILIAR?

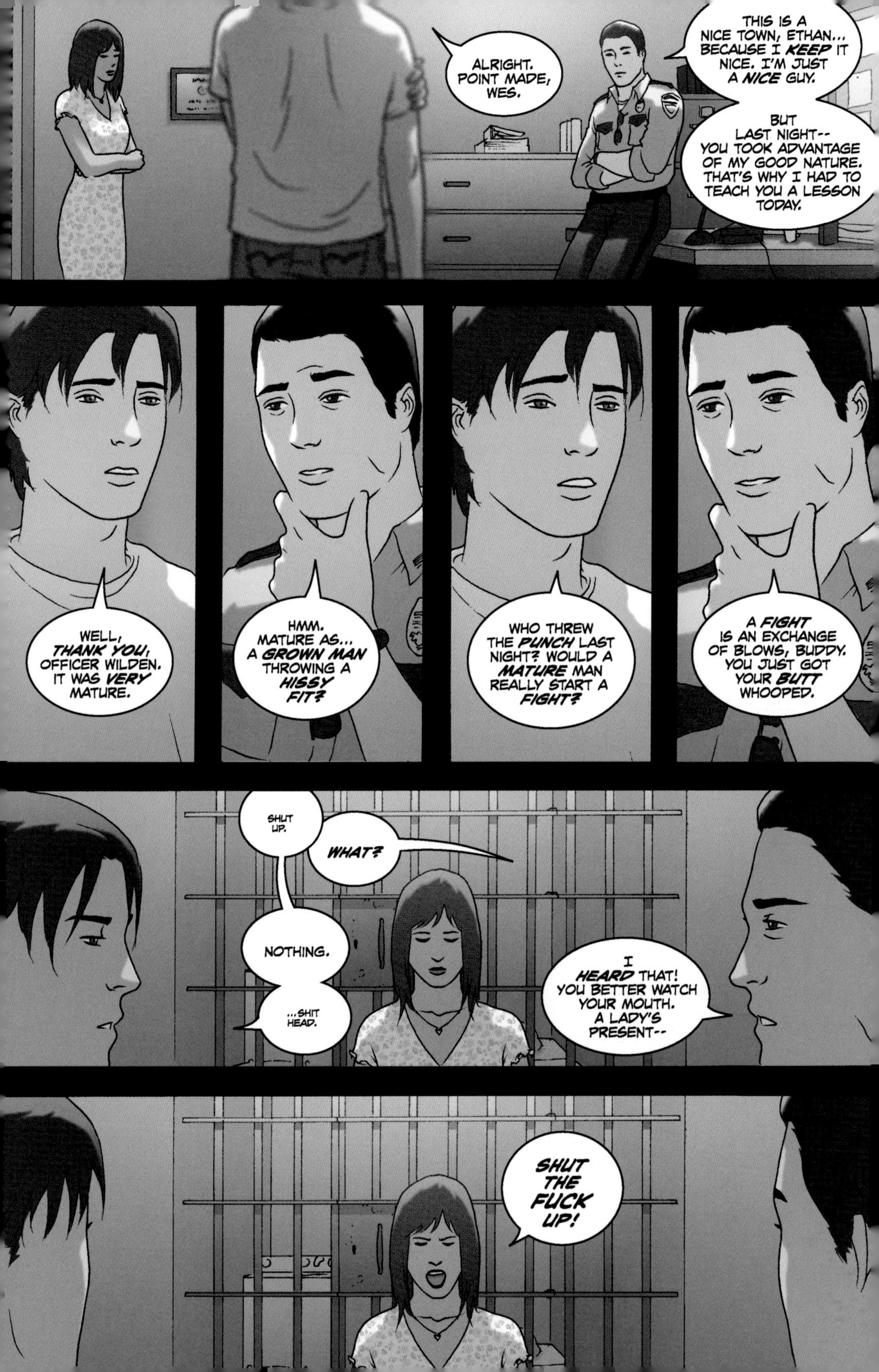
ALRIGHT. POINT MADE, WES.
THIS IS A NICE TOWN, ETHAN... BECAUSE I KEEP IT NICE. I'M JUST A NICE GUY.
BUT LAST NIGHT-- YOU TOOK ADVANTAGE OF MY GOOD NATURE. THAT'S WHY I HAD TO TEACH YOU A LESSON TODAY.
WELL, THANK YOU, OFFICER WILDEN. IT WAS VERY MATURE.
HMM. MATURE AS... A GROWN MAN THROWING A HISSY FIT?
WHO THREW THE PUNCH LAST NIGHT? WOULD A MATURE MAN REALLY START A FIGHT?
A FIGHT IS AN EXCHANGE OF BLOWS, BUDDY. YOU JUST GOT YOUR BUTT WHOOPED.
SHUT UP.
WHAT?
NOTHING.
...SHIT HEAD.
I HEARD THAT! YOU BETTER WATCH YOUR MOUTH. A LADY'S PRESENT--
SHUT THE FUCK UP!

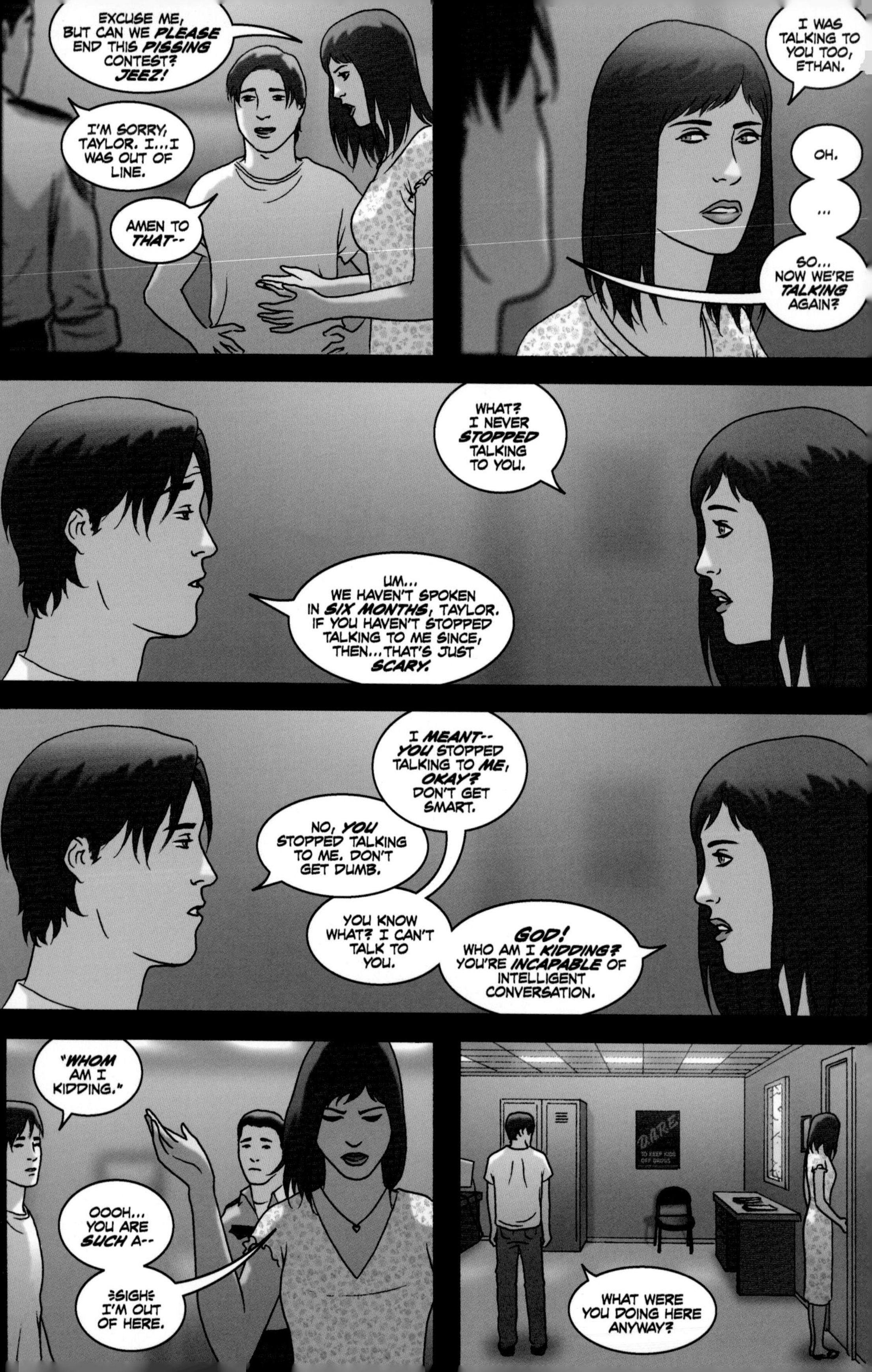
EXCUSE ME, BUT CAN WE PLEASE END THIS PISSING CONTEST? JEEZ!
I'M SORRY, TAYLOR. I...I WAS OUT OF LINE.
AMEN TO THAT--
I WAS TALKING TO YOU TOO, ETHAN.
OH.
...
SO... NOW WE'RE TALKING AGAIN?
WHAT? I NEVER STOPPED TALKING TO YOU.
UM... WE HAVEN'T SPOKEN IN SIX MONTHS, TAYLOR. IF YOU HAVEN'T STOPPED TALKING TO ME SINCE, THEN...THAT'S JUST SCARY.
I MEANT-- YOU STOPPED TALKING TO ME, OKAY? DON'T GET SMART.
NO, YOU STOPPED TALKING TO ME. DON'T GET DUMB.
YOU KNOW WHAT? I CAN'T TALK TO YOU.
GOD! WHO AM I KIDDING? YOU'RE INCAPABLE OF INTELLIGENT CONVERSATION.
"WHOM AM I KIDDING."
OOOH... YOU ARE SUCH A--
SIGH I'M OUT OF HERE.
D.A.R.E. TO KEEP KIDS OFF DRUGS
WHAT WERE YOU DOING HERE ANYWAY?

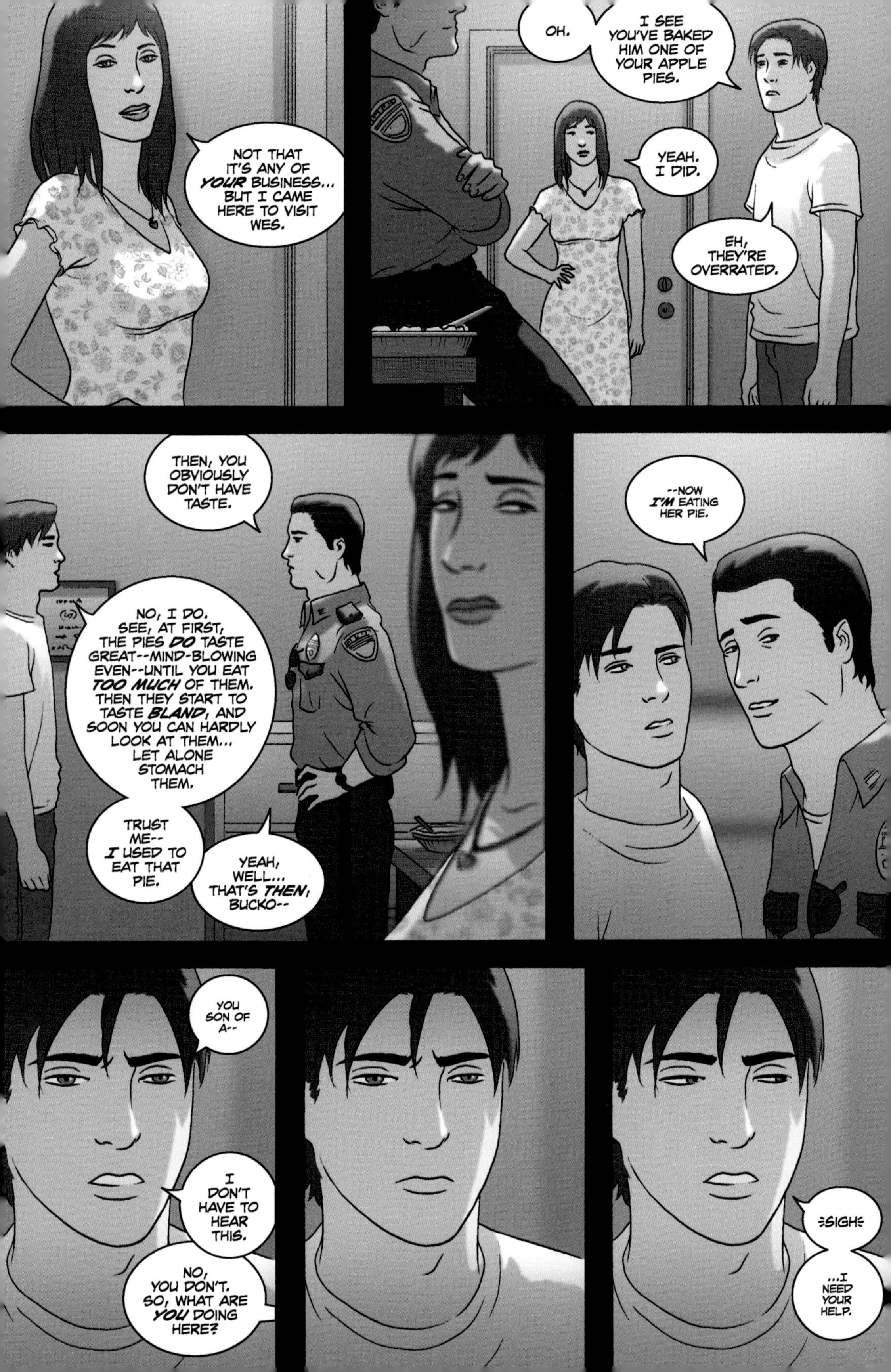
NOT THAT IT'S ANY OF YOUR BUSINESS... BUT I CAME HERE TO VISIT WES.
OH.
I SEE YOU'VE BAKED HIM ONE OF YOUR APPLE PIES.
YEAH. I DID.
EH, THEY'RE OVERRATED.
THEN, YOU OBVIOUSLY DON'T HAVE TASTE.
NO, I DO. SEE, AT FIRST, THE PIES DO TASTE GREAT--MIND-BLOWING EVEN--UNTIL YOU EAT TOO MUCH OF THEM. THEN THEY START TO TASTE BLAND, AND SOON YOU CAN HARDLY LOOK AT THEM... LET ALONE STOMACH THEM.
TRUST ME-- I USED TO EAT THAT PIE.
YEAH, WELL... THAT'S THEN, BUCKO--
--NOW I'M EATING HER PIE.
YOU SON OF A--
I DON'T HAVE TO HEAR THIS.
NO, YOU DON'T. SO, WHAT ARE YOU DOING HERE?
SIGH
...I NEED YOUR HELP.

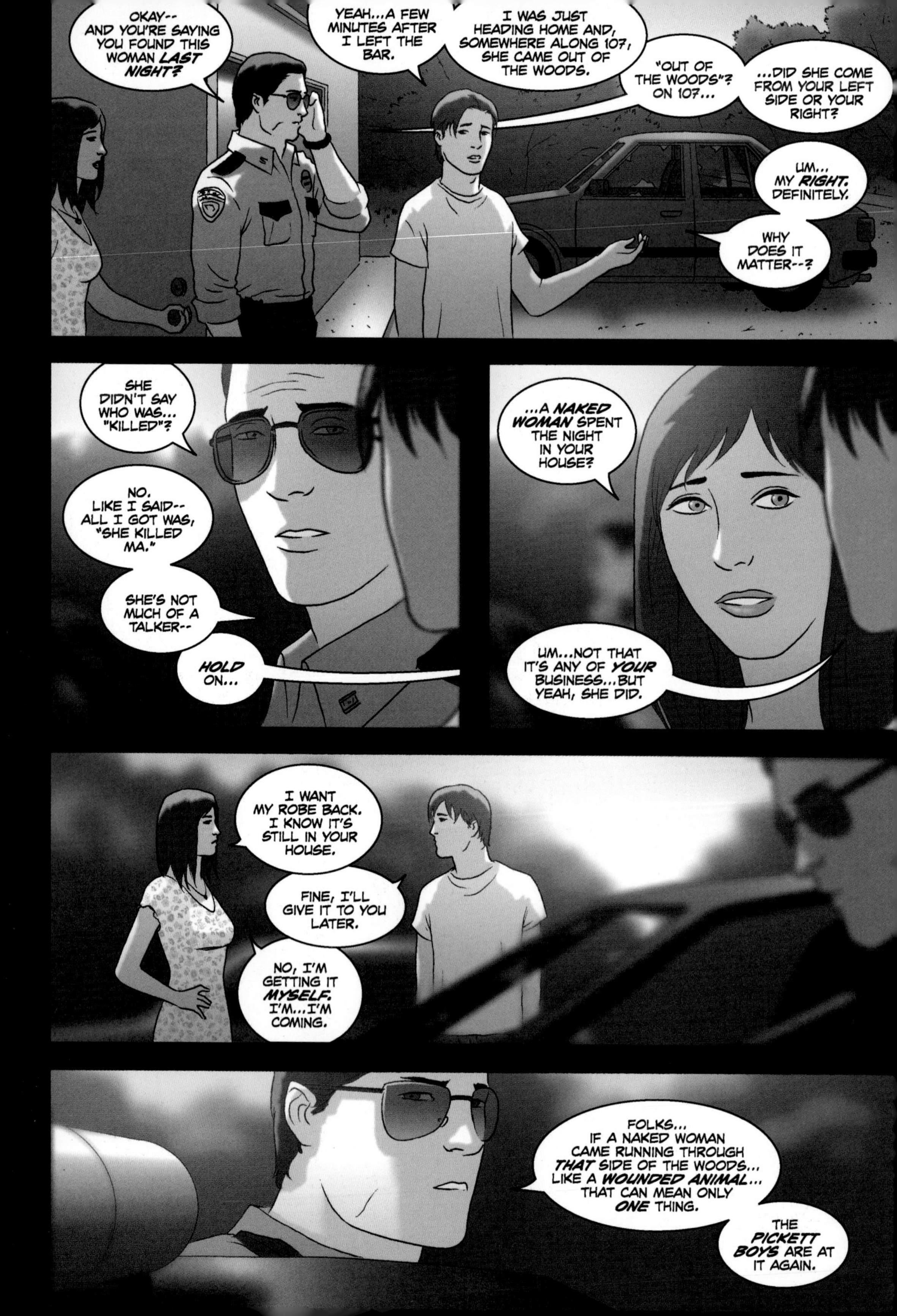
OKAY-- AND YOU'RE SAYING YOU FOUND THIS WOMAN LAST NIGHT?
YEAH...A FEW MINUTES AFTER I LEFT THE BAR.
I WAS JUST HEADING HOME AND, SOMEWHERE ALONG 107, SHE CAME OUT OF THE WOODS.
"OUT OF THE WOODS"? ON 107...
...DID SHE COME FROM YOUR LEFT SIDE OR YOUR RIGHT?
UM... MY RIGHT. DEFINITELY.
WHY DOES IT MATTER--?
SHE DIDN'T SAY WHO WAS... "KILLED"?
NO. LIKE I SAID-- ALL I GOT WAS, "SHE KILLED MA."
SHE'S NOT MUCH OF A TALKER--
HOLD ON...
...A NAKED WOMAN SPENT THE NIGHT IN YOUR HOUSE?
UM...NOT THAT IT'S ANY OF YOUR BUSINESS...BUT YEAH, SHE DID.
I WANT MY ROBE BACK. I KNOW IT'S STILL IN YOUR HOUSE.
FINE, I'LL GIVE IT TO YOU LATER.
NO, I'M GETTING IT MYSELF. I'M...I'M COMING.
FOLKS... IF A NAKED WOMAN CAME RUNNING THROUGH THAT SIDE OF THE WOODS... LIKE A WOUNDED ANIMAL... THAT CAN MEAN ONLY ONE THING.
THE PICKETT BOYS ARE AT IT AGAIN.

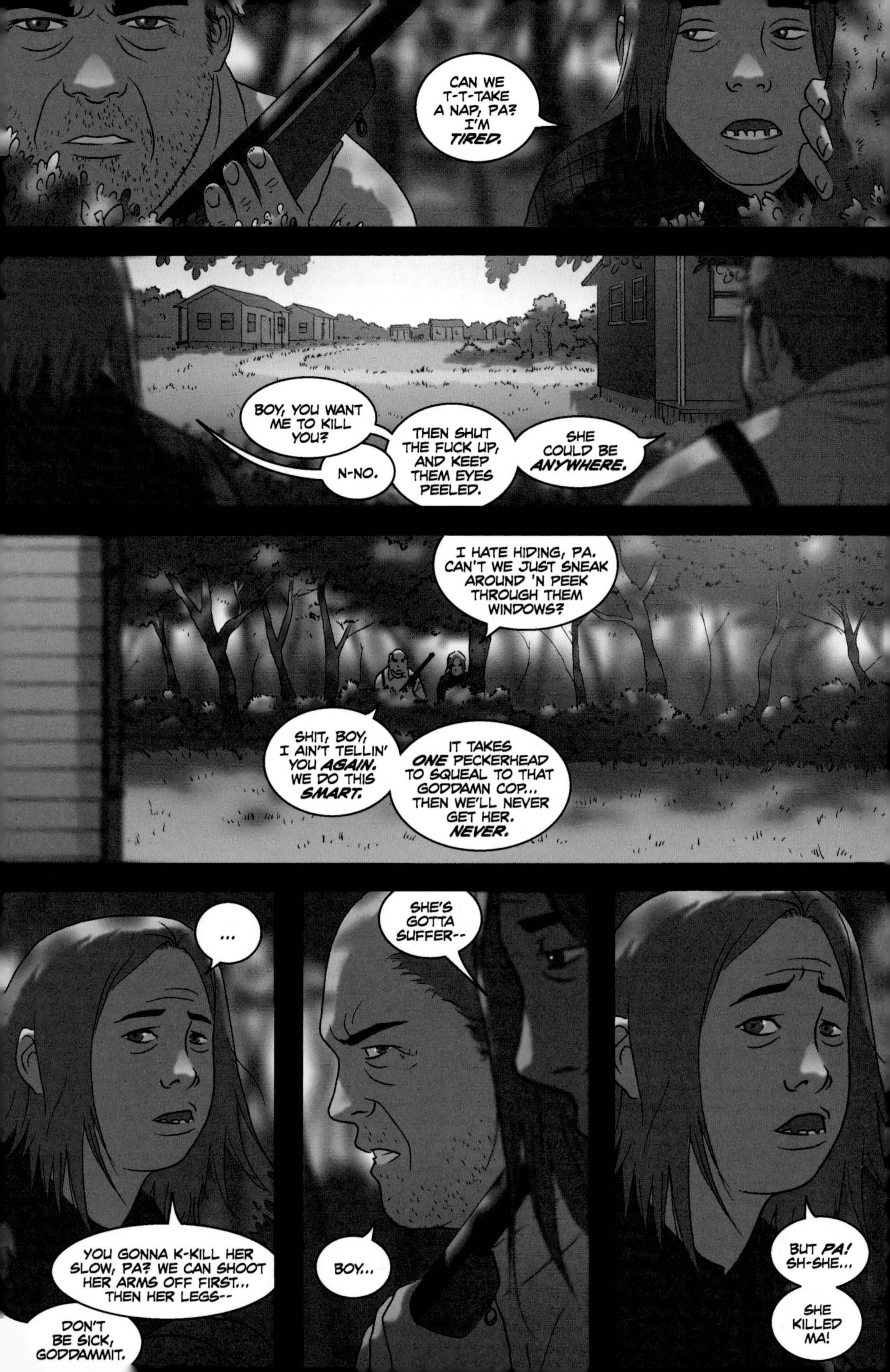
CAN WE T-T-TAKE A NAP, PA? I'M *TIRED.*
BOY, YOU WANT ME TO KILL YOU?
N-NO.
THEN SHUT THE FUCK UP, AND KEEP THEM EYES PEELED.
SHE COULD BE *ANYWHERE.*
I HATE HIDING, PA. CAN'T WE JUST SNEAK AROUND 'N PEEK THROUGH THEM WINDOWS?
SHIT, BOY, I AIN'T TELLIN' YOU *AGAIN.* WE DO THIS *SMART.*
IT TAKES *ONE* PECKERHEAD TO SQUEAL TO THAT GODDAMN COP... THEN WE'LL NEVER GET HER. *NEVER.*
...
YOU GONNA K-KILL HER SLOW, PA? WE CAN SHOOT HER ARMS OFF FIRST... THEN HER LEGS--
DON'T BE SICK, GODDAMMIT.
SHE'S GOTTA SUFFER--
BOY...
BUT *PA!* SH-SHE...
SHE KILLED MA!

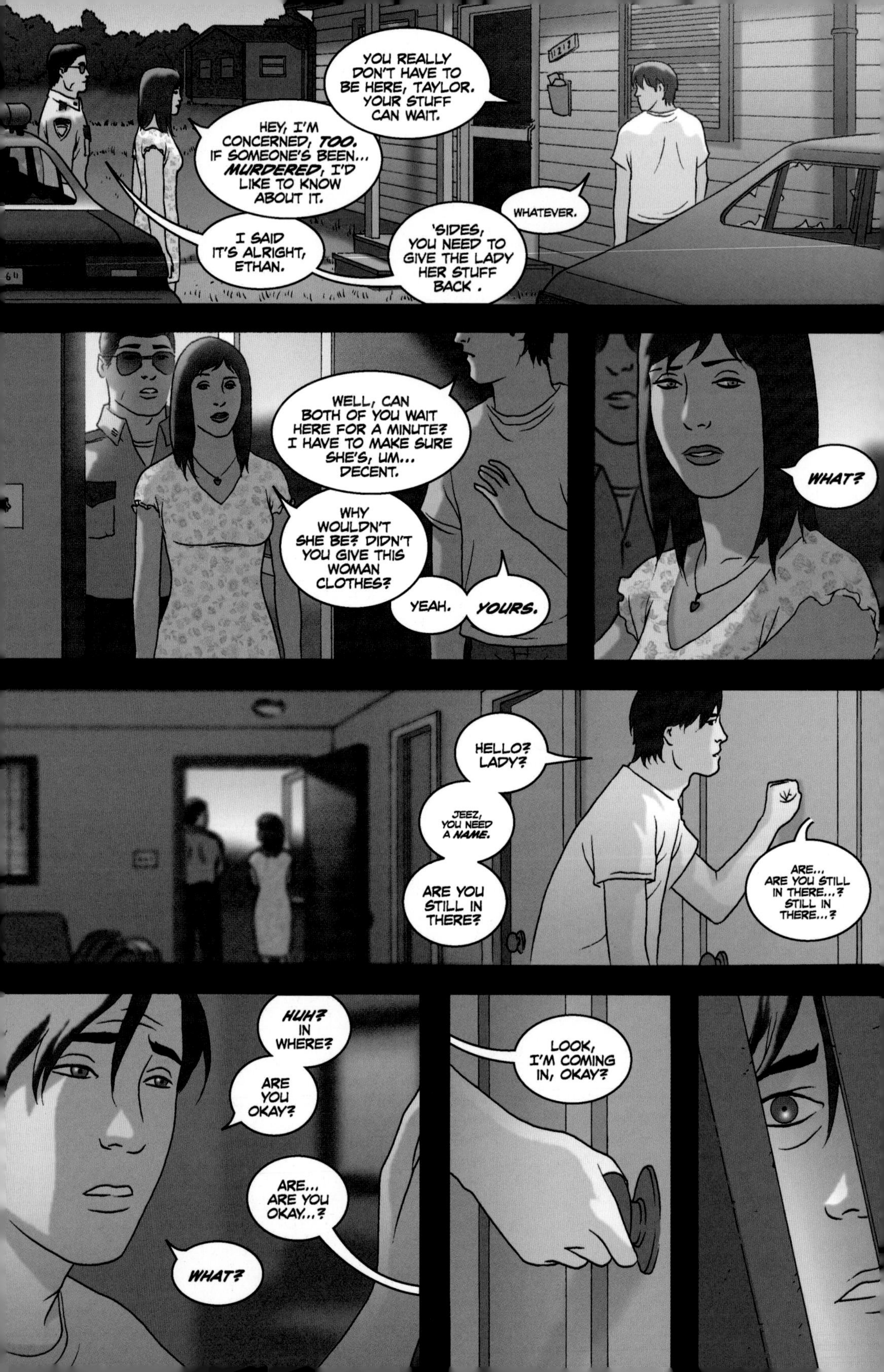
YOU REALLY DON'T HAVE TO BE HERE, TAYLOR. YOUR STUFF CAN WAIT.
HEY, I'M CONCERNED, TOO. IF SOMEONE'S BEEN... MURDERED, I'D LIKE TO KNOW ABOUT IT.
WHATEVER.
I SAID IT'S ALRIGHT, ETHAN.
'SIDES, YOU NEED TO GIVE THE LADY HER STUFF BACK .
WELL, CAN BOTH OF YOU WAIT HERE FOR A MINUTE? I HAVE TO MAKE SURE SHE'S, UM... DECENT.
WHY WOULDN'T SHE BE? DIDN'T YOU GIVE THIS WOMAN CLOTHES?
YEAH.
YOURS.
WHAT?
HELLO? LADY?
JEEZ, YOU NEED A NAME.
ARE YOU STILL IN THERE?
ARE... ARE YOU STILL IN THERE...? STILL IN THERE...?
HUH? IN WHERE?
ARE YOU OKAY?
ARE... ARE YOU OKAY...?
WHAT?
LOOK, I'M COMING IN, OKAY?

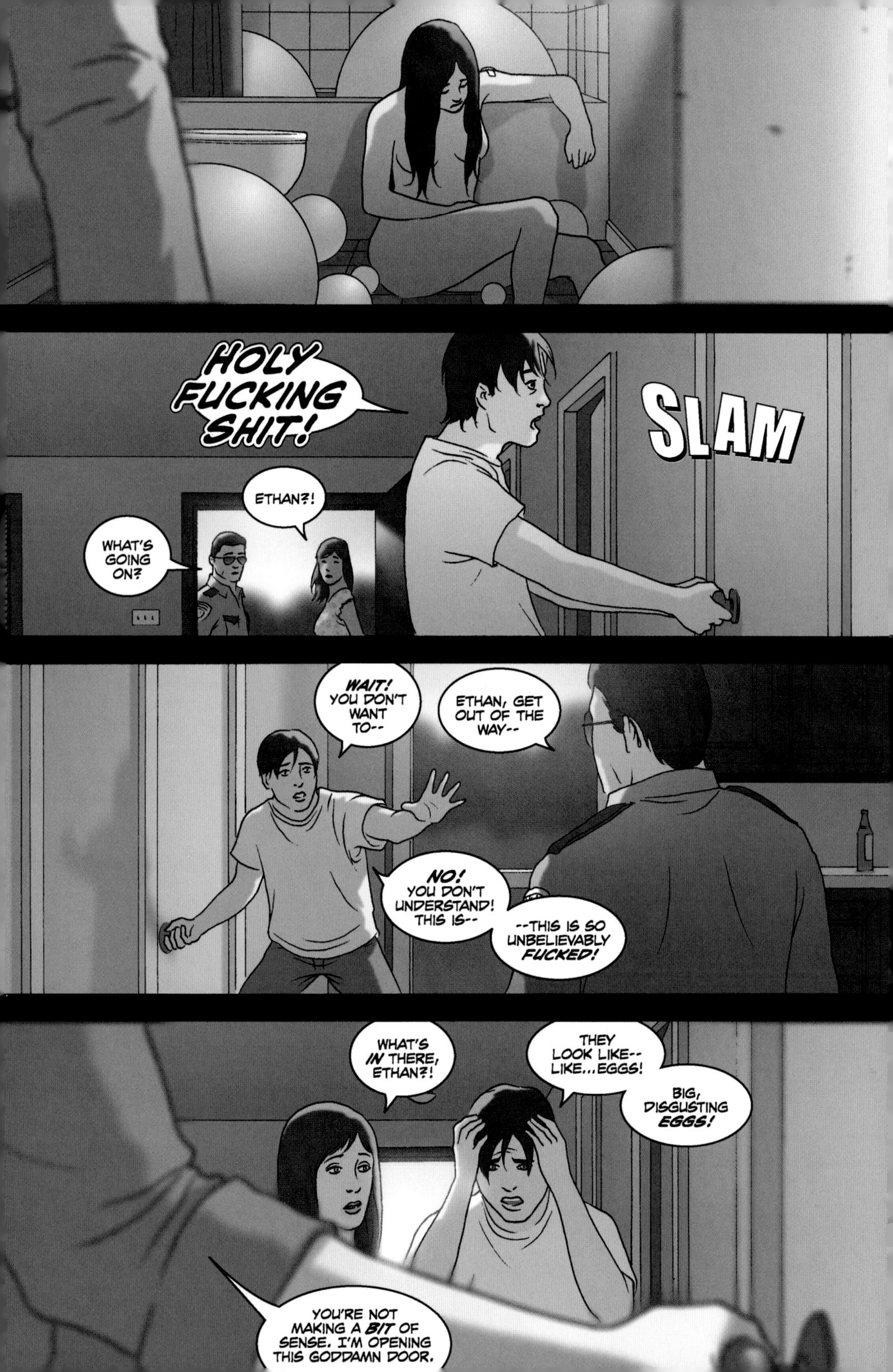

HOLY FUCKING SHIT!
SLAM
ETHAN?!
WHAT'S GOING ON?
WAIT! YOU DON'T WANT TO--
ETHAN, GET OUT OF THE WAY--
NO! YOU DON'T UNDERSTAND! THIS IS--
--THIS IS SO UNBELIEVABLY FUCKED!
WHAT'S IN THERE, ETHAN?!
THEY LOOK LIKE-- LIKE...EGGS!
BIG, DISGUSTING EGGS!
YOU'RE NOT MAKING A BIT OF SENSE. I'M OPENING THIS GODDAMN DOOR.

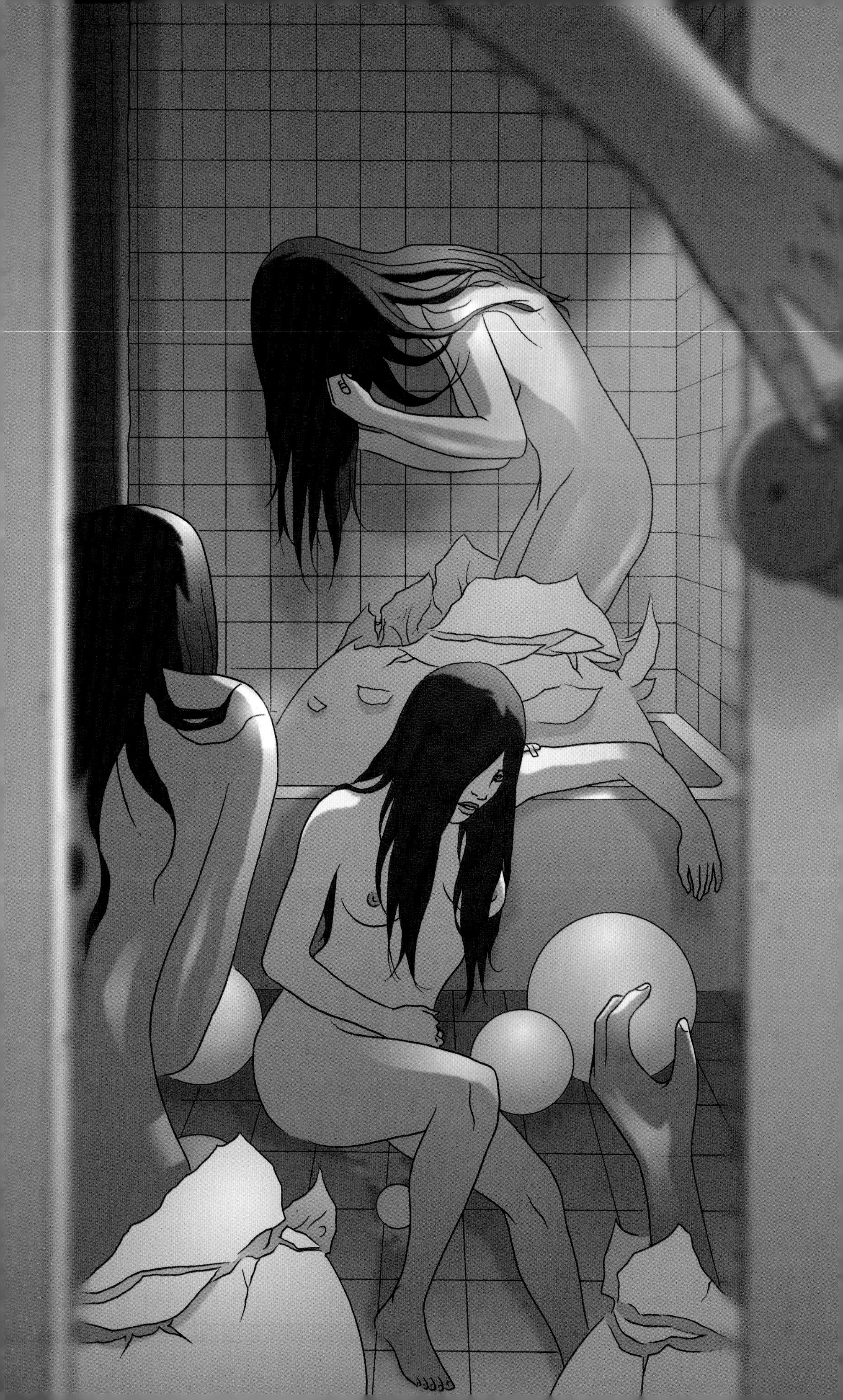

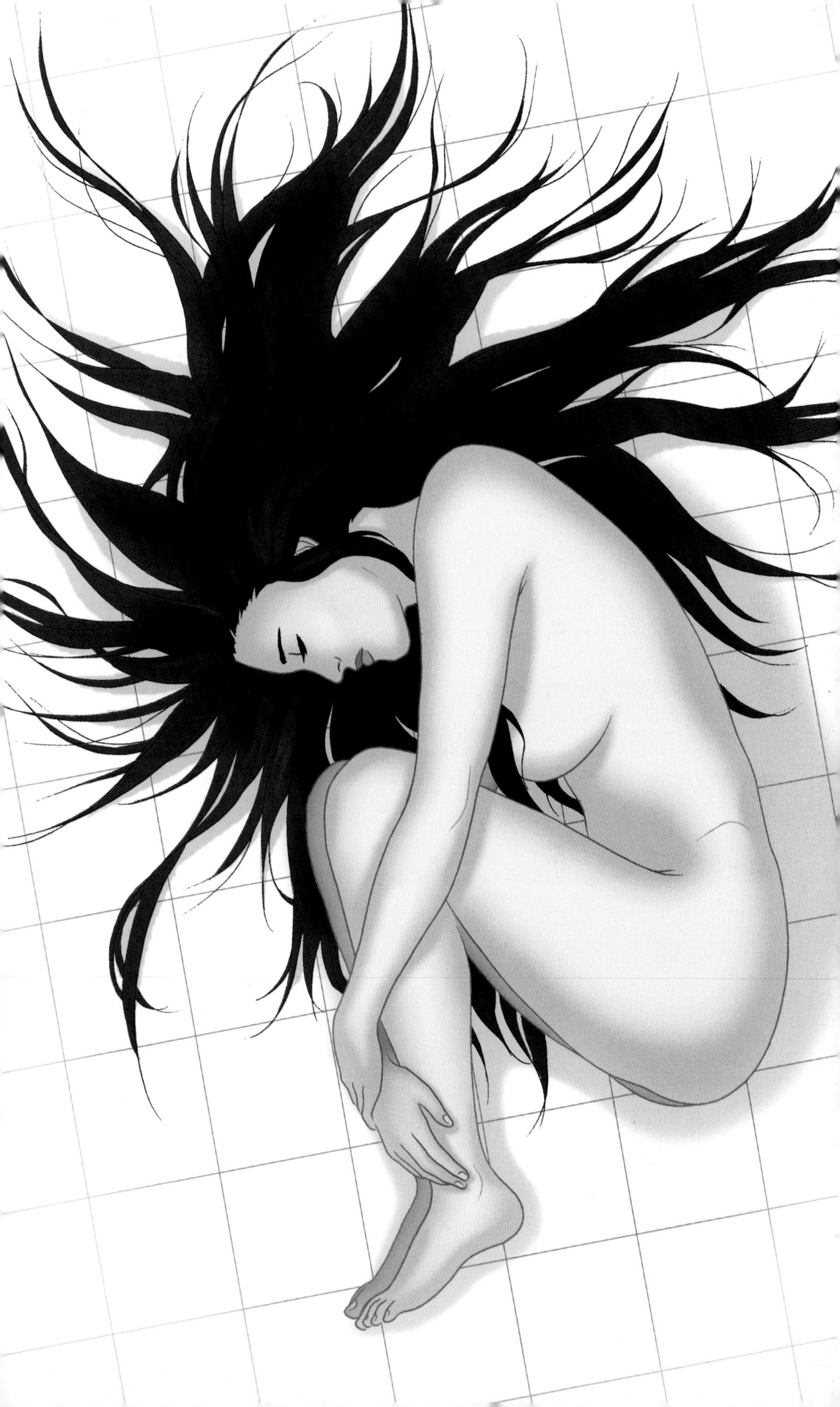

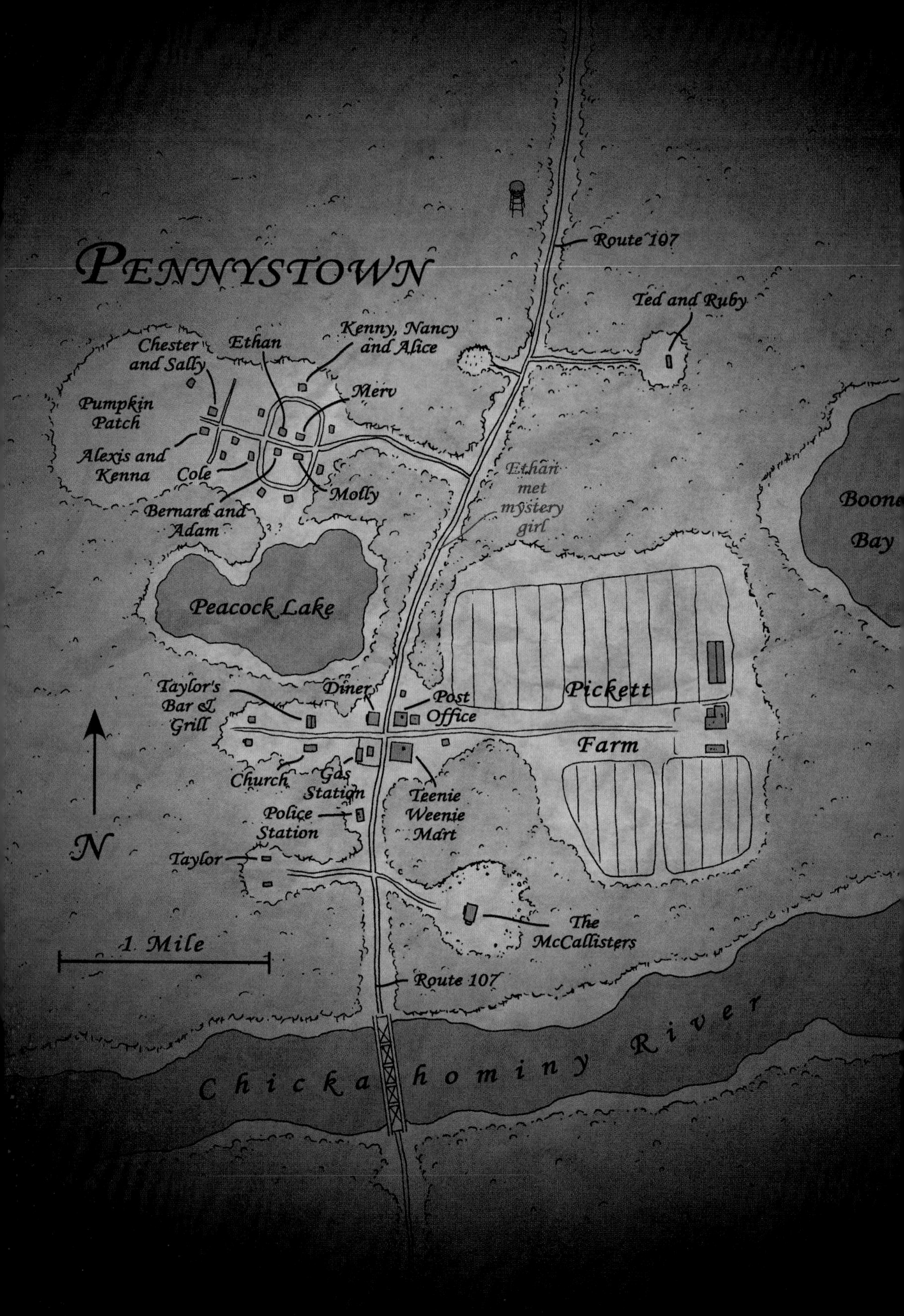
Pennystown
Route 107
Ted and Ruby
Kenny, Nancy and Alice
Chester and Sally
Ethan
Merv
Pumpkin Patch
Alexis and Kenna
Cole
Molly
Bernard and Adam
Ethan met mystery girl
Boone Bay
Peacock Lake
Taylor's Bar & Grill
Diner
Post Office
Pickett Farm
Church
Gas Station
Teenie Weenie Mart
Police Station
N
Taylor
The McCallisters
1 Mile
Route 107
Chickahominy River

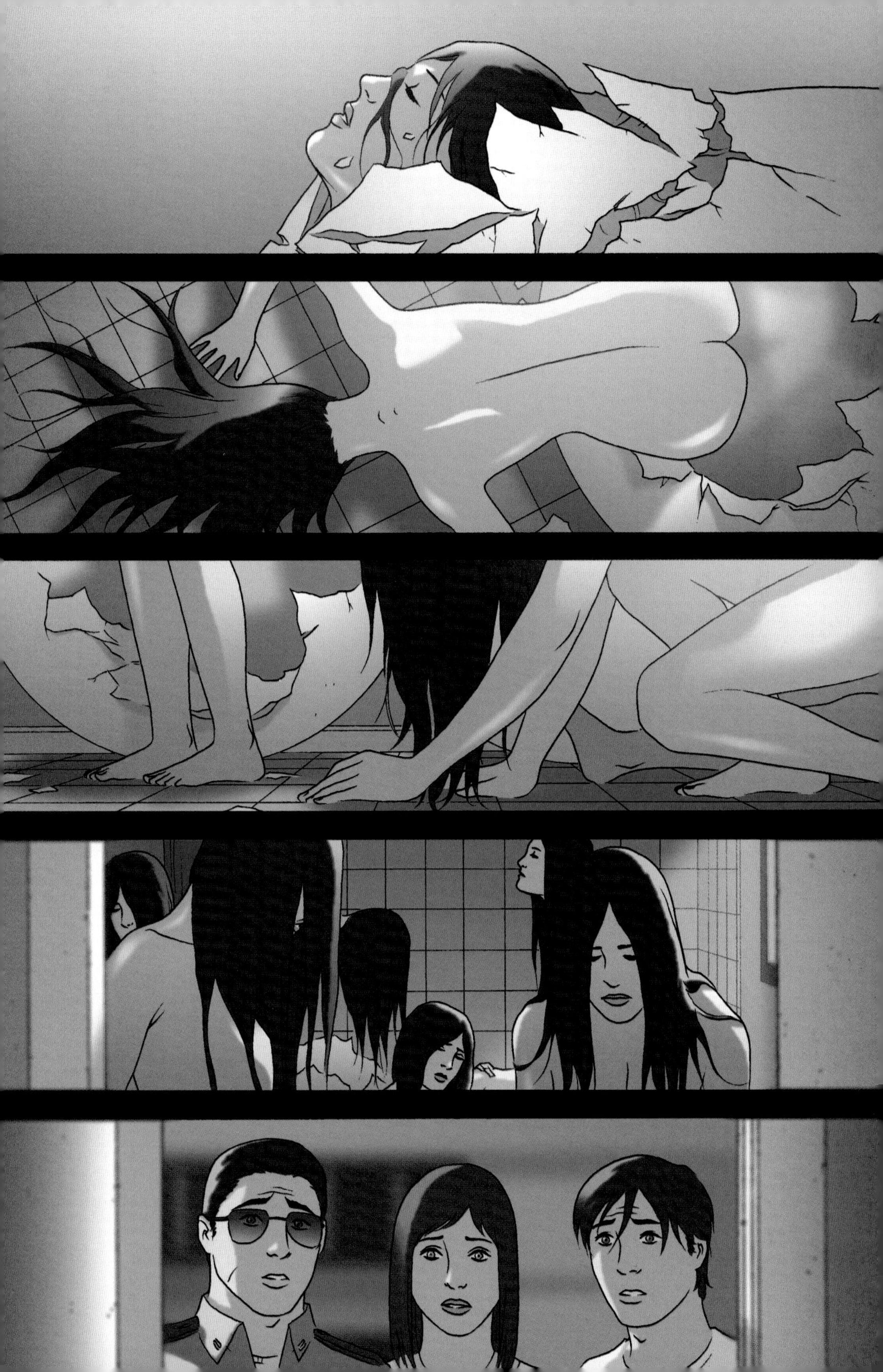

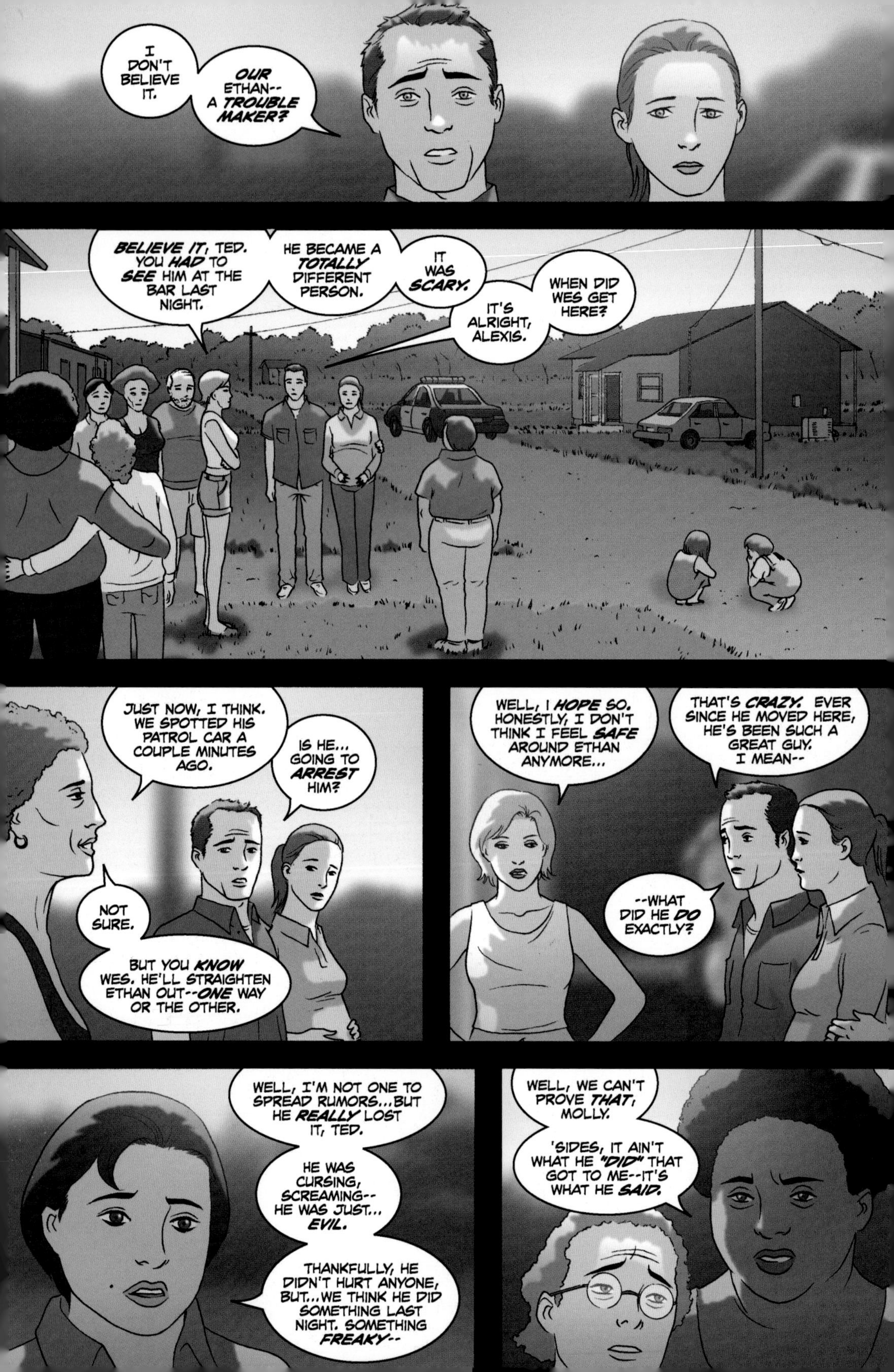
I DON'T BELIEVE IT.
OUR ETHAN-- A TROUBLE MAKER?
BELIEVE IT, TED. YOU HAD TO SEE HIM AT THE BAR LAST NIGHT.
HE BECAME A TOTALLY DIFFERENT PERSON.
IT WAS SCARY.
IT'S ALRIGHT, ALEXIS.
WHEN DID WES GET HERE?
JUST NOW, I THINK. WE SPOTTED HIS PATROL CAR A COUPLE MINUTES AGO.
IS HE... GOING TO ARREST HIM?
NOT SURE.
BUT YOU KNOW WES. HE'LL STRAIGHTEN ETHAN OUT--ONE WAY OR THE OTHER.
WELL, I HOPE SO. HONESTLY, I DON'T THINK I FEEL SAFE AROUND ETHAN ANYMORE...
THAT'S CRAZY. EVER SINCE HE MOVED HERE, HE'S BEEN SUCH A GREAT GUY. I MEAN--
--WHAT DID HE DO EXACTLY?
WELL, I'M NOT ONE TO SPREAD RUMORS...BUT HE REALLY LOST IT, TED.
HE WAS CURSING, SCREAMING-- HE WAS JUST... EVIL.
THANKFULLY, HE DIDN'T HURT ANYONE, BUT...WE THINK HE DID SOMETHING LAST NIGHT. SOMETHING FREAKY--
WELL, WE CAN'T PROVE THAT, MOLLY.
'SIDES, IT AIN'T WHAT HE "DID" THAT GOT TO ME--IT'S WHAT HE SAID.

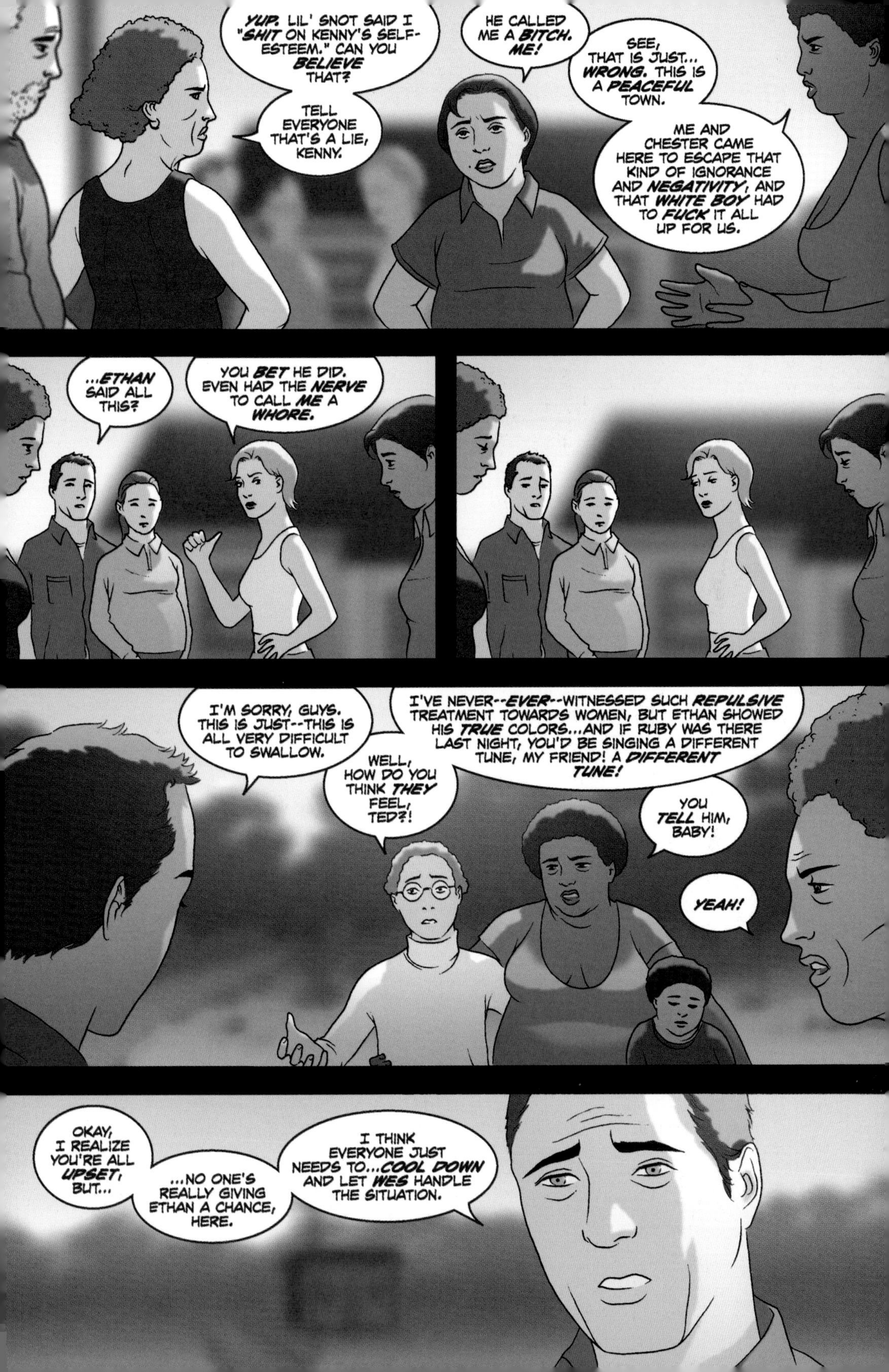
YUP. LIL' SNOT SAID I "SHIT ON KENNY'S SELF-ESTEEM." CAN YOU BELIEVE THAT?
TELL EVERYONE THAT'S A LIE, KENNY.
HE CALLED ME A BITCH. ME!
SEE, THAT IS JUST... WRONG. THIS IS A PEACEFUL TOWN.
ME AND CHESTER CAME HERE TO ESCAPE THAT KIND OF IGNORANCE AND NEGATIVITY, AND THAT WHITE BOY HAD TO FUCK IT ALL UP FOR US.
...ETHAN SAID ALL THIS?
YOU BET HE DID. EVEN HAD THE NERVE TO CALL ME A WHORE.
I'M SORRY, GUYS. THIS IS JUST--THIS IS ALL VERY DIFFICULT TO SWALLOW.
WELL, HOW DO YOU THINK THEY FEEL, TED?!
I'VE NEVER--EVER--WITNESSED SUCH REPULSIVE TREATMENT TOWARDS WOMEN, BUT ETHAN SHOWED HIS TRUE COLORS...AND IF RUBY WAS THERE LAST NIGHT, YOU'D BE SINGING A DIFFERENT TUNE, MY FRIEND! A DIFFERENT TUNE!
YOU TELL HIM, BABY!
YEAH!
OKAY, I REALIZE YOU'RE ALL UPSET, BUT...
...NO ONE'S REALLY GIVING ETHAN A CHANCE, HERE.
I THINK EVERYONE JUST NEEDS TO...COOL DOWN AND LET WES HANDLE THE SITUATION.

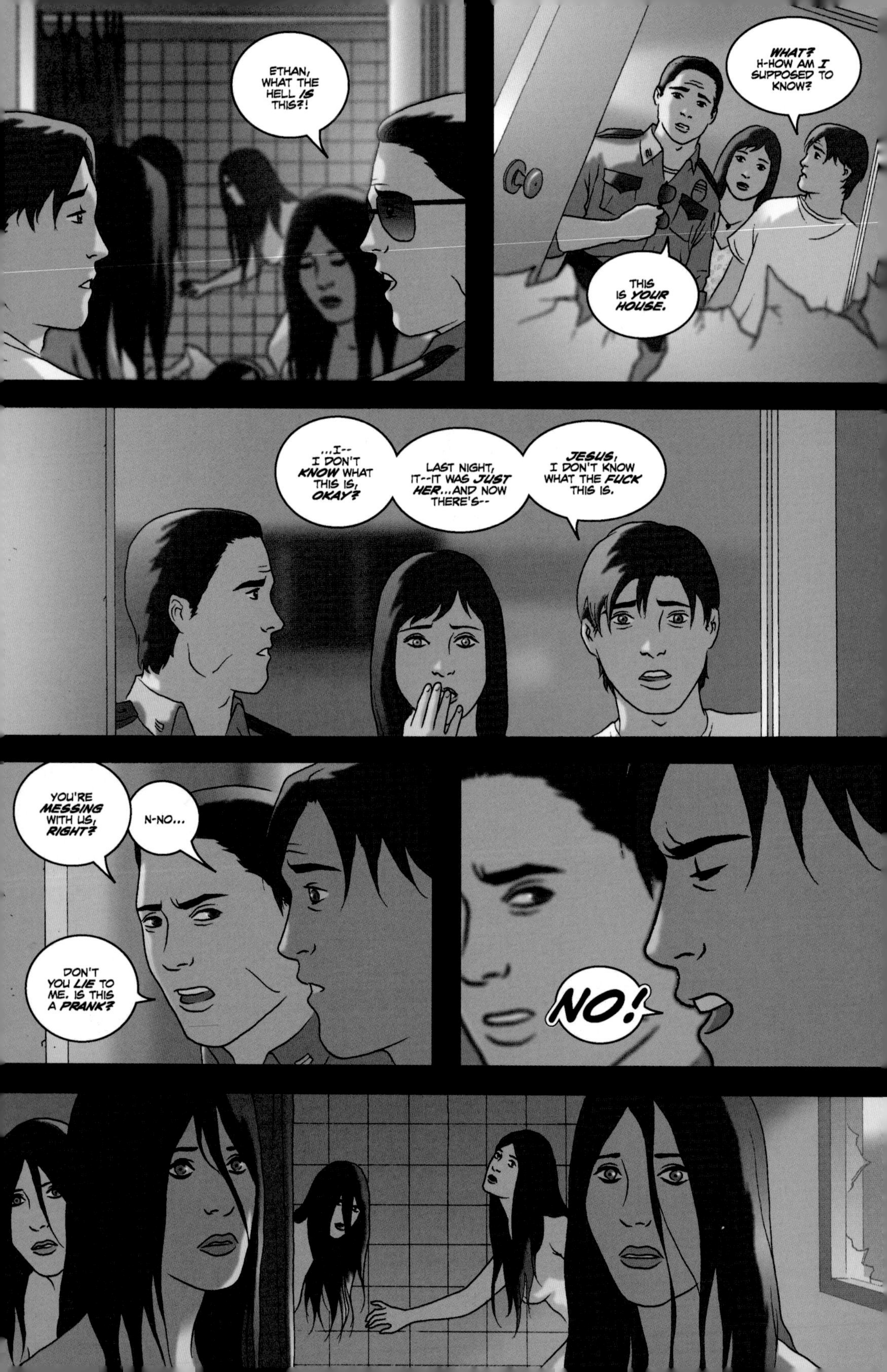
ETHAN, WHAT THE HELL IS THIS?!
WHAT? H-HOW AM I SUPPOSED TO KNOW?
THIS IS YOUR HOUSE.
...I-- I DON'T KNOW WHAT THIS IS, OKAY?
LAST NIGHT, IT--IT WAS JUST HER...AND NOW THERE'S--
JESUS, I DON'T KNOW WHAT THE FUCK THIS IS.
YOU'RE MESSING WITH US, RIGHT?
N-NO...
DON'T YOU LIE TO ME. IS THIS A PRANK?
NO!

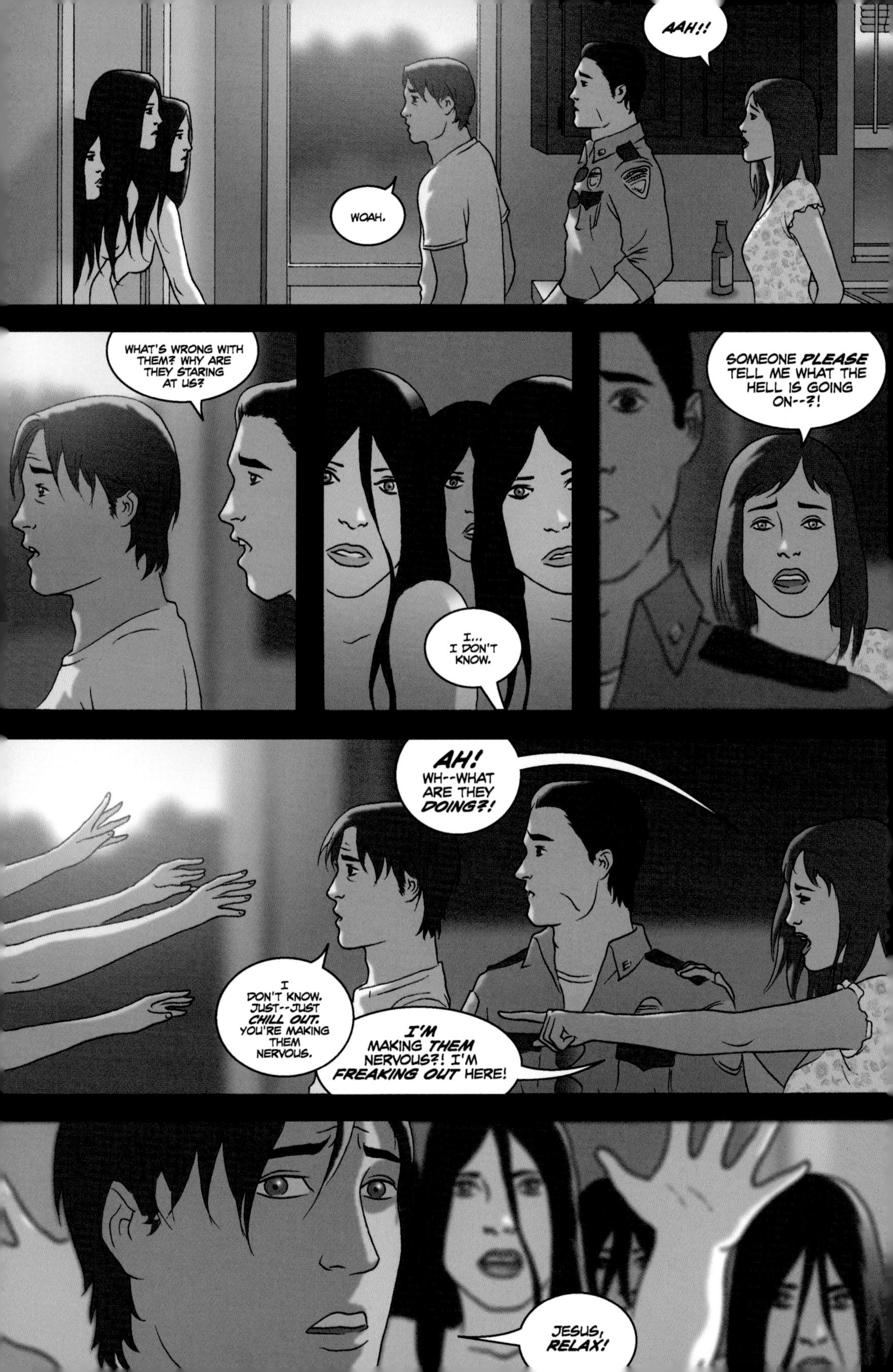
AAH!!
WOAH.
WHAT'S WRONG WITH THEM? WHY ARE THEY STARING AT US?
I... I DON'T KNOW.
SOMEONE PLEASE TELL ME WHAT THE HELL IS GOING ON--?!
AH! WH--WHAT ARE THEY DOING?!
I DON'T KNOW. JUST--JUST CHILL OUT. YOU'RE MAKING THEM NERVOUS.
I'M MAKING THEM NERVOUS?! I'M FREAKING OUT HERE!
JESUS, RELAX!

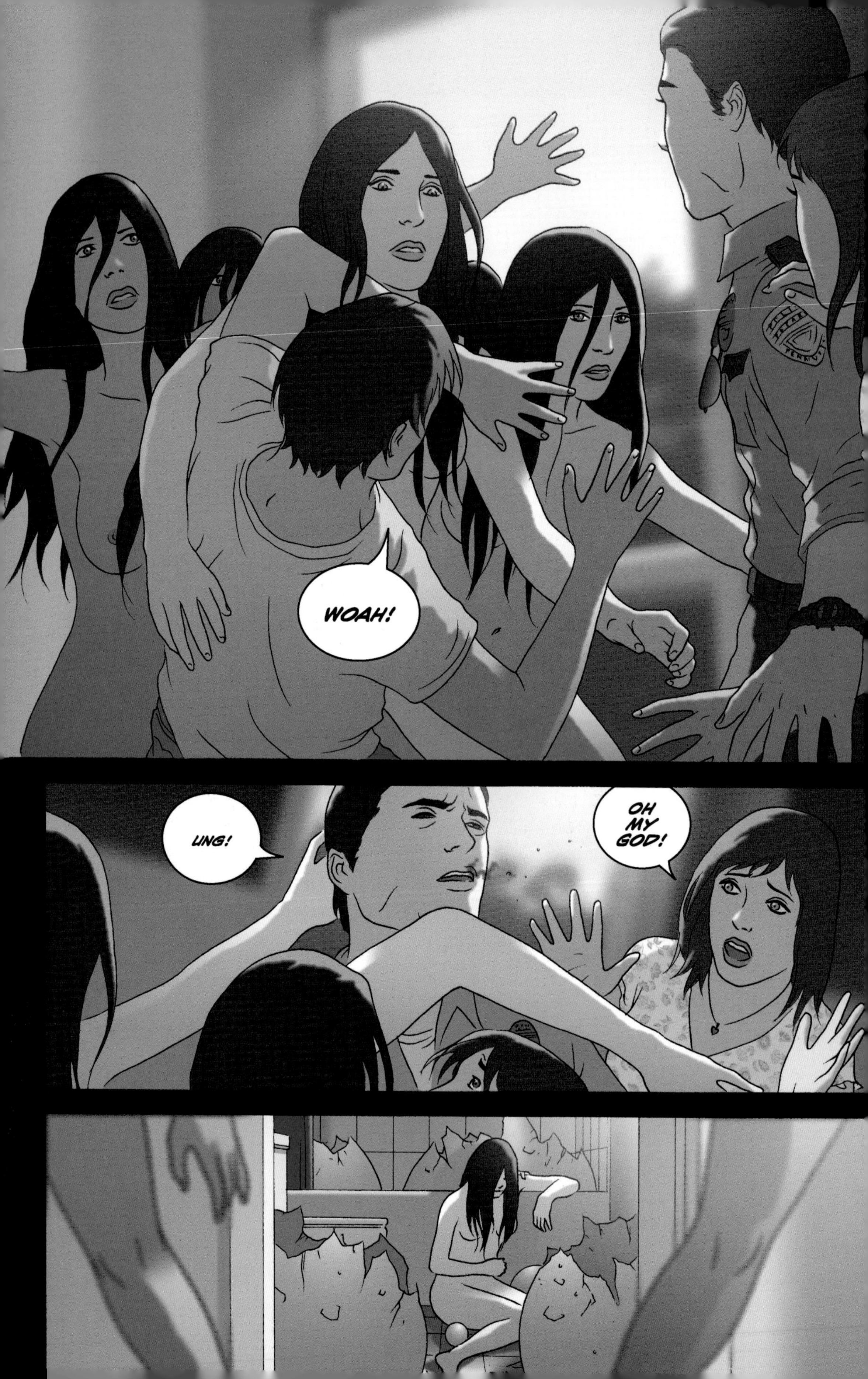
WOAH!
UNG!
OH MY GOD!

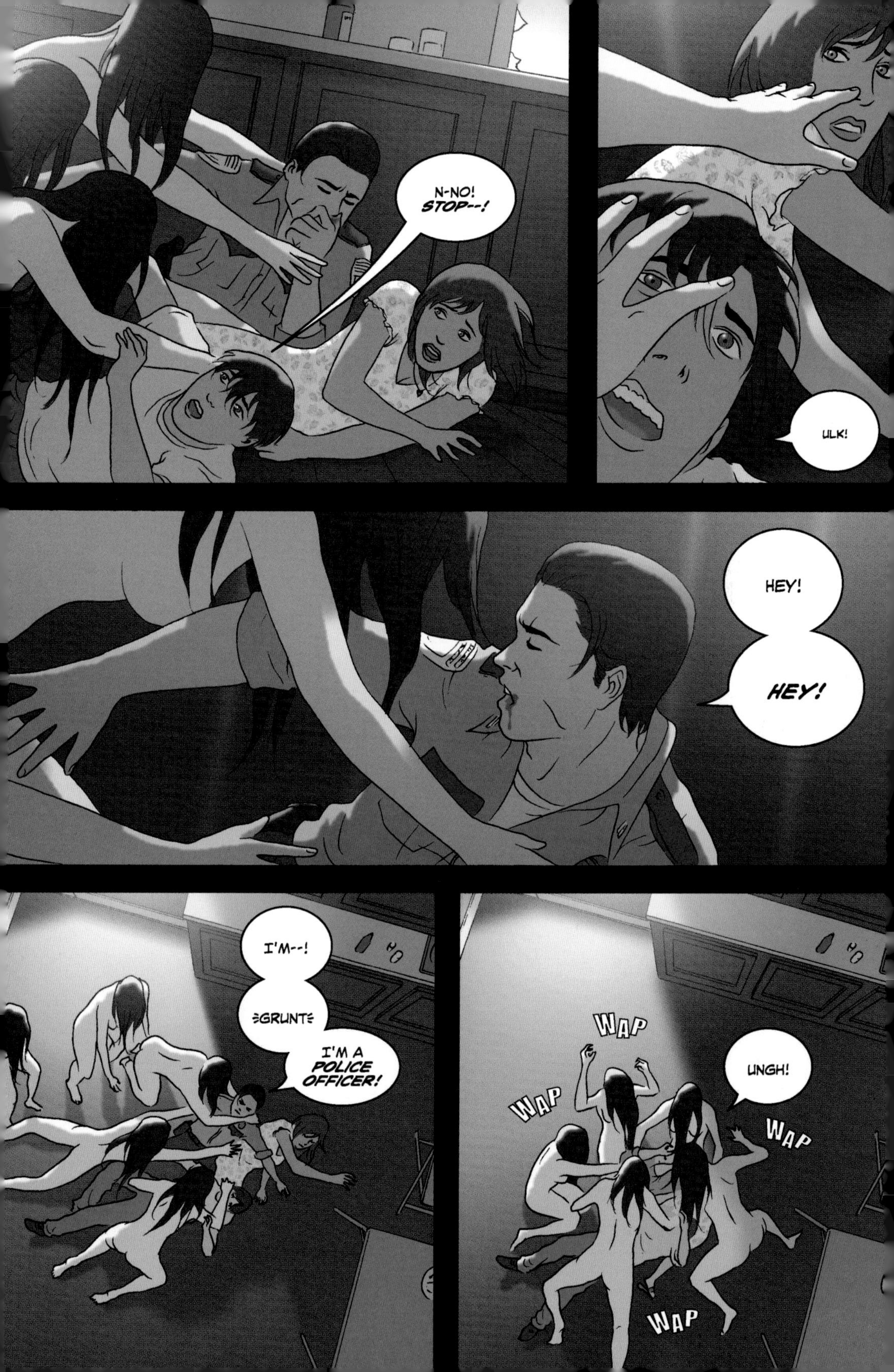
N-NO! STOP--!
ULK!
HEY!
HEY!
I'M--!
GRUNT
I'M A POLICE OFFICER!
WAP
WAP
UNGH!
WAP
WAP

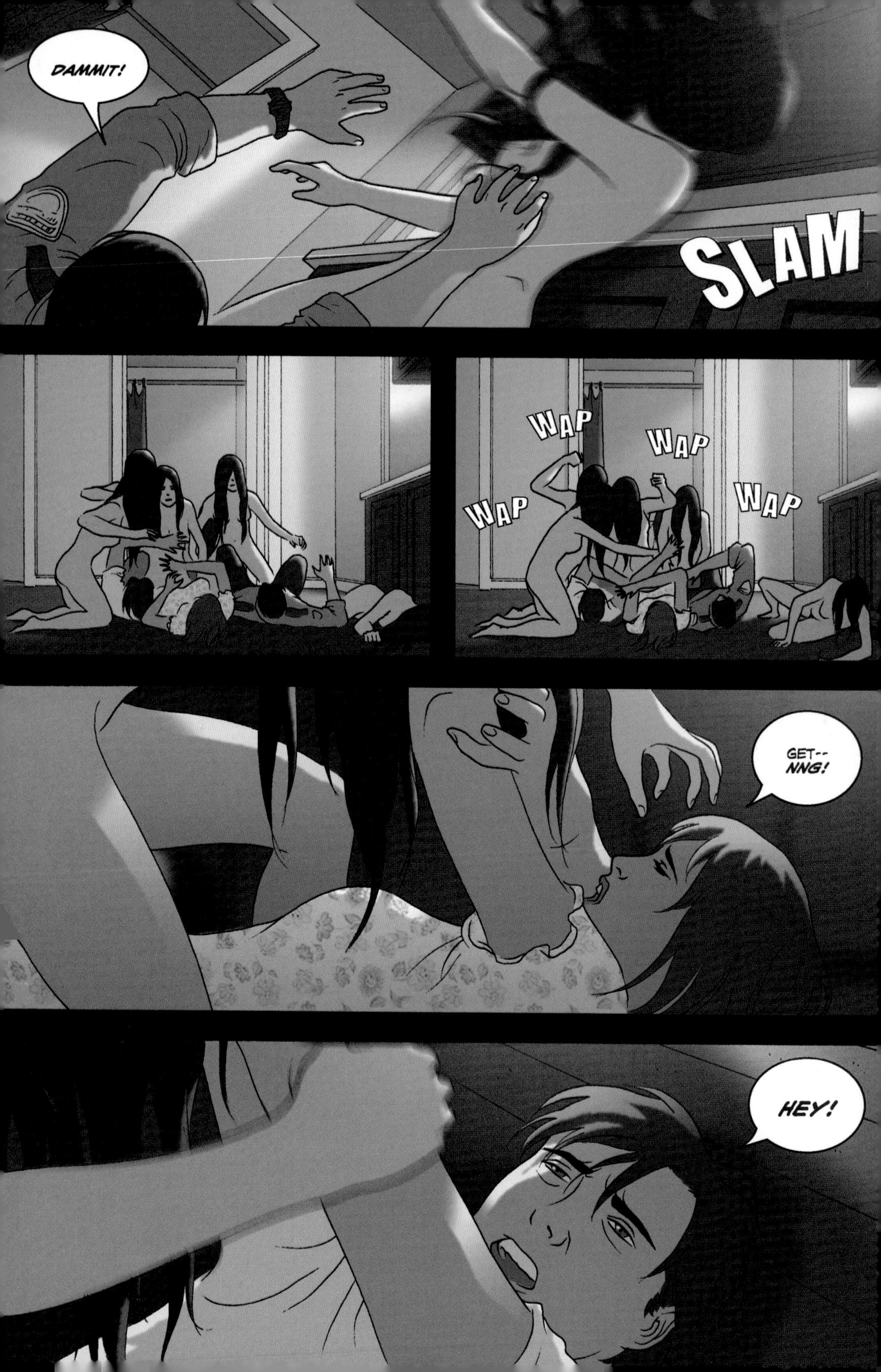
DAMMIT!
SLAM
WAP
WAP
WAP
WAP
GET--
NNG!
HEY!

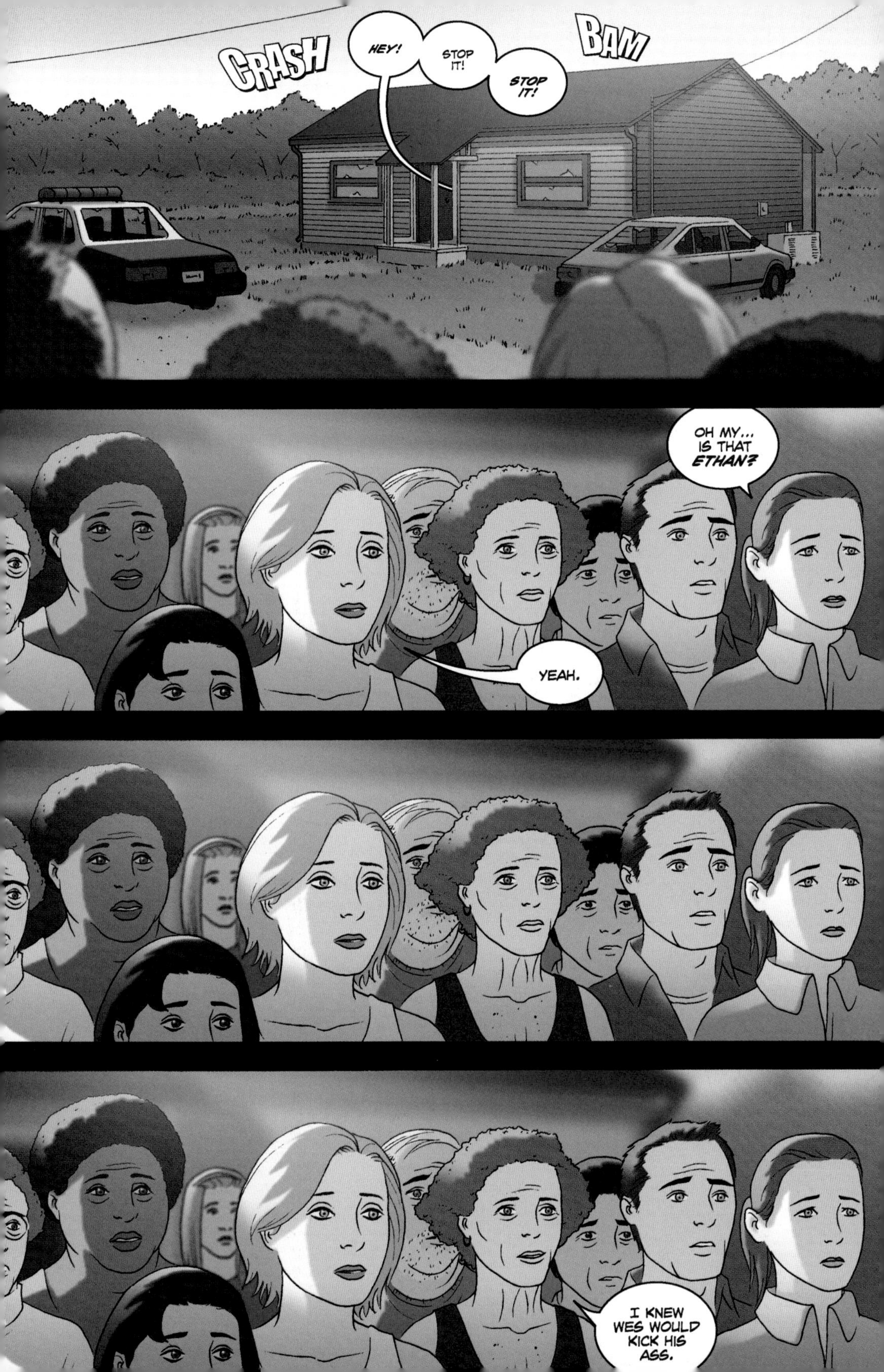
CRASH
HEY!
STOP IT!
STOP IT!
BAM
OH MY... IS THAT ETHAN?
YEAH.
I KNEW WES WOULD KICK HIS ASS.

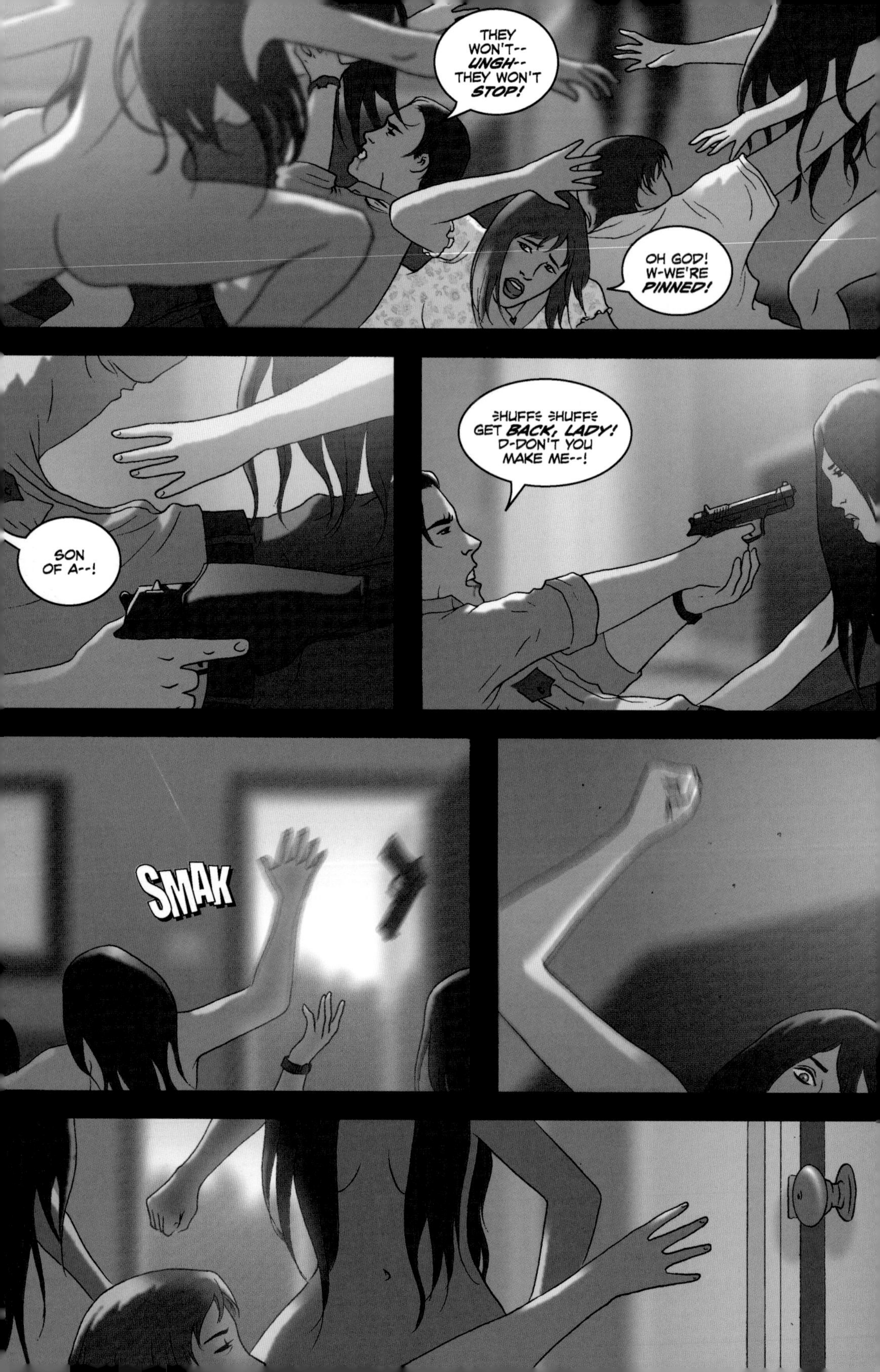
THEY WON'T-- UNGH-- THEY WON'T STOP!
OH GOD! W-WE'RE PINNED!
SON OF A--!
HUFF HUFF GET BACK, LADY! D-DON'T YOU MAKE ME--!
SMAK

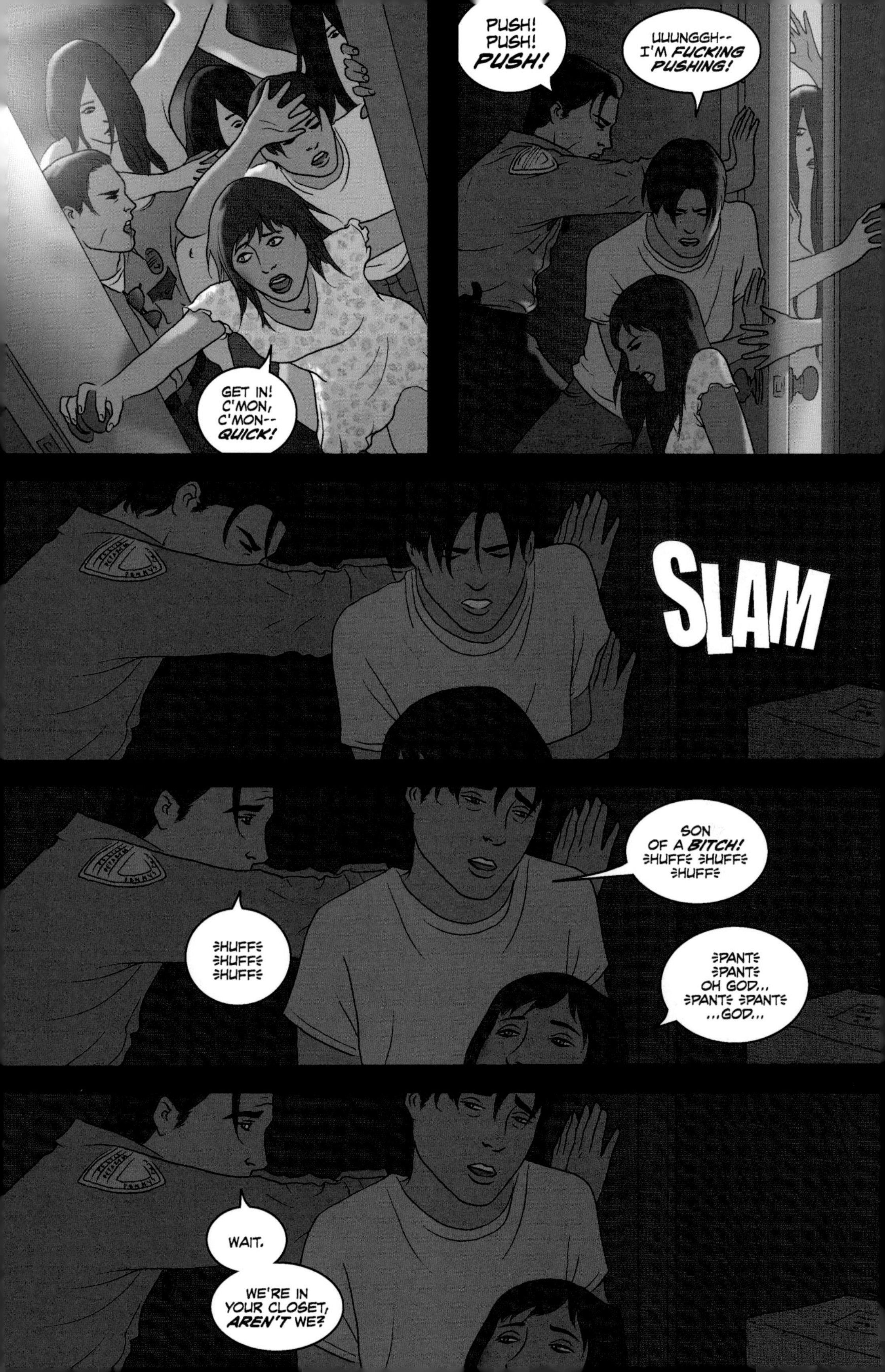
GET IN! C'MON, C'MON-- QUICK!
PUSH! PUSH! PUSH!
UUUNGGH-- I'M FUCKING PUSHING!
SLAM
SON OF A BITCH! HUFF HUFF HUFF
HUFF HUFF HUFF
PANT PANT OH GOD... PANT PANT ...GOD...
WAIT.
WE'RE IN YOUR CLOSET, AREN'T WE?

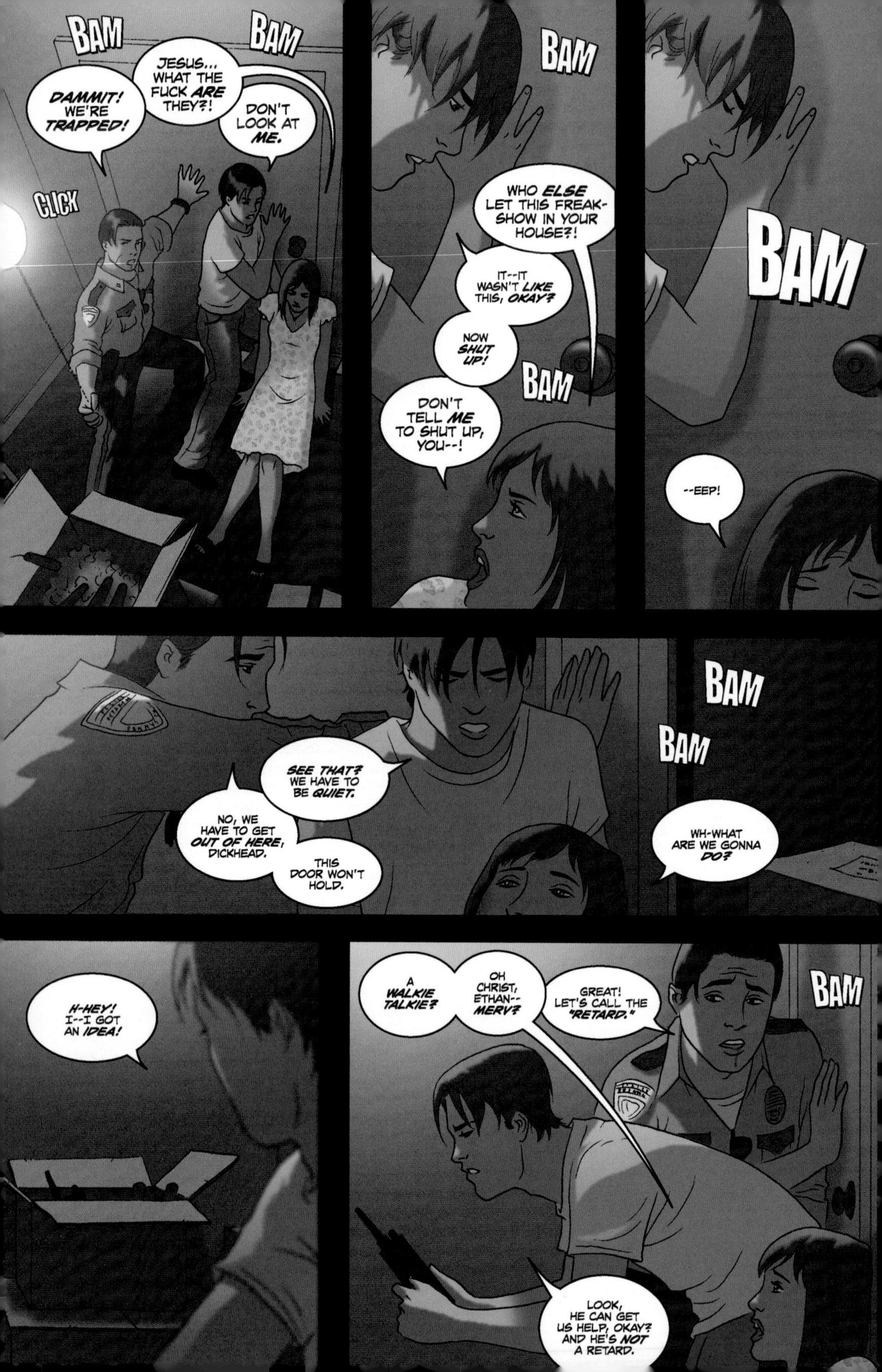
BAM
BAM
DAMMIT! WE'RE TRAPPED!
JESUS... WHAT THE FUCK ARE THEY?!
DON'T LOOK AT ME.
CLICK
BAM
WHO ELSE LET THIS FREAK-SHOW IN YOUR HOUSE?!
IT--IT WASN'T LIKE THIS, OKAY?
NOW SHUT UP!
BAM
DON'T TELL ME TO SHUT UP, YOU--!
BAM
--EEP!
BAM
BAM
SEE THAT? WE HAVE TO BE QUIET.
NO, WE HAVE TO GET OUT OF HERE, DICKHEAD.
THIS DOOR WON'T HOLD.
WH-WHAT ARE WE GONNA DO?
H-HEY! I--I GOT AN IDEA!
A WALKIE TALKIE?
OH CHRIST, ETHAN--MERV?
GREAT! LET'S CALL THE "RETARD."
BAM
LOOK, HE CAN GET US HELP, OKAY? AND HE'S NOT A RETARD.

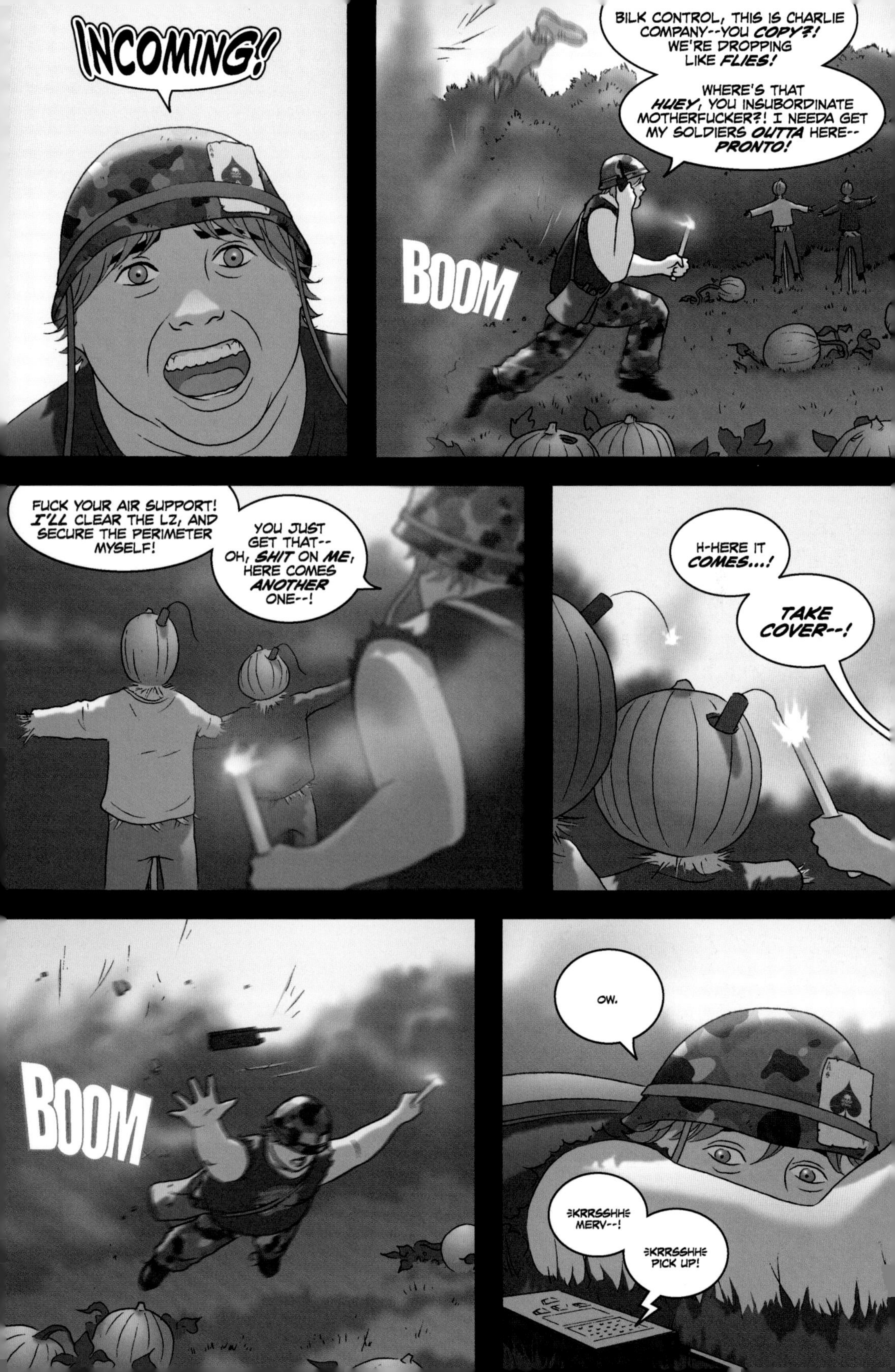
INCOMING!
BILK CONTROL, THIS IS CHARLIE COMPANY--YOU COPY?! WE'RE DROPPING LIKE FLIES!
WHERE'S THAT HUEY, YOU INSUBORDINATE MOTHERFUCKER?! I NEEDA GET MY SOLDIERS OUTTA HERE-- PRONTO!
BOOM
FUCK YOUR AIR SUPPORT! I'LL CLEAR THE LZ, AND SECURE THE PERIMETER MYSELF!
YOU JUST GET THAT-- OH, SHIT ON ME, HERE COMES ANOTHER ONE--!
H-HERE IT COMES...!
TAKE COVER--!
BOOM
OW.
KRRSSHH MERV--!
KRRSSHH PICK UP!

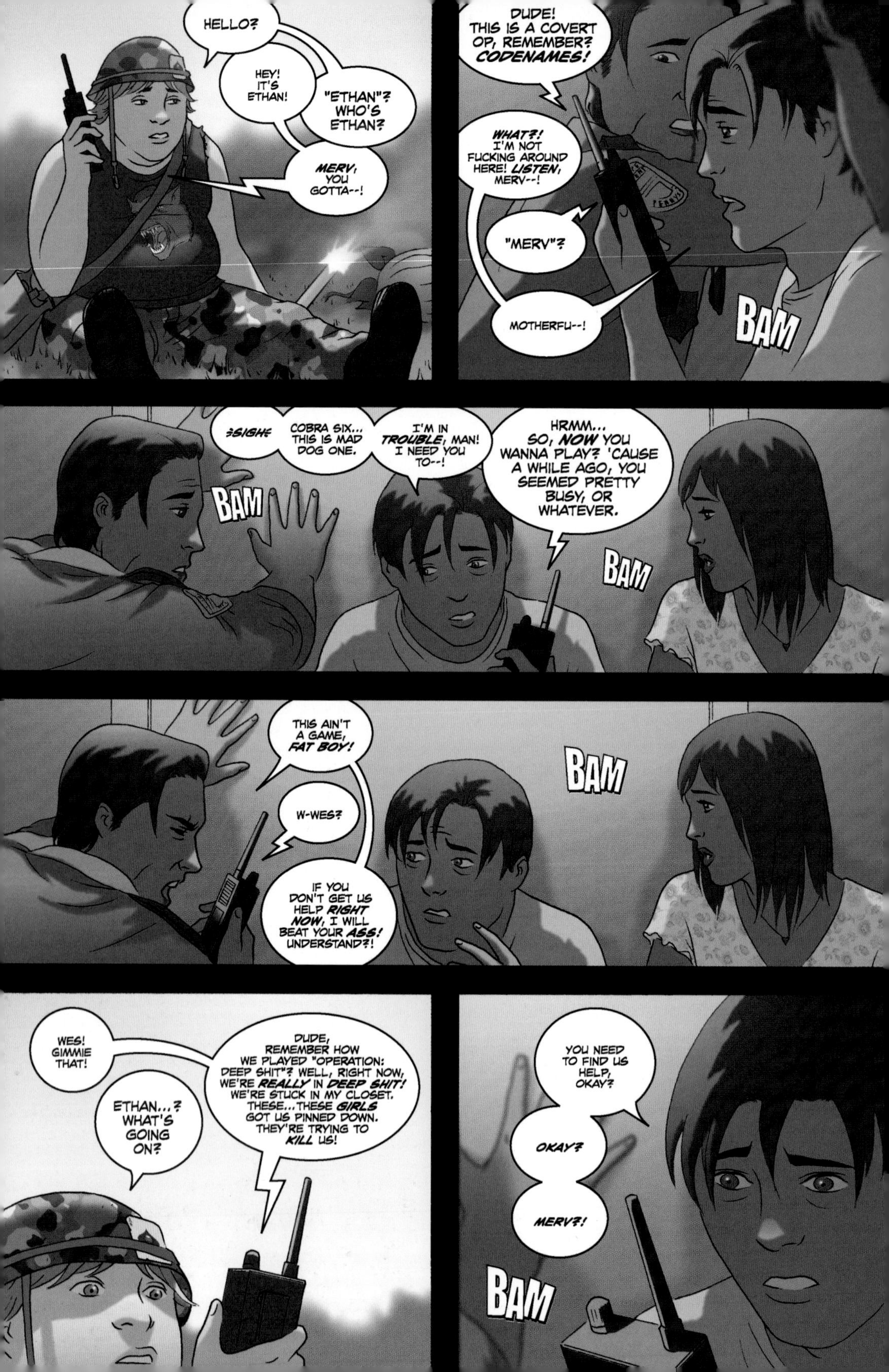

HELLO?
HEY! IT'S ETHAN!
"ETHAN"? WHO'S ETHAN?
MERV, YOU GOTTA--!
DUDE! THIS IS A COVERT OP, REMEMBER? CODENAMES!
WHAT?! I'M NOT FUCKING AROUND HERE! LISTEN, MERV--!
"MERV"?
MOTHERFU--!
BAM
⋨SIGH⋩
COBRA SIX... THIS IS MAD DOG ONE.
I'M IN TROUBLE, MAN! I NEED YOU TO--!
HRMM... SO, NOW YOU WANNA PLAY? 'CAUSE A WHILE AGO, YOU SEEMED PRETTY BUSY, OR WHATEVER.
BAM
BAM
THIS AIN'T A GAME, FAT BOY!
W-WES?
IF YOU DON'T GET US HELP RIGHT NOW, I WILL BEAT YOUR ASS! UNDERSTAND?!
BAM
WES! GIMMIE THAT!
ETHAN...? WHAT'S GOING ON?
DUDE, REMEMBER HOW WE PLAYED "OPERATION: DEEP SHIT"? WELL, RIGHT NOW, WE'RE REALLY IN DEEP SHIT! WE'RE STUCK IN MY CLOSET. THESE...THESE GIRLS GOT US PINNED DOWN. THEY'RE TRYING TO KILL US!
YOU NEED TO FIND US HELP, OKAY?
OKAY?
MERV?!
BAM

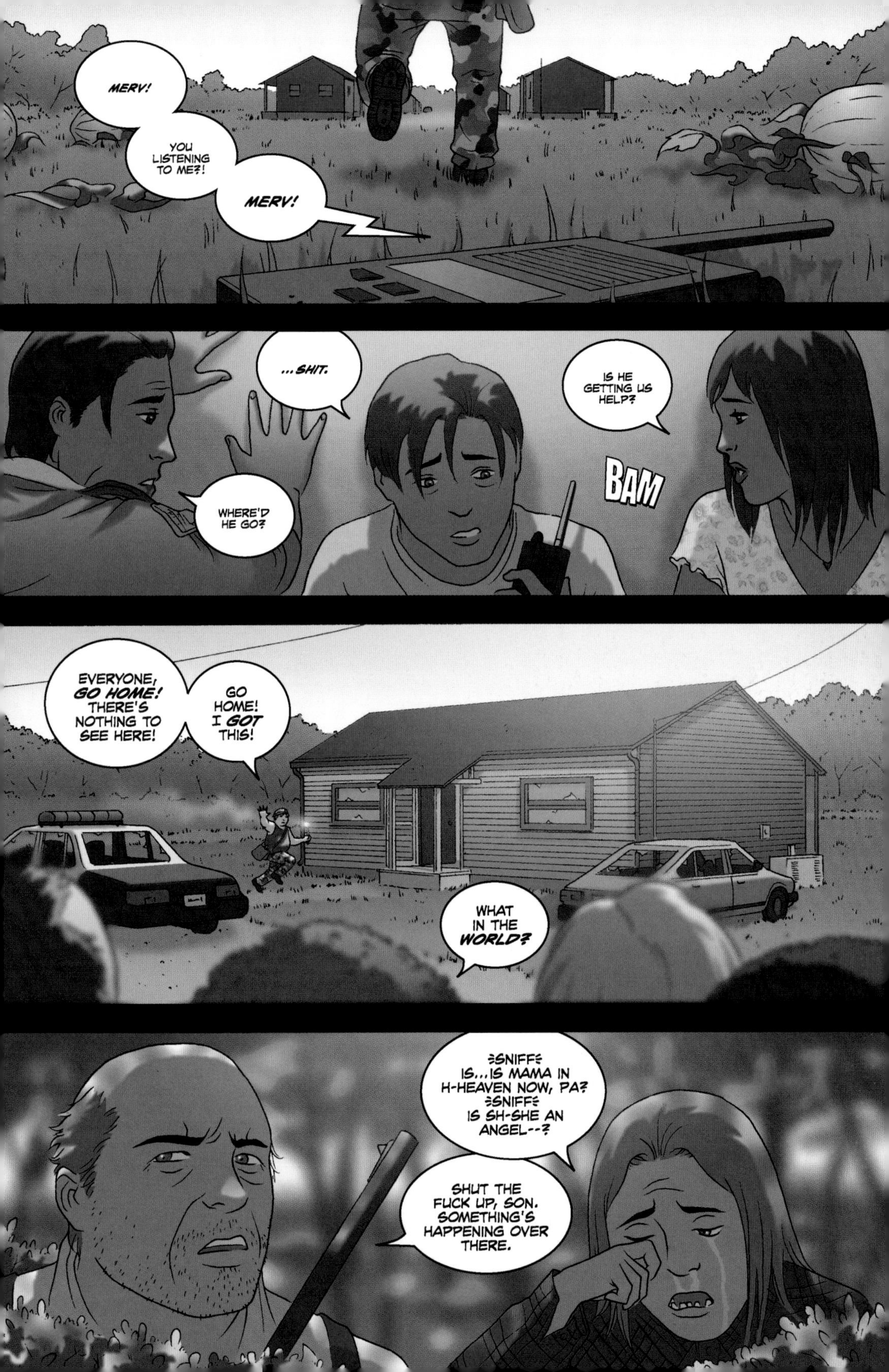
MERV!
YOU LISTENING TO ME?!
MERV!
...SHIT.
IS HE GETTING US HELP?
WHERE'D HE GO?
BAM
EVERYONE, GO HOME! THERE'S NOTHING TO SEE HERE!
GO HOME! I GOT THIS!
WHAT IN THE WORLD?
=SNIFF= IS...IS MAMA IN H-HEAVEN NOW, PA? =SNIFF= IS SH-SHE AN ANGEL--?
SHUT THE FUCK UP, SON. SOMETHING'S HAPPENING OVER THERE.

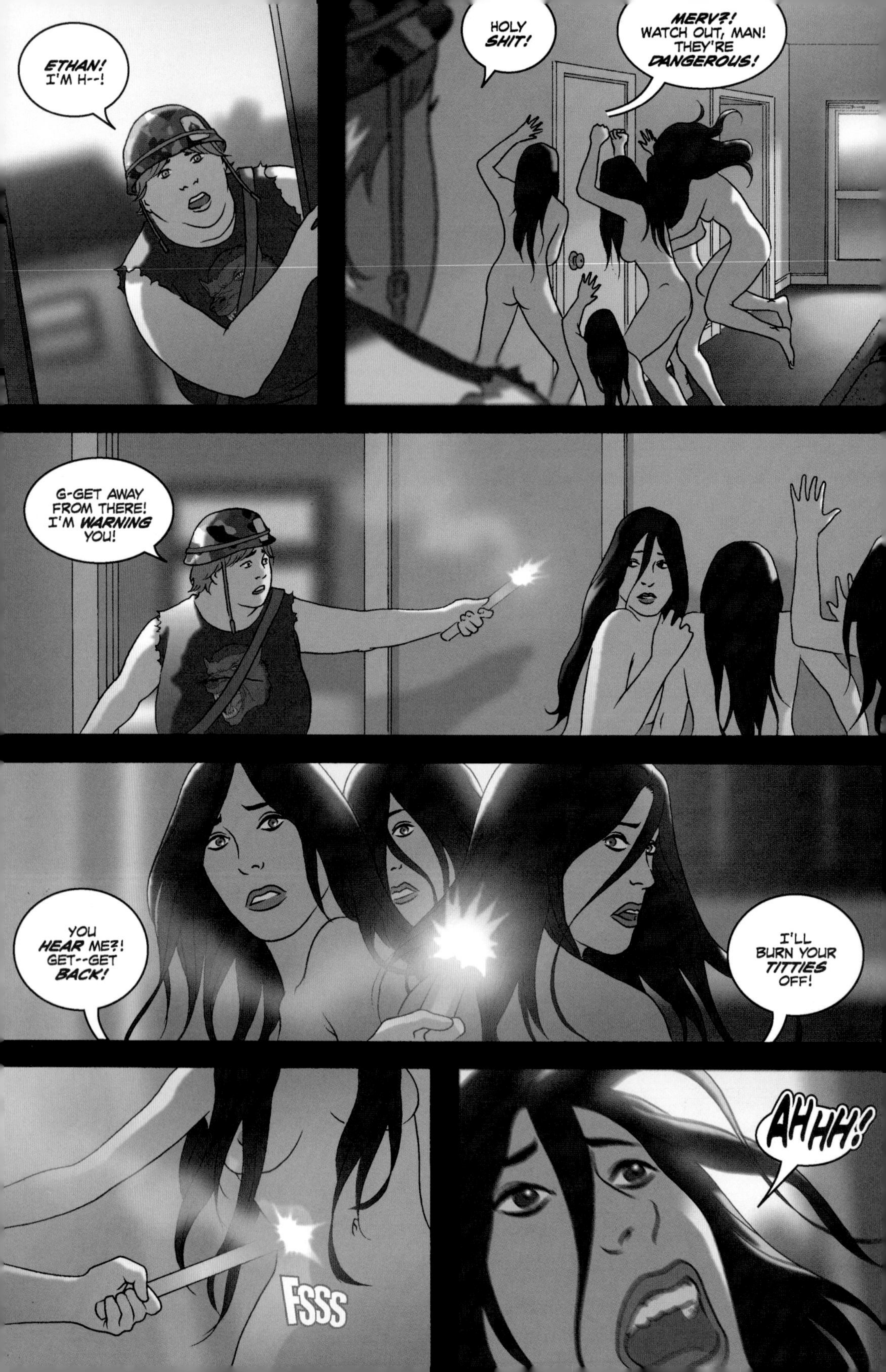
ETHAN! I'M H--!
HOLY SHIT!
MERV?! WATCH OUT, MAN! THEY'RE DANGEROUS!
G-GET AWAY FROM THERE! I'M WARNING YOU!
YOU HEAR ME?! GET--GET BACK!
I'LL BURN YOUR TITTIES OFF!
FSSS
AHHH!

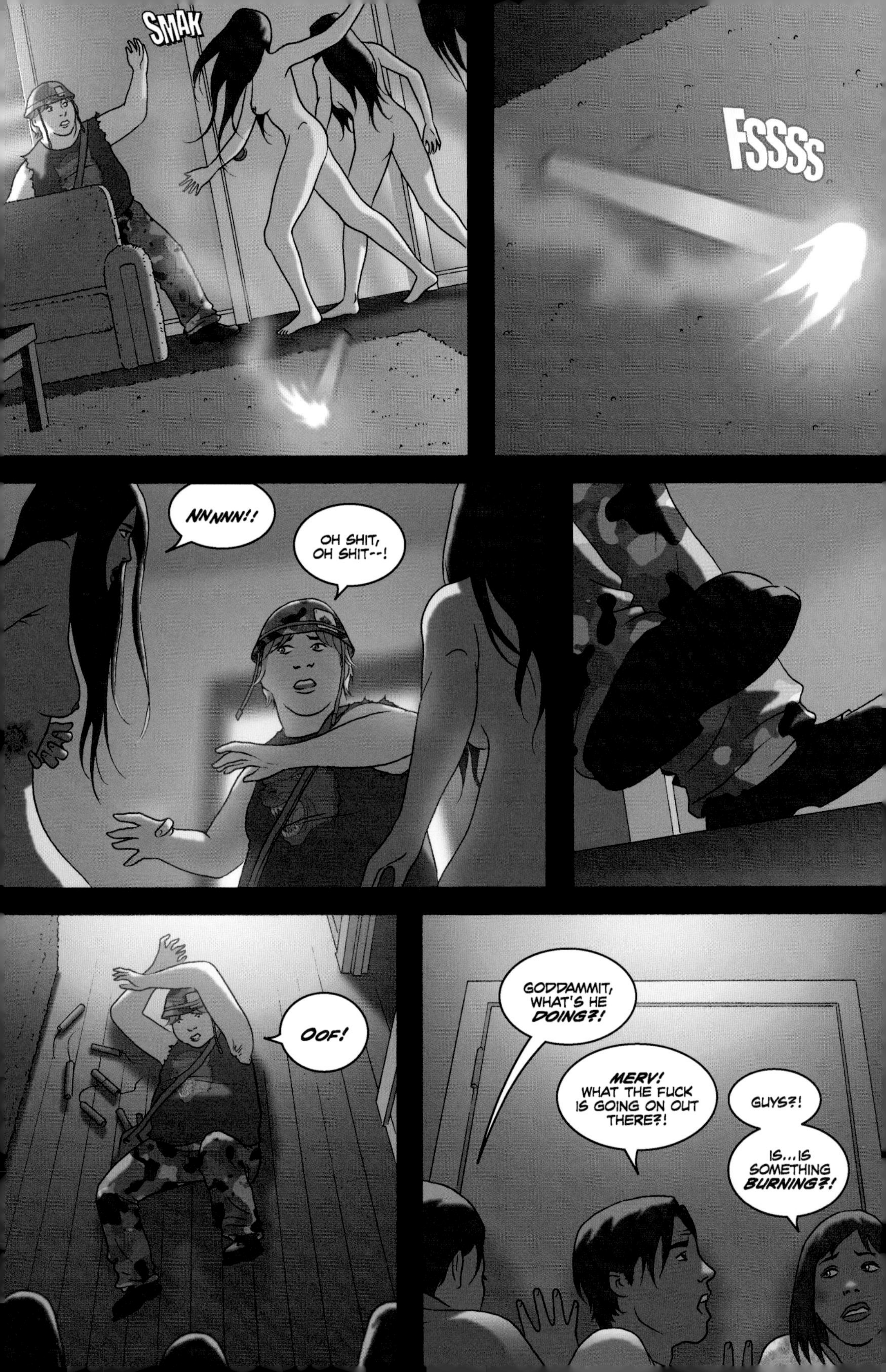
SMAK
FSSSS
NNNNN!!
OH SHIT, OH SHIT--!
OOF!
GODDAMMIT, WHAT'S HE DOING?!
MERV! WHAT THE FUCK IS GOING ON OUT THERE?!
GUYS?!
IS...IS SOMETHING BURNING?!

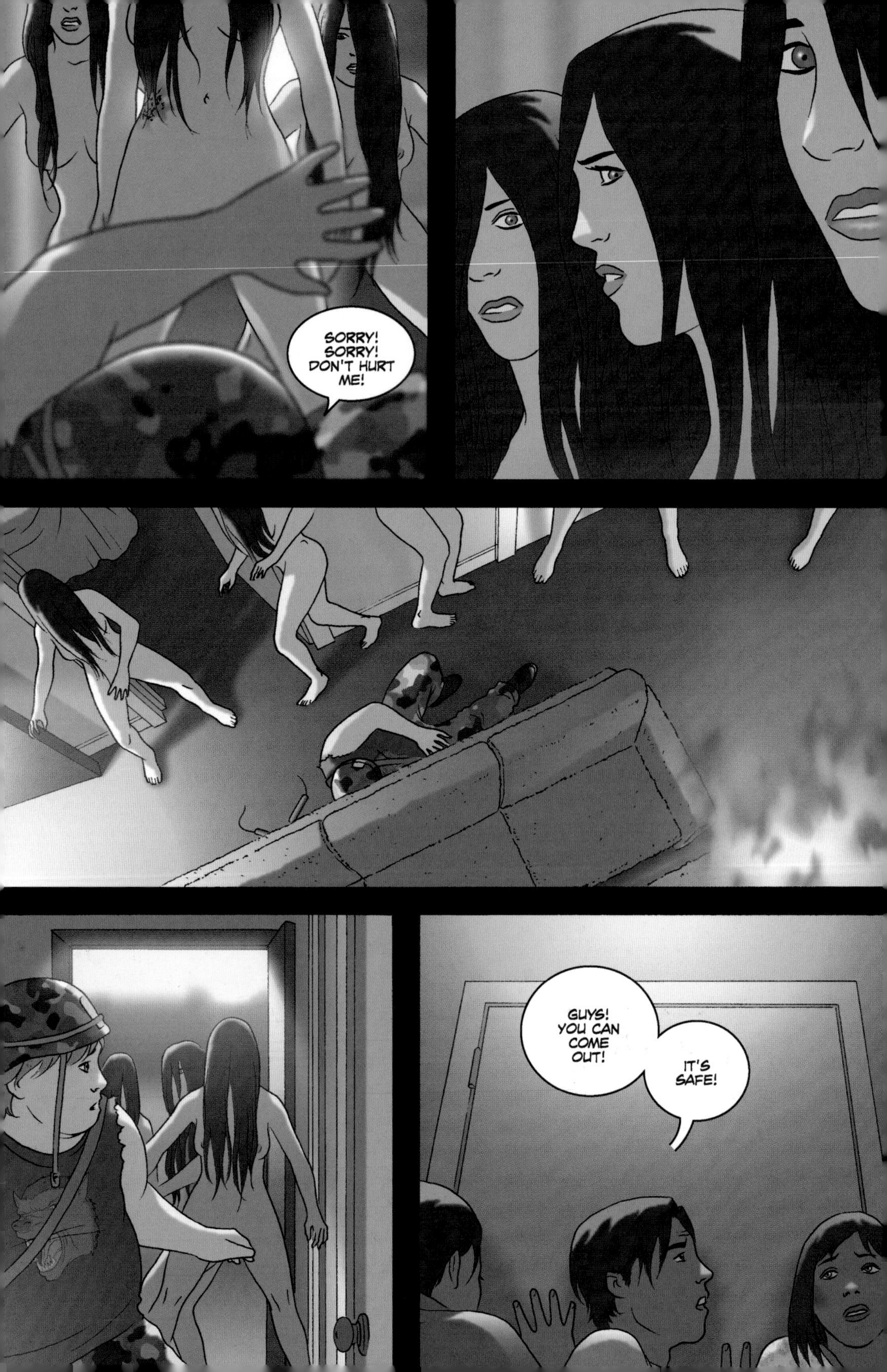
SORRY! SORRY! DON'T HURT ME!
GUYS! YOU CAN COME OUT!
IT'S SAFE!

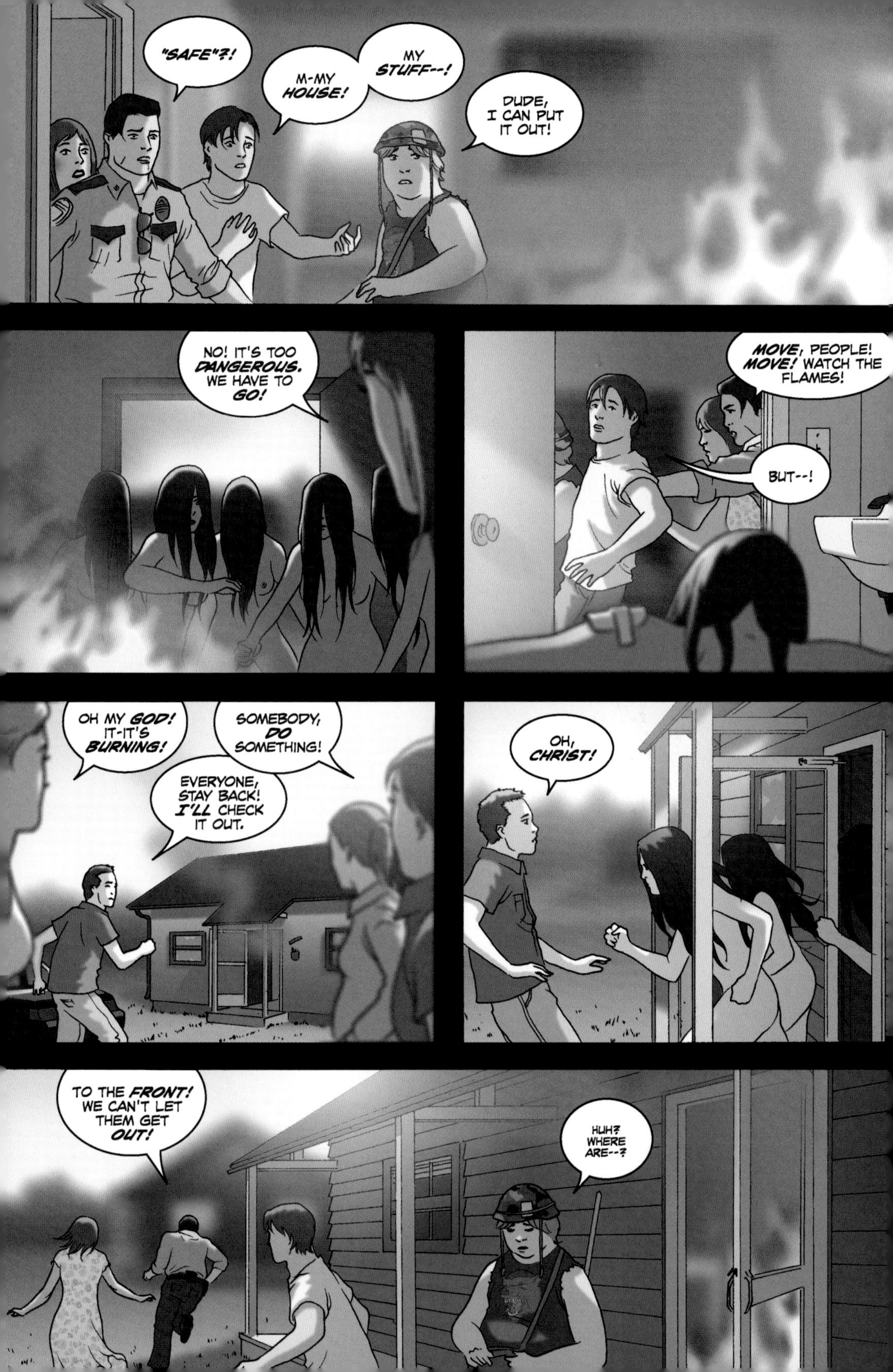
"SAFE"?!
M-MY HOUSE!
MY STUFF--!
DUDE, I CAN PUT IT OUT!
NO! IT'S TOO DANGEROUS. WE HAVE TO GO!
MOVE, PEOPLE! MOVE! WATCH THE FLAMES!
BUT--!
OH MY GOD! IT-IT'S BURNING!
SOMEBODY, DO SOMETHING!
EVERYONE, STAY BACK! I'LL CHECK IT OUT.
OH, CHRIST!
TO THE FRONT! WE CAN'T LET THEM GET OUT!
HUH? WHERE ARE--?

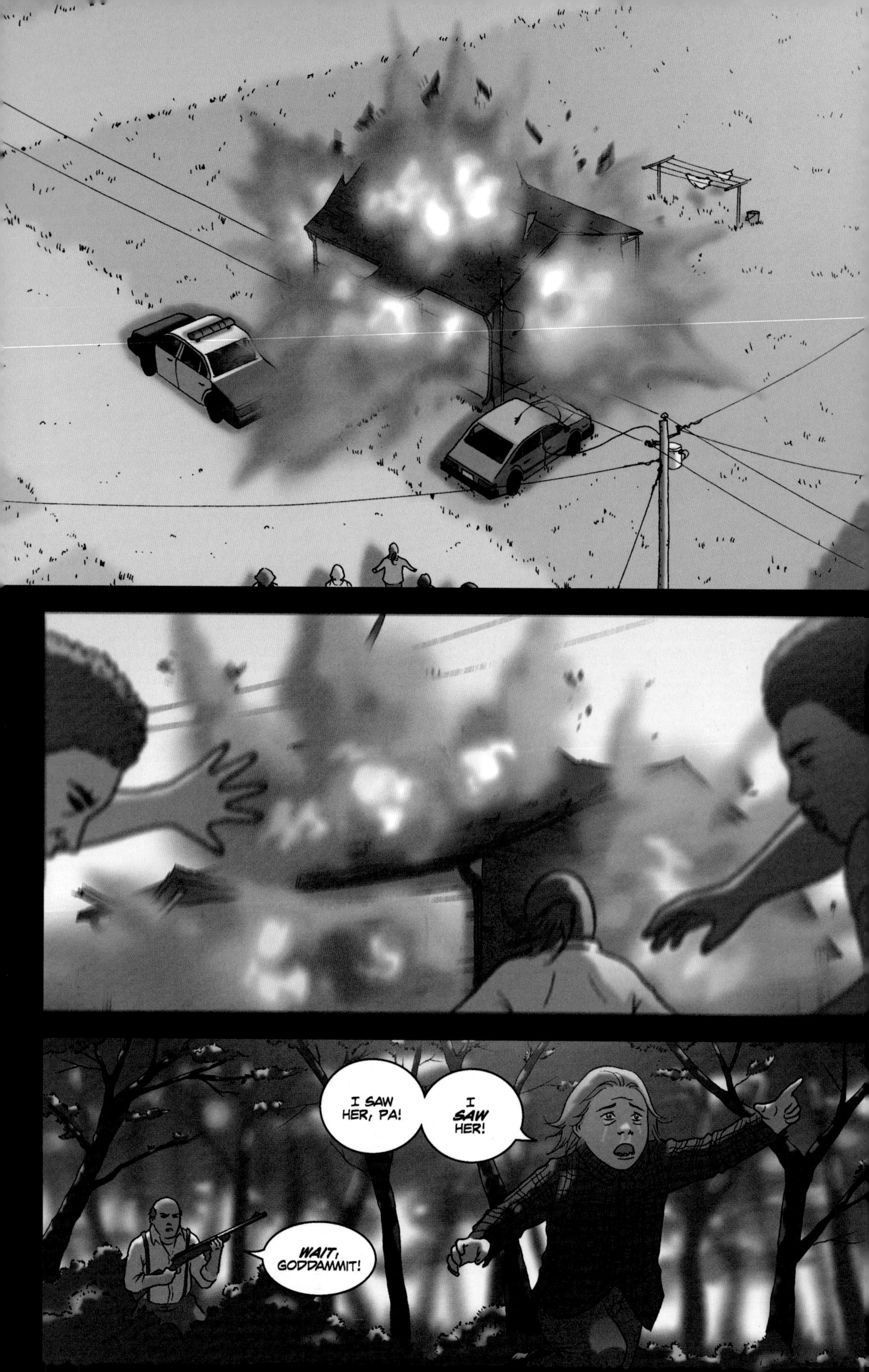
I SAW HER, PA!
I *SAW* HER!
WAIT, GODDAMMIT!

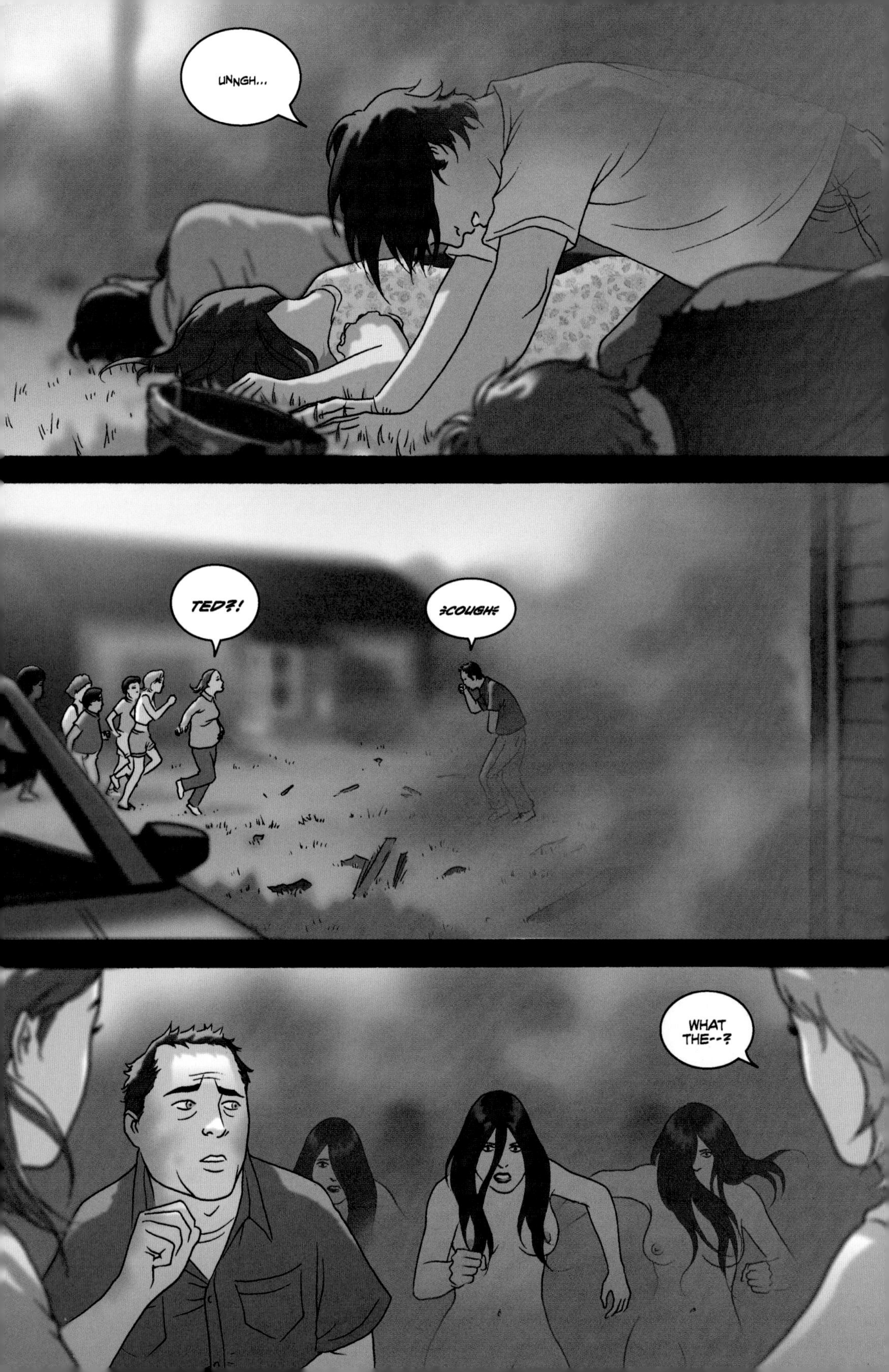
UNNGH...
TED?!
COUGH
WHAT THE--?

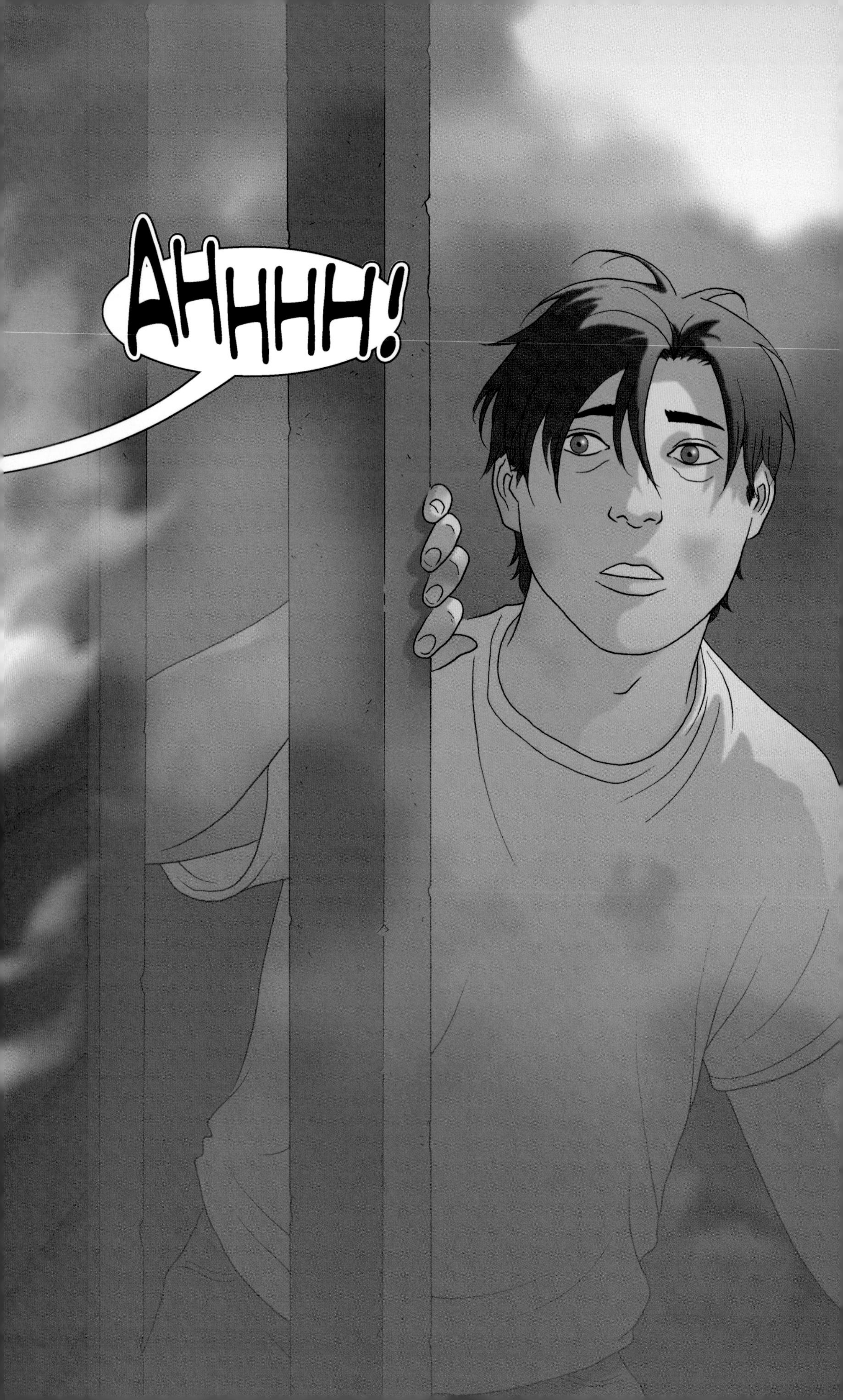
AHHHH!

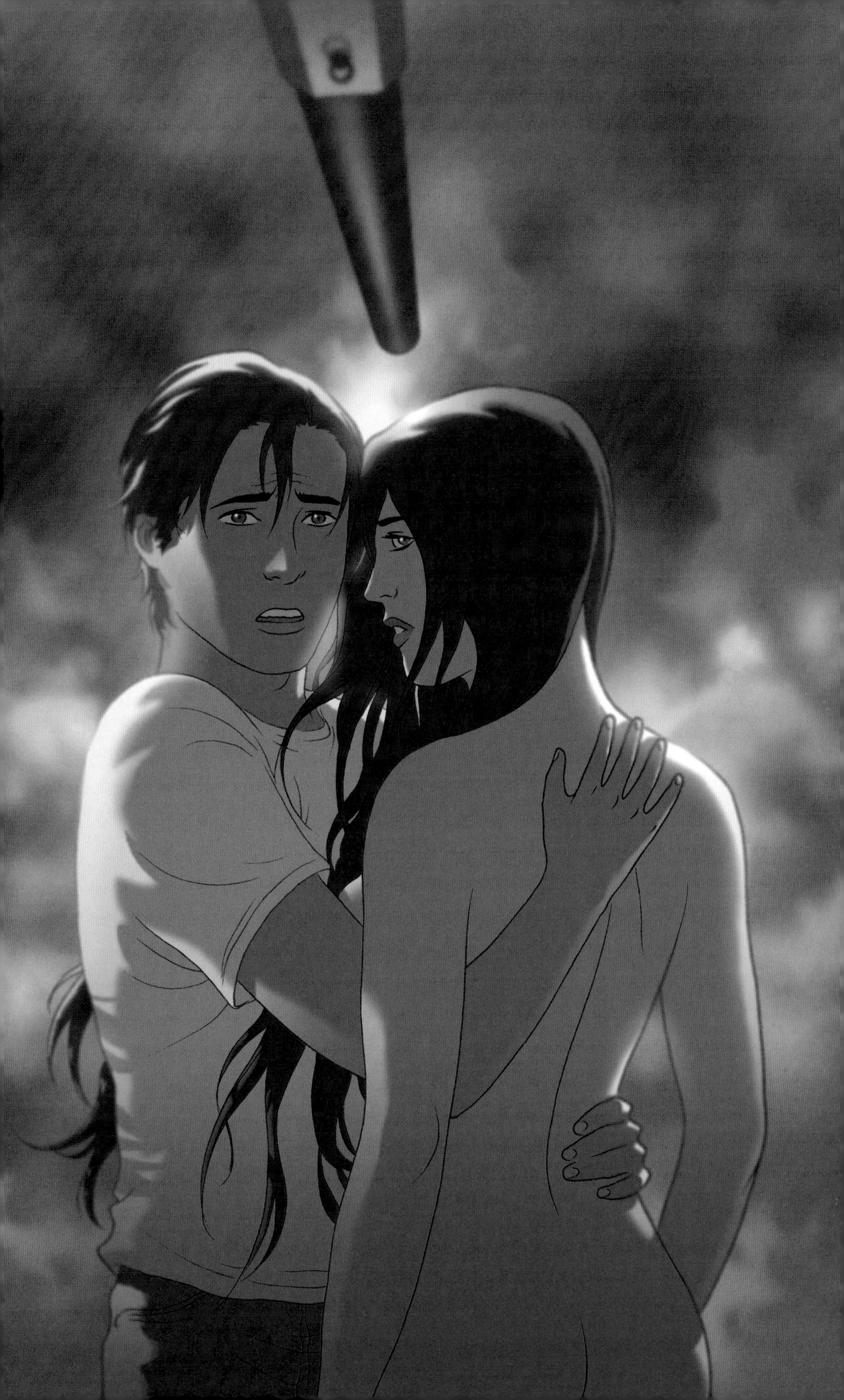

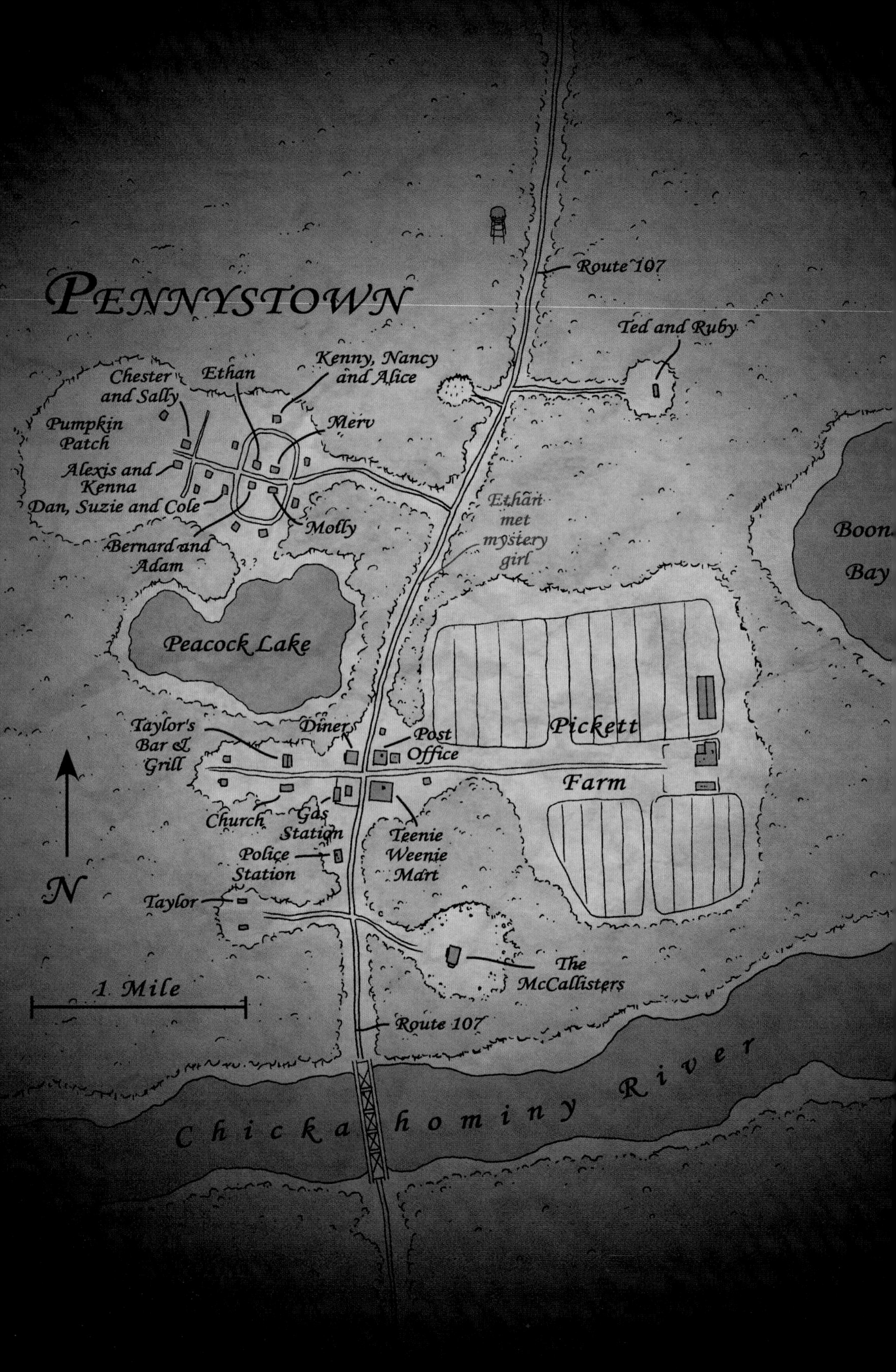

Pennystown
Route 107
Ted and Ruby
Kenny, Nancy and Alice
Chester and Sally
Ethan
Pumpkin Patch
Merv
Alexis and Kenna
Dan, Suzie and Cole
Molly
Bernard and Adam
Ethan met mystery girl
Boon. Bay
Peacock Lake
Taylor's Bar & Grill
Diner
Post Office
Pickett Farm
Church
Gas Station
Teenie Weenie Mart
Police Station
N
Taylor
The McCallisters
1 Mile
Route 107
Chickahominy River

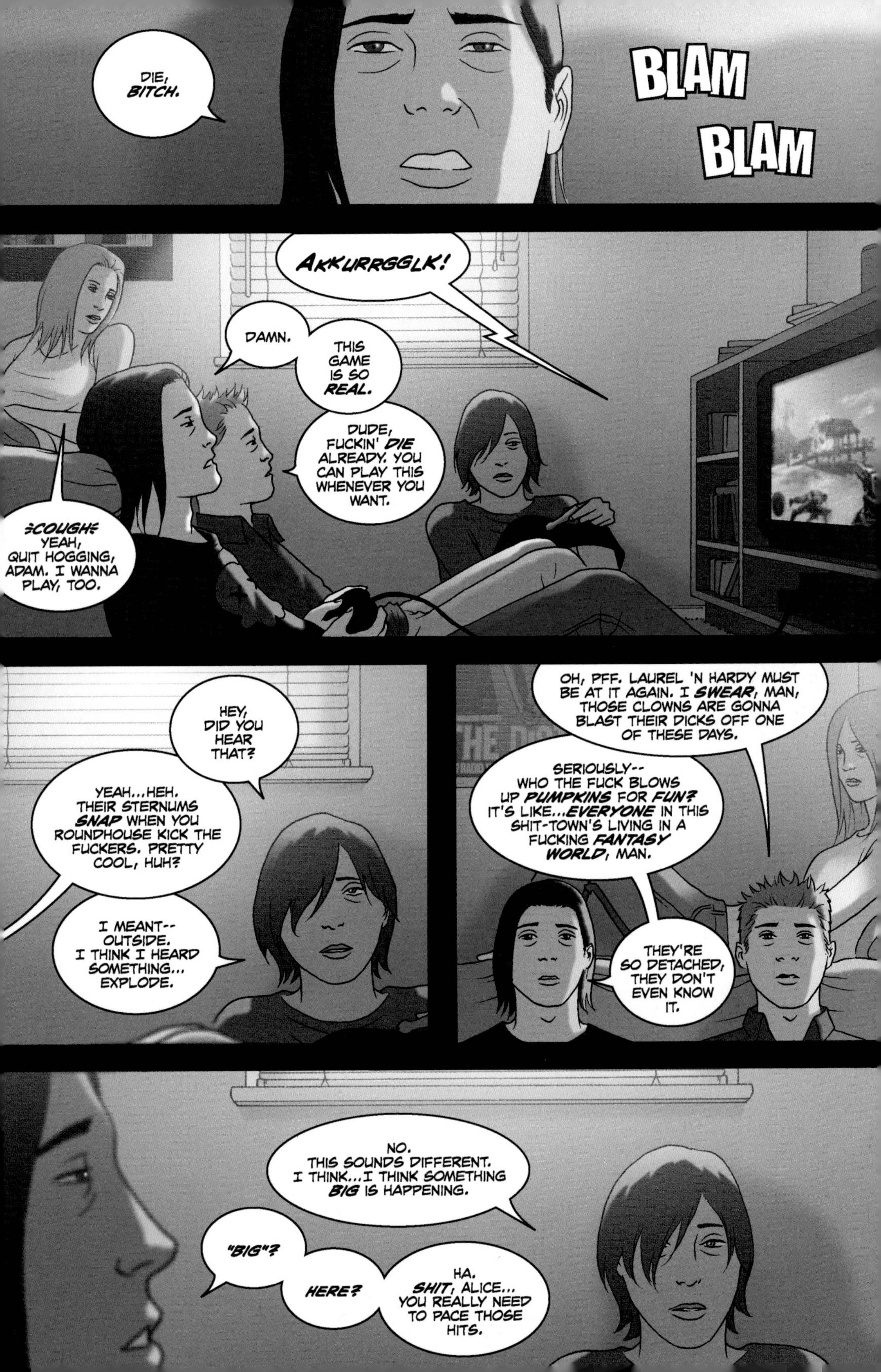
DIE, BITCH.
BLAM
BLAM
AKKURRGGLK!
DAMN.
THIS GAME IS SO REAL.
DUDE, FUCKIN' DIE ALREADY. YOU CAN PLAY THIS WHENEVER YOU WANT.
:COUGH: YEAH, QUIT HOGGING, ADAM. I WANNA PLAY, TOO.
HEY, DID YOU HEAR THAT?
YEAH...HEH. THEIR STERNUMS SNAP WHEN YOU ROUNDHOUSE KICK THE FUCKERS. PRETTY COOL, HUH?
I MEANT-- OUTSIDE. I THINK I HEARD SOMETHING... EXPLODE.
OH, PFF. LAUREL 'N HARDY MUST BE AT IT AGAIN. I SWEAR, MAN, THOSE CLOWNS ARE GONNA BLAST THEIR DICKS OFF ONE OF THESE DAYS.
SERIOUSLY-- WHO THE FUCK BLOWS UP PUMPKINS FOR FUN? IT'S LIKE...EVERYONE IN THIS SHIT-TOWN'S LIVING IN A FUCKING FANTASY WORLD, MAN.
THEY'RE SO DETACHED, THEY DON'T EVEN KNOW IT.
NO. THIS SOUNDS DIFFERENT. I THINK...I THINK SOMETHING BIG IS HAPPENING.
"BIG"?
HERE?
HA. SHIT, ALICE... YOU REALLY NEED TO PACE THOSE HITS.

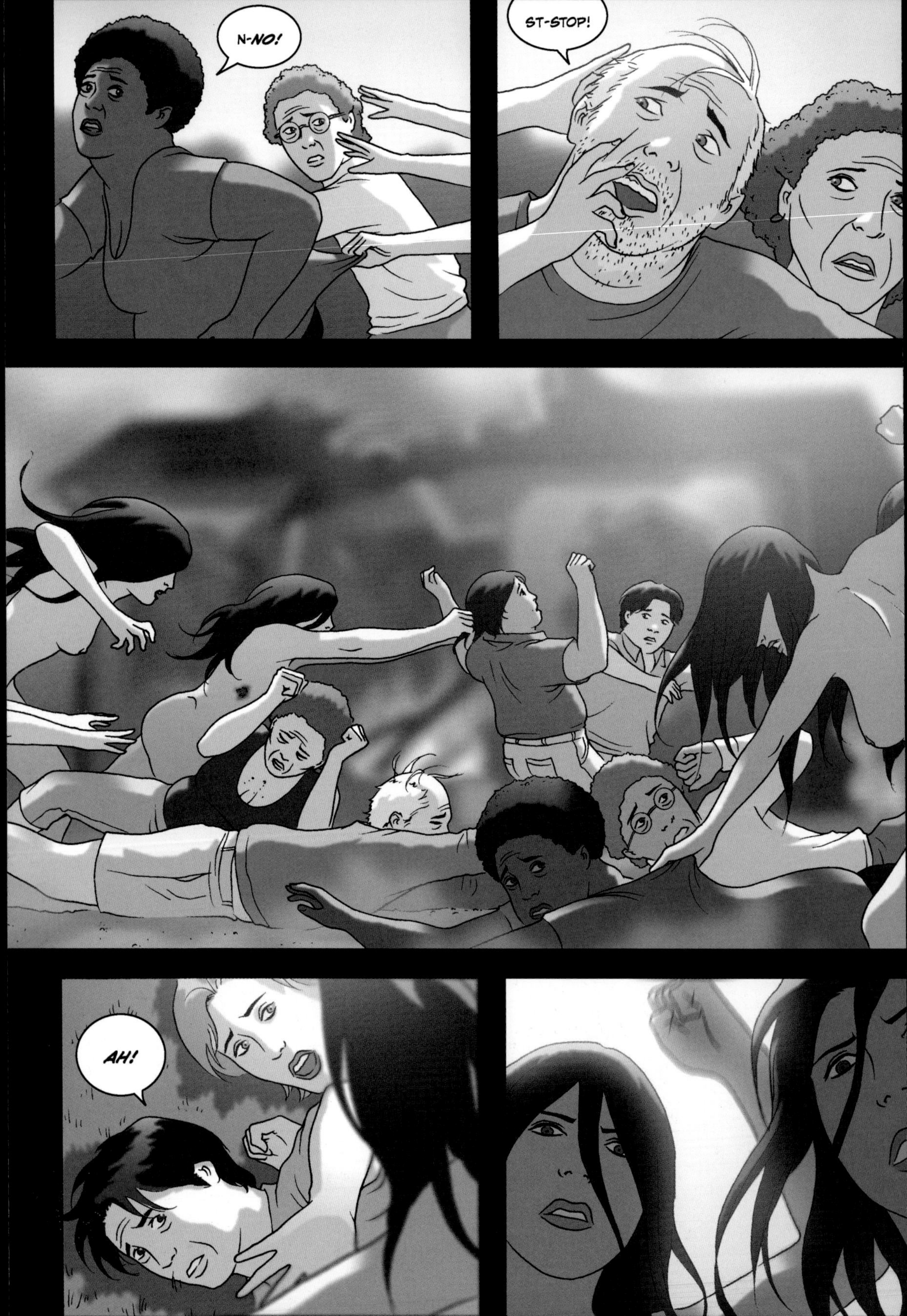
N-NO!
ST-STOP!
AH!

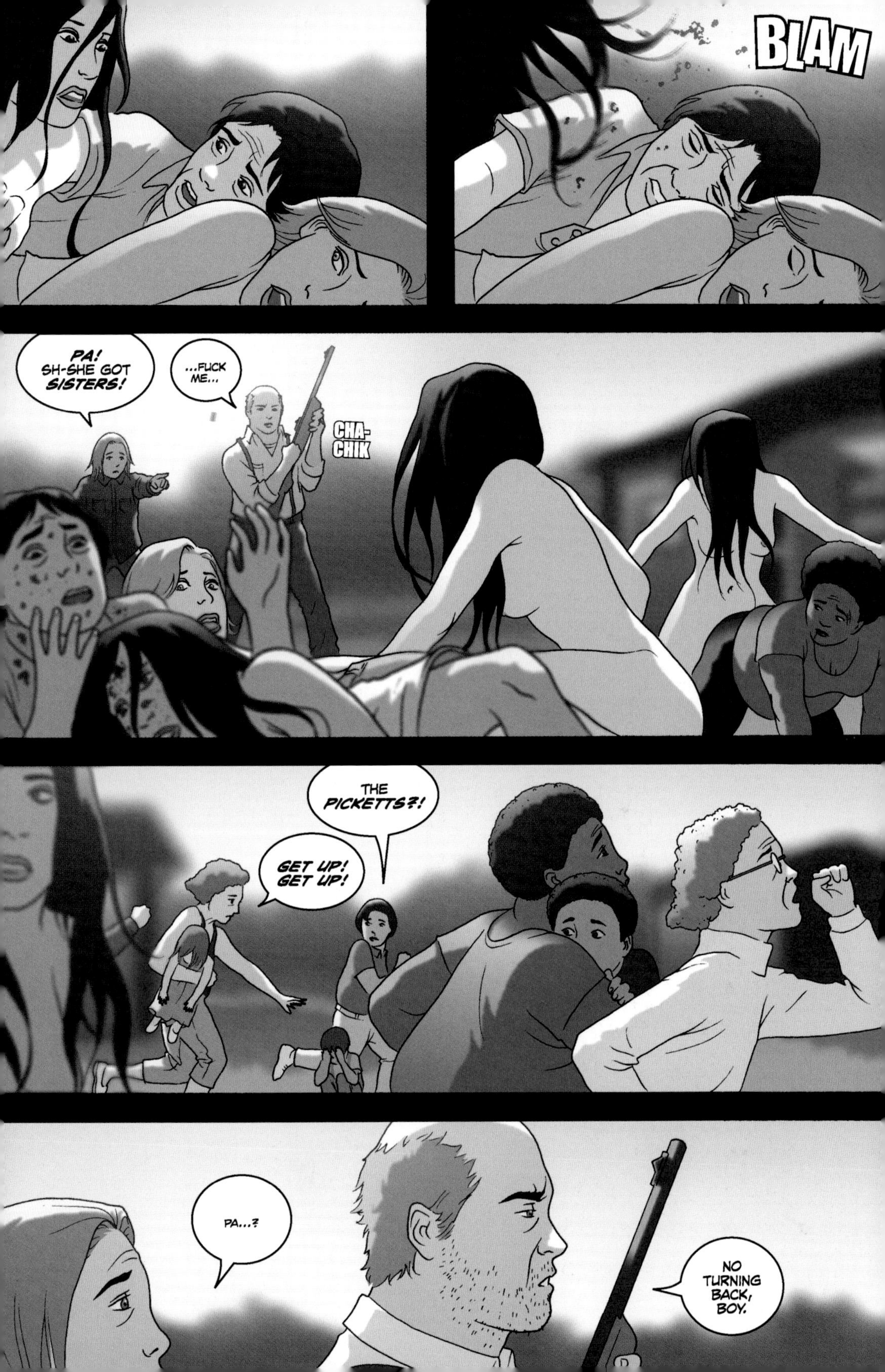
BLAM
PA! SH-SHE GOT SISTERS!
...FUCK ME...
CHA-CHIK
THE PICKETTS?!
GET UP! GET UP!
PA...?
NO TURNING BACK, BOY.

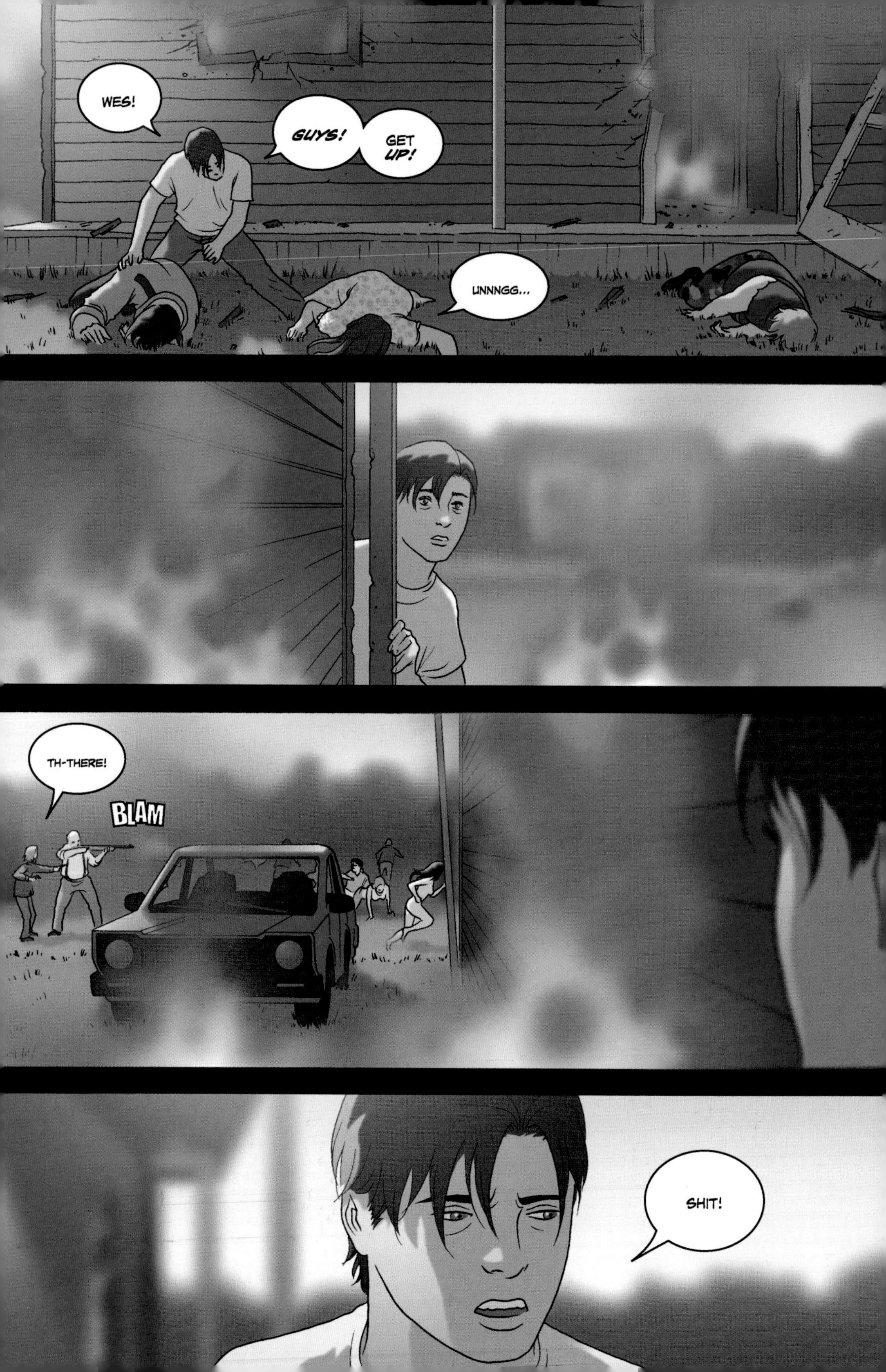
WES!
GUYS!
GET UP!
UNNNGG...
TH-THERE!
BLAM
SHIT!

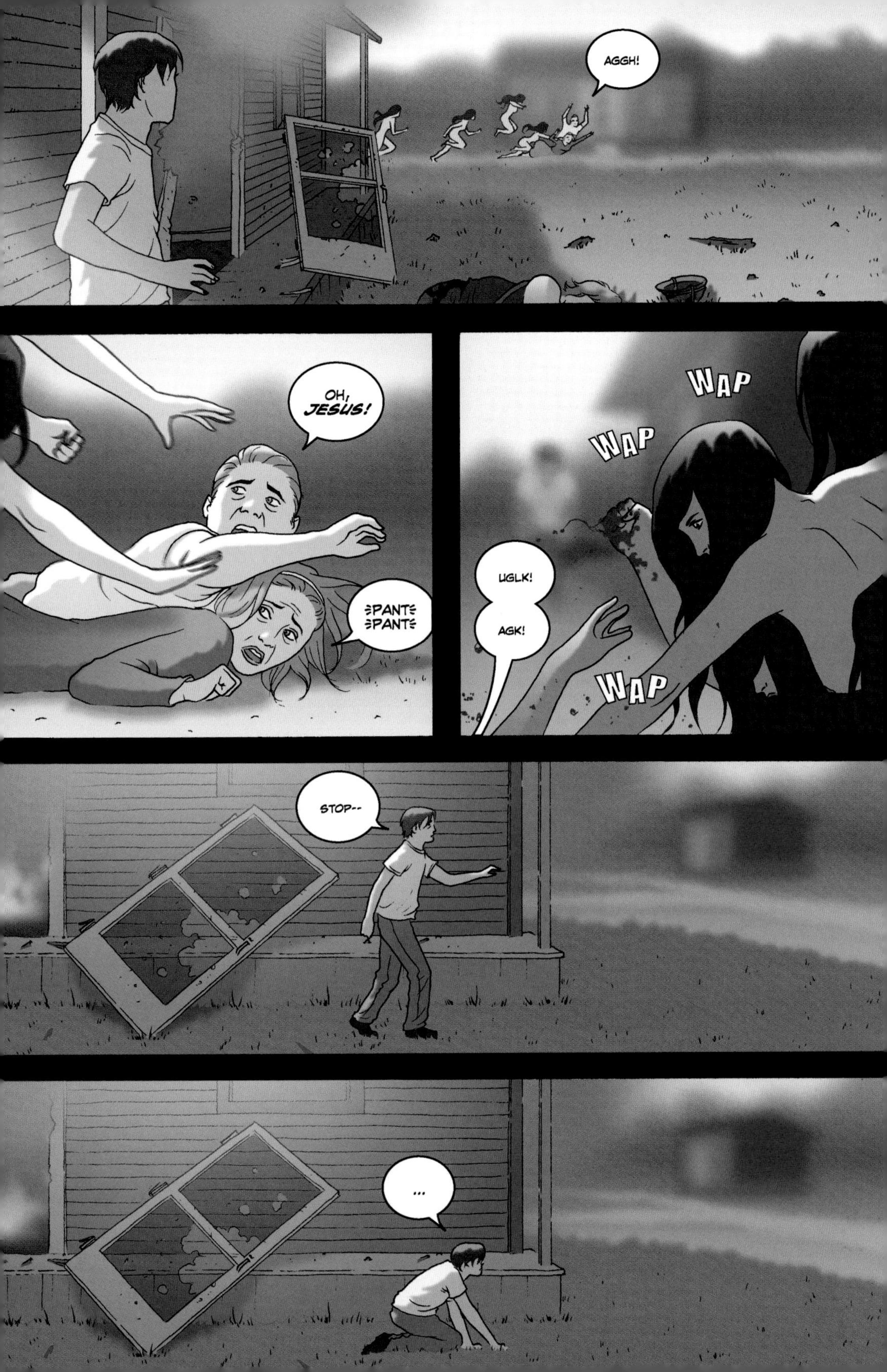
AGGH!
OH, JESUS!
PANT PANT
WAP
WAP
UGLK!
AGK!
WAP
STOP--
...

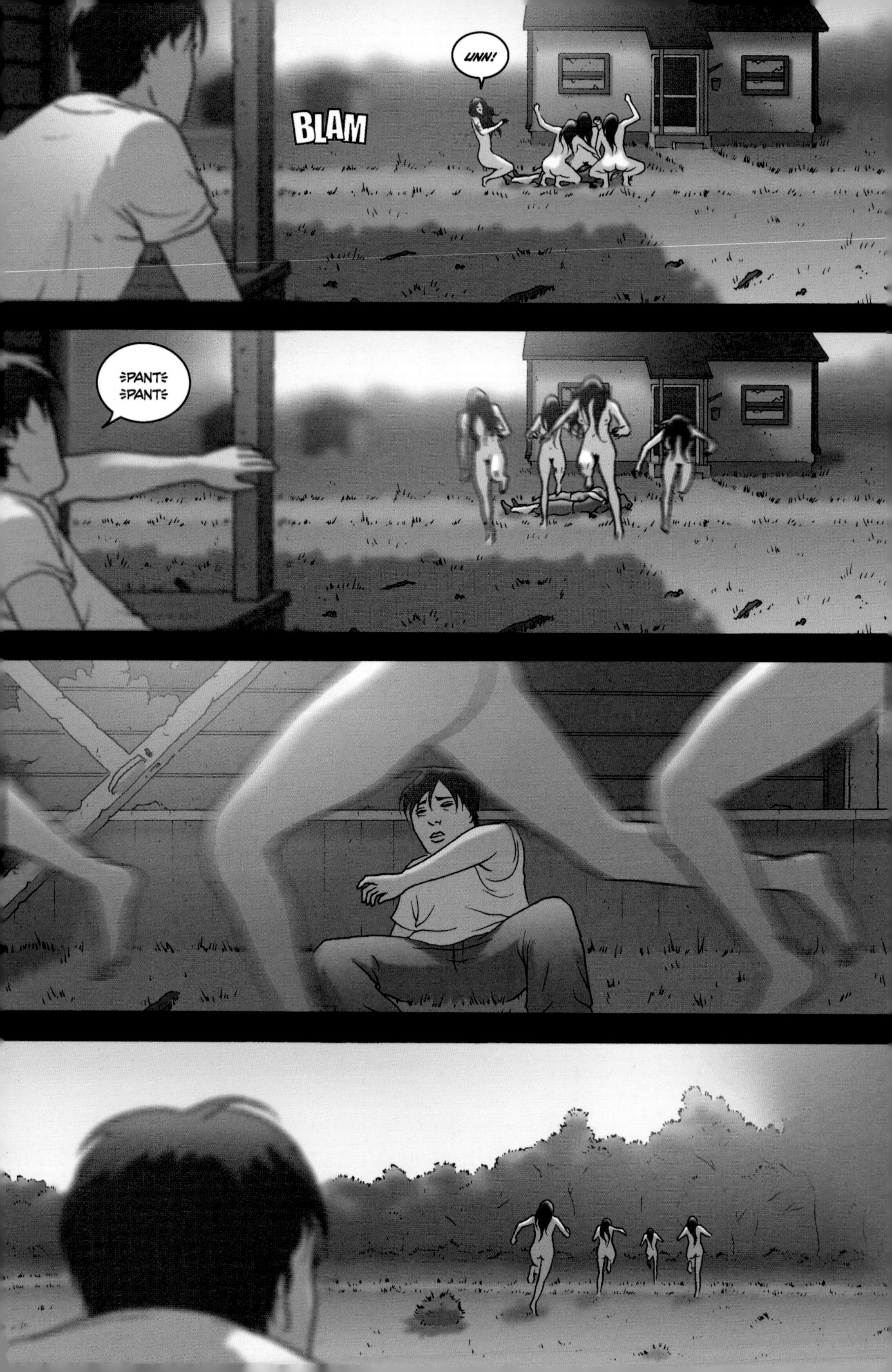

UNN!
BLAM
PANT
PANT

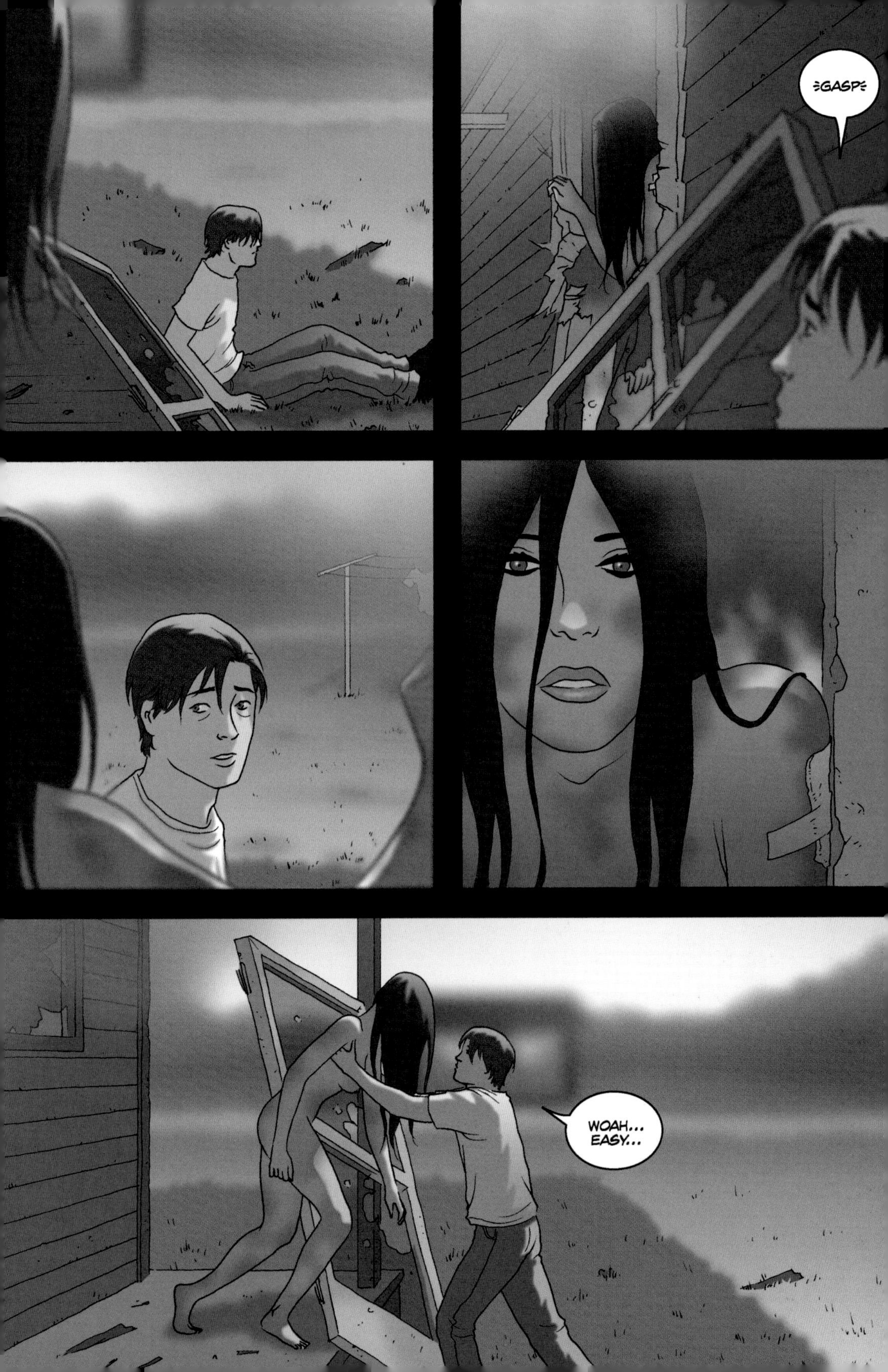

GASP
WOAH... EASY...

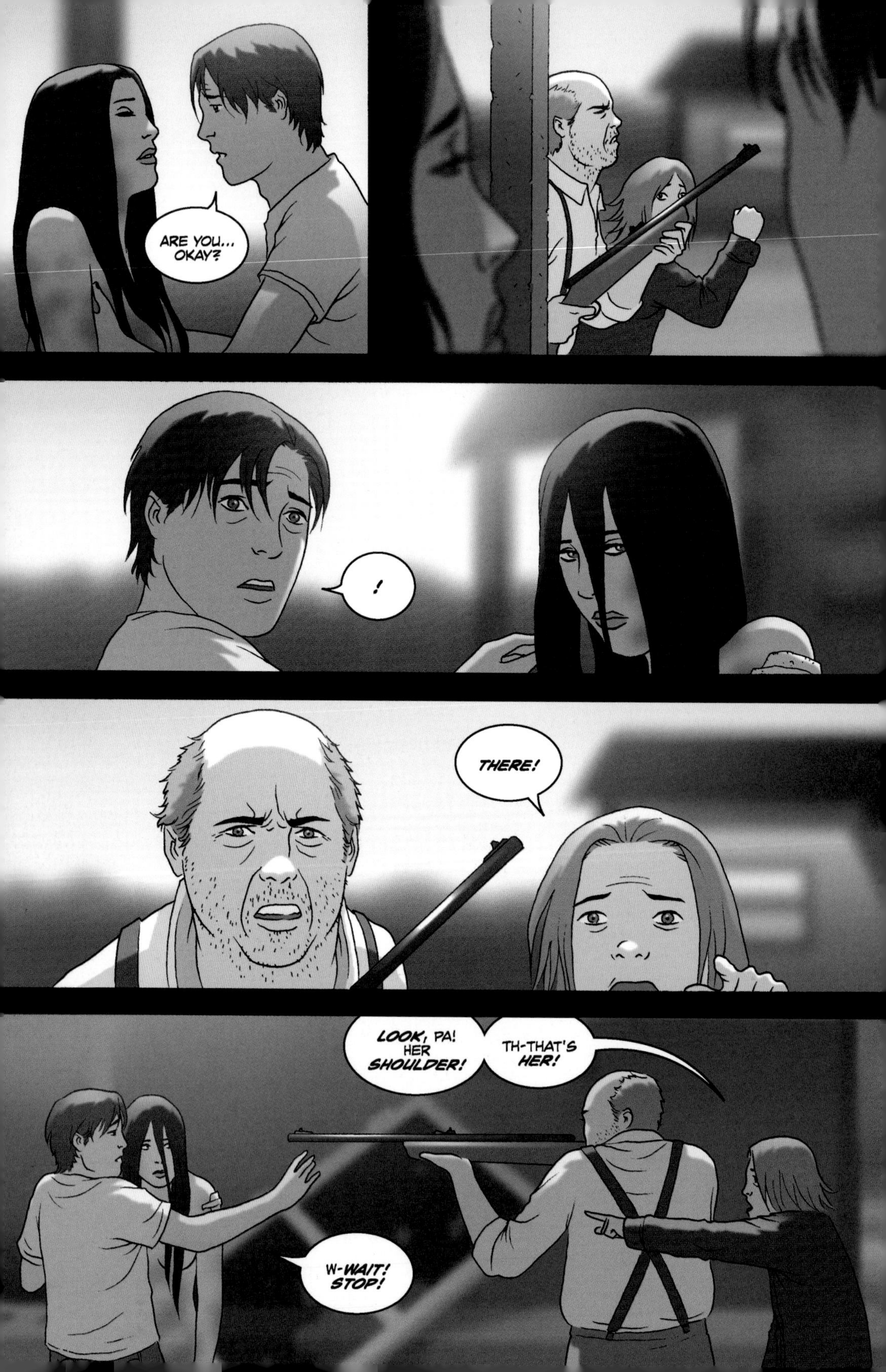
ARE YOU... OKAY?
!
THERE!
LOOK, PA! HER SHOULDER!
TH-THAT'S HER!
W-WAIT! STOP!

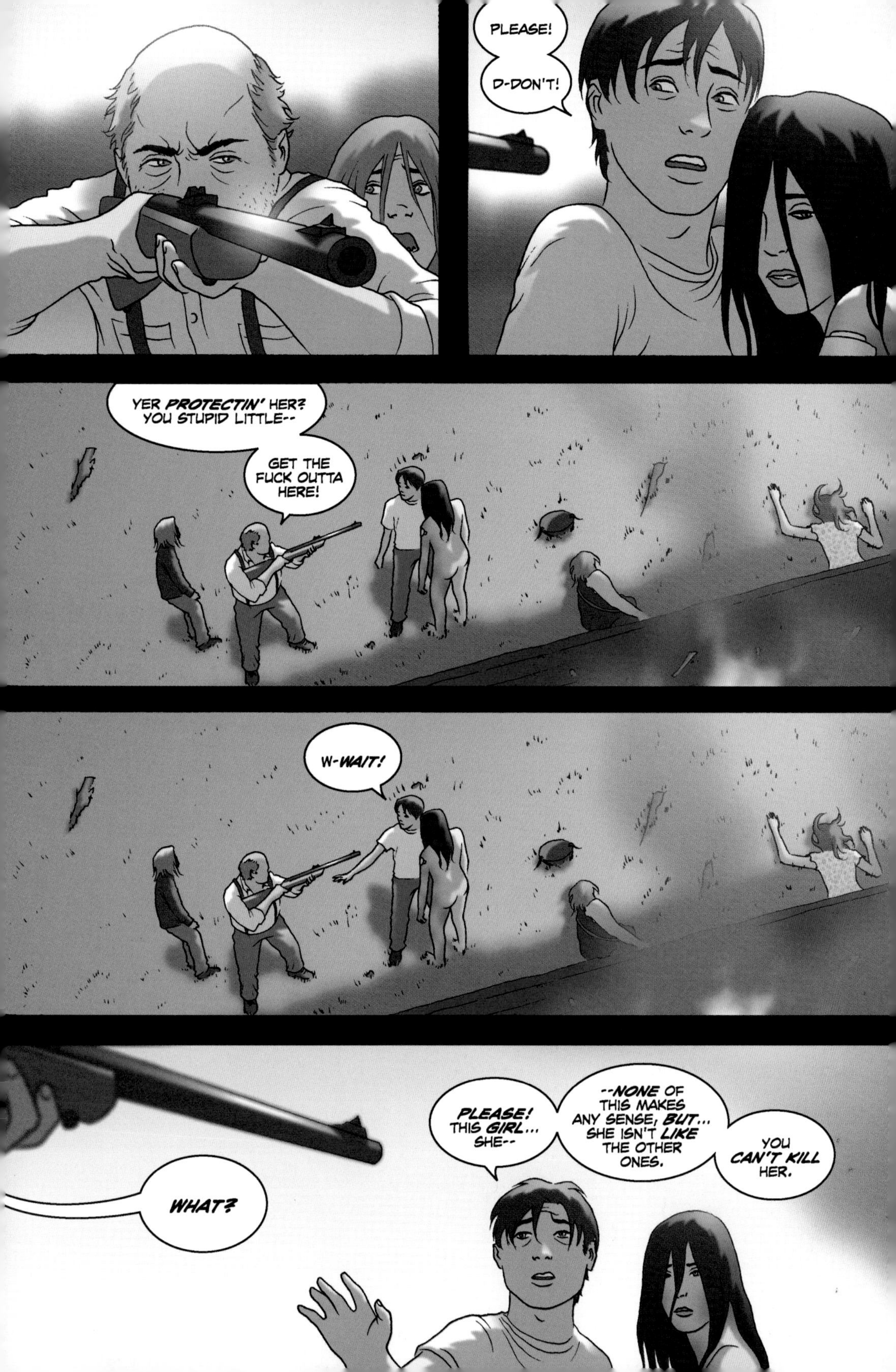
PLEASE!
D-DON'T!
YER PROTECTIN' HER? YOU STUPID LITTLE--
GET THE FUCK OUTTA HERE!
W-WAIT!
PLEASE! THIS GIRL... SHE--
--NONE OF THIS MAKES ANY SENSE, BUT... SHE ISN'T LIKE THE OTHER ONES.
YOU CAN'T KILL HER.
WHAT?

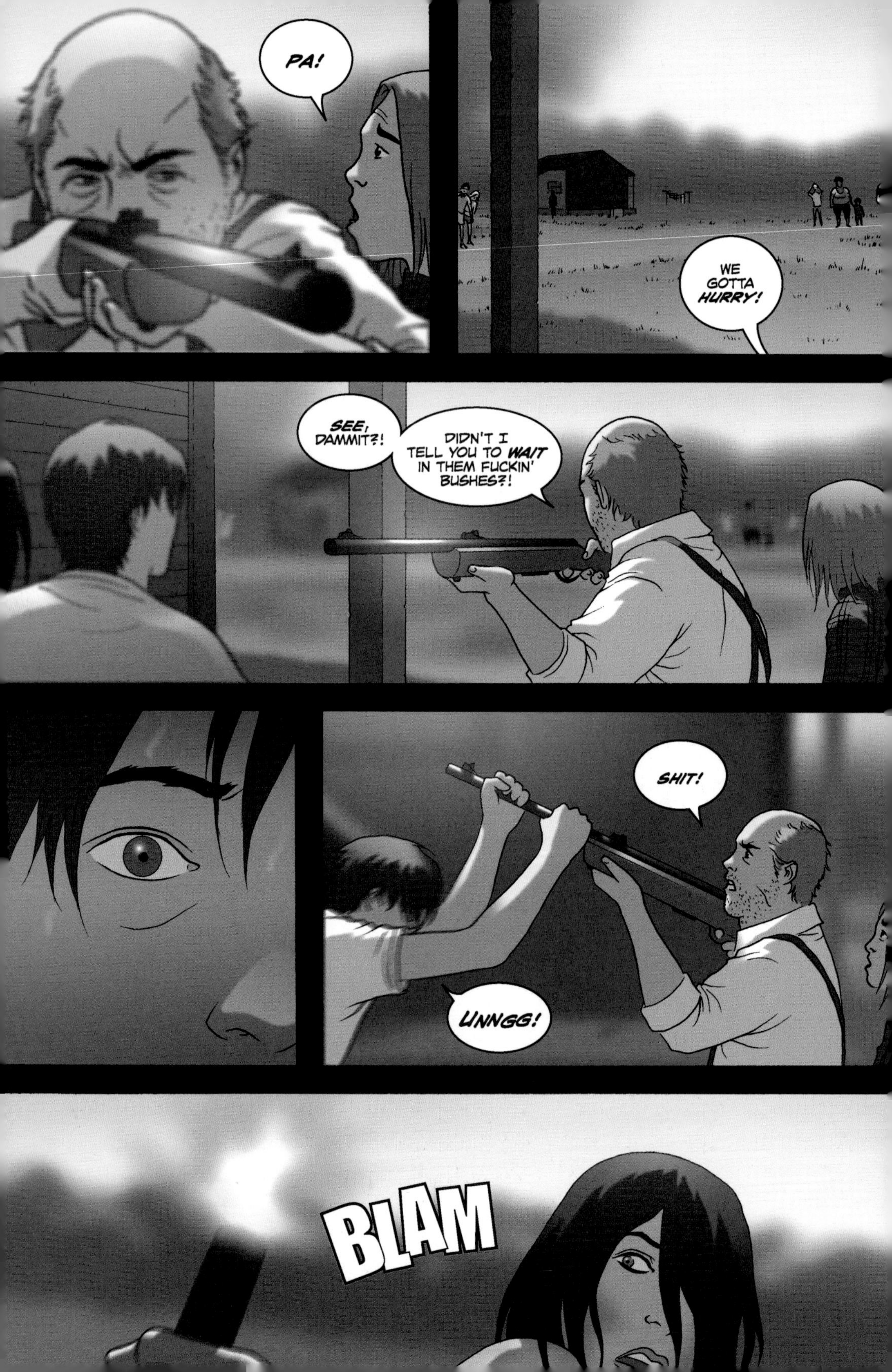
PA!
WE GOTTA HURRY!
SEE, DAMMIT?!
DIDN'T I TELL YOU TO WAIT IN THEM FUCKIN' BUSHES?!
SHIT!
UNNGG!
BLAM

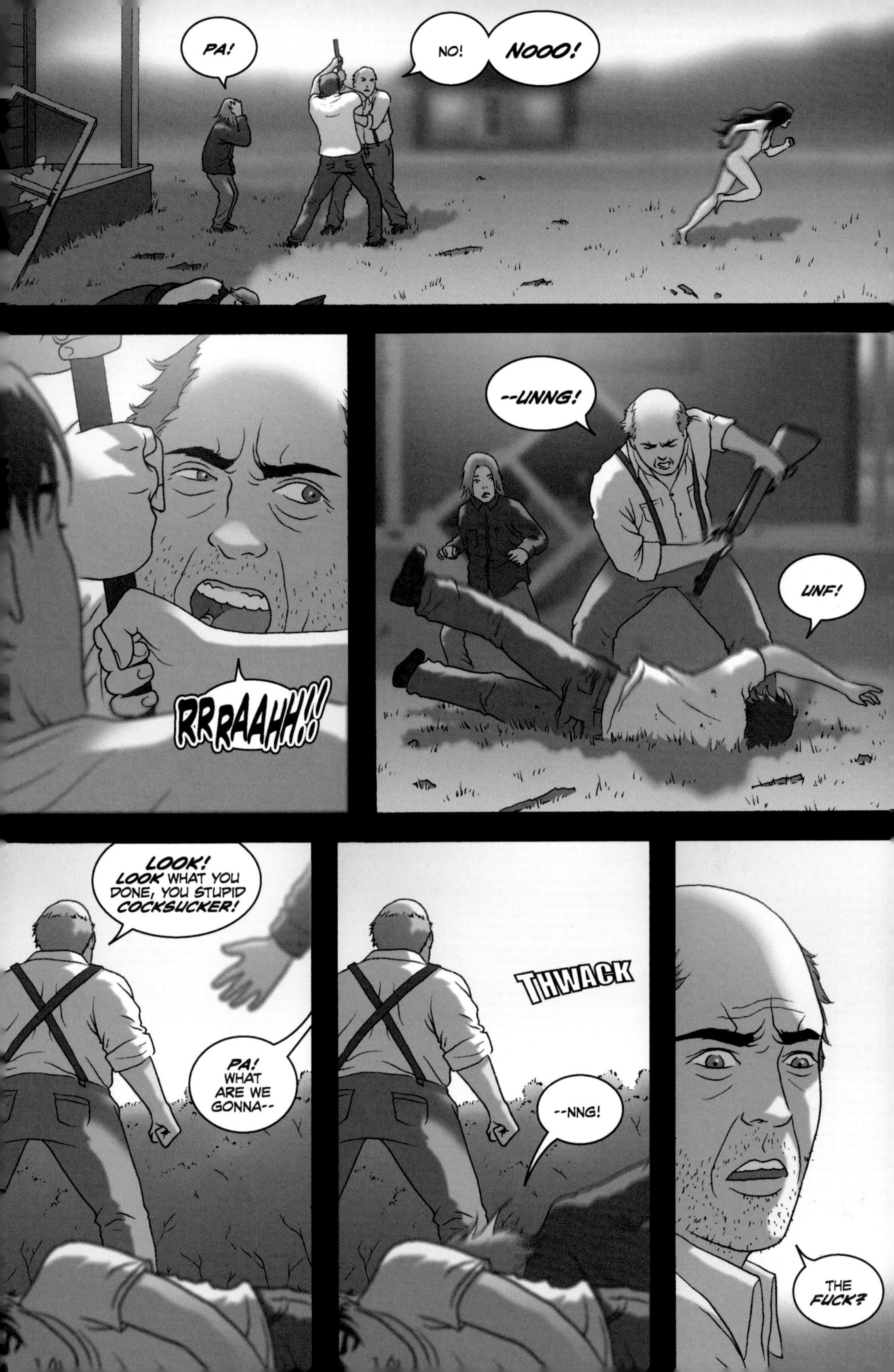
PA!
NO!
NOOO!
RRRAAHH!!
--UNNG!
UNF!
LOOK! LOOK WHAT YOU DONE, YOU STUPID COCKSUCKER!
PA! WHAT ARE WE GONNA--
THWACK
--NNG!
THE FUCK?

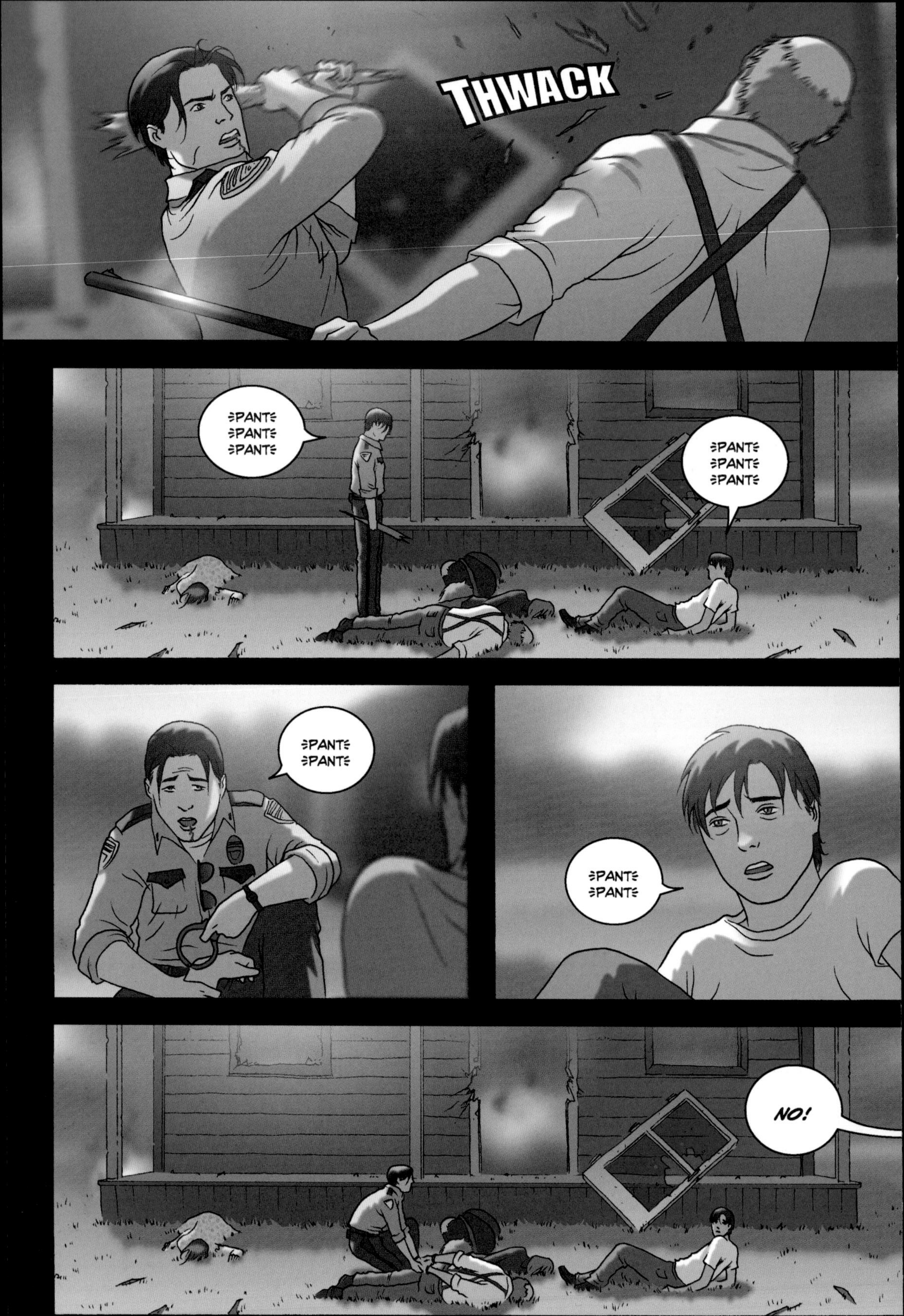
THWACK
PANT PANT PANT
PANT PANT PANT
PANT PANT
PANT PANT
NO!

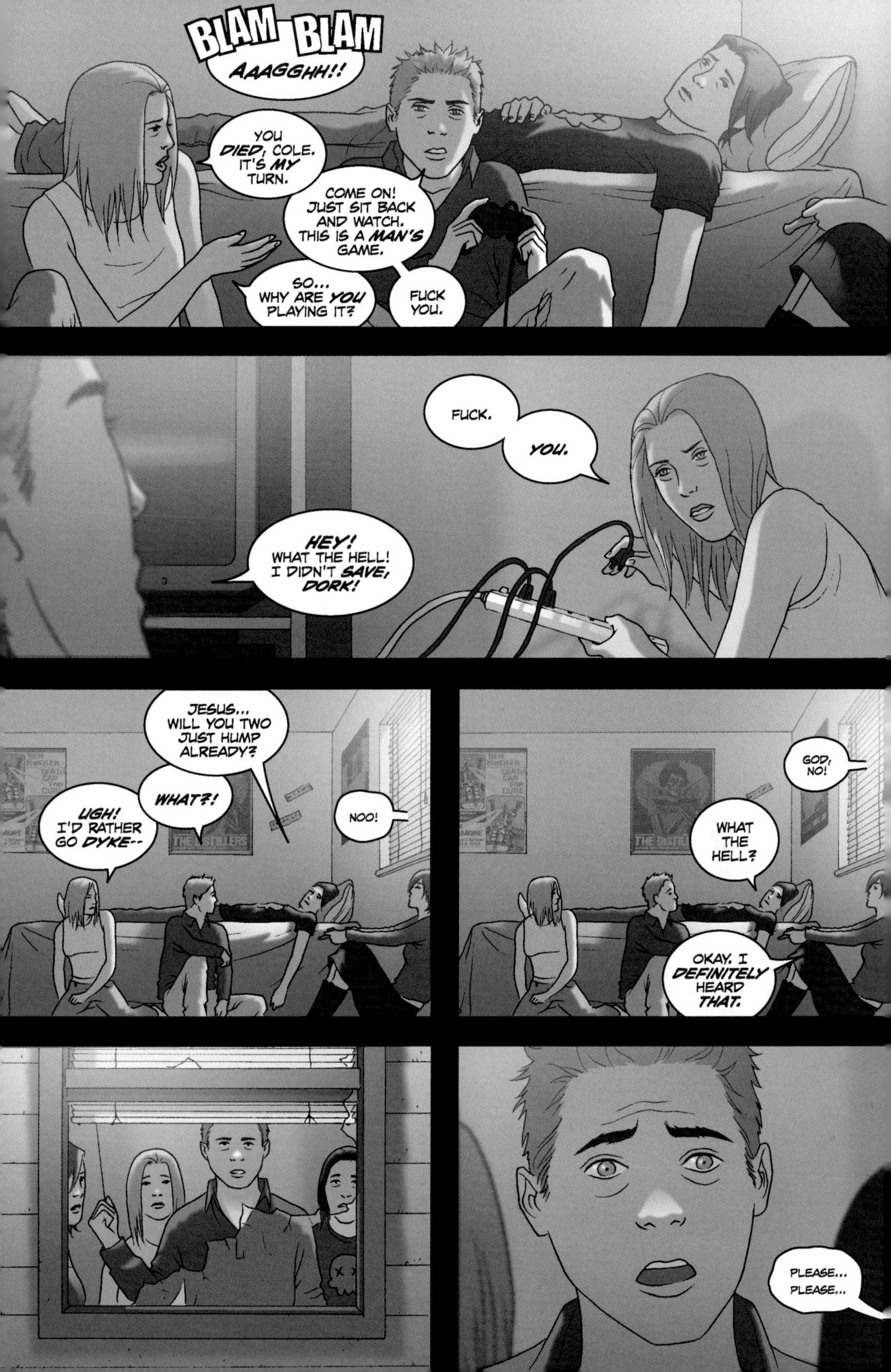
BLAM BLAM
AAAGGHH!!
YOU DIED, COLE. IT'S MY TURN.
COME ON! JUST SIT BACK AND WATCH. THIS IS A MAN'S GAME.
SO... WHY ARE YOU PLAYING IT?
FUCK YOU.
FUCK.
YOU.
HEY! WHAT THE HELL! I DIDN'T SAVE, DORK!
JESUS... WILL YOU TWO JUST HUMP ALREADY?
WHAT?!
UGH! I'D RATHER GO DYKE--
NOO!
THE DISTILLERS
GOD, NO!
WHAT THE HELL?
OKAY. I DEFINITELY HEARD THAT.
PLEASE...
PLEASE...

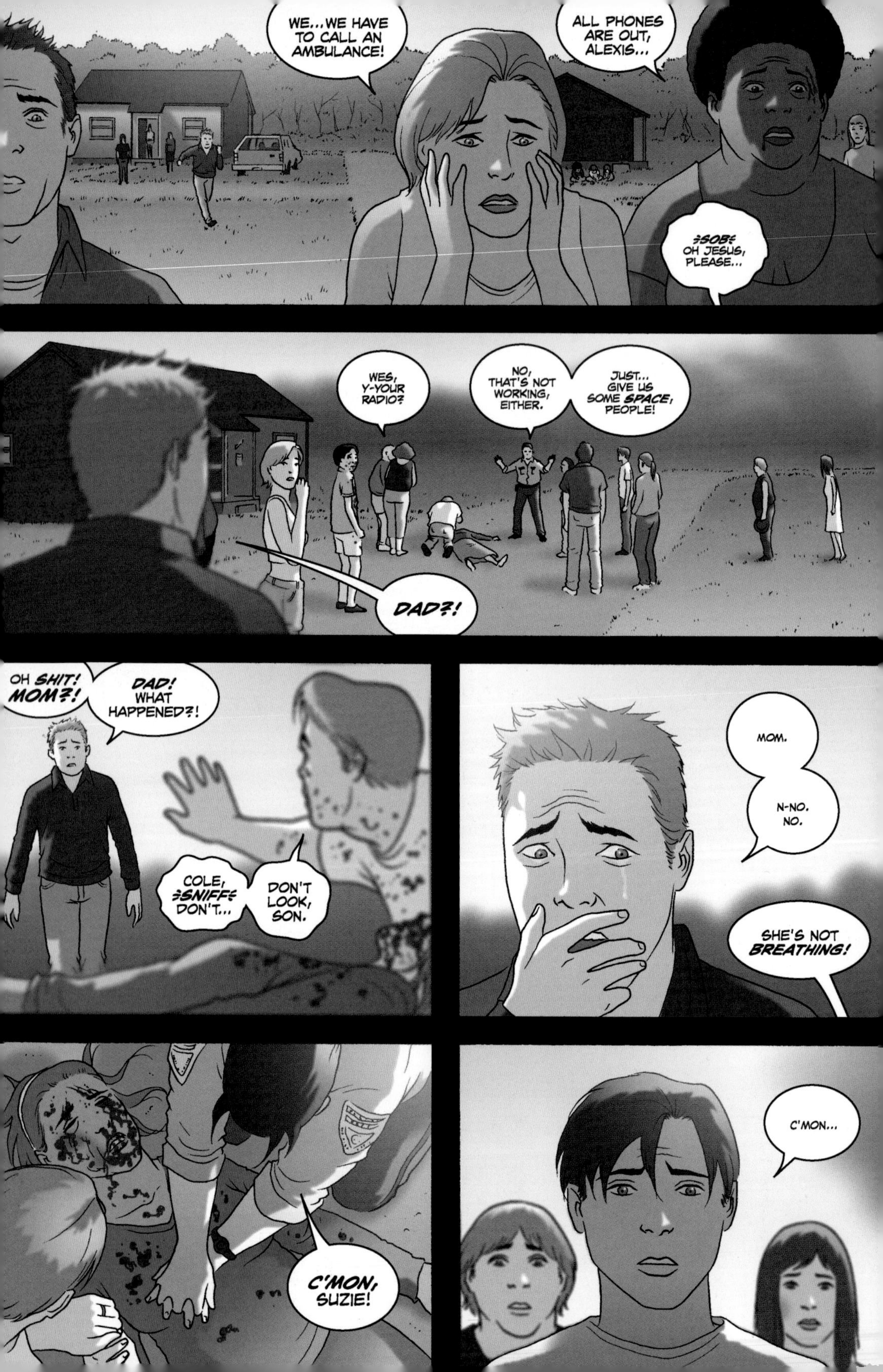
WE...WE HAVE TO CALL AN AMBULANCE!
ALL PHONES ARE OUT, ALEXIS...
SOB OH JESUS, PLEASE...
WES, Y-YOUR RADIO?
NO, THAT'S NOT WORKING, EITHER.
JUST... GIVE US SOME SPACE, PEOPLE!
DAD?!
OH SHIT! MOM?!
DAD! WHAT HAPPENED?!
COLE, SNIFF DON'T...
DON'T LOOK, SON.
MOM.
N-NO. NO.
SHE'S NOT BREATHING!
C'MON, SUZIE!
C'MON...

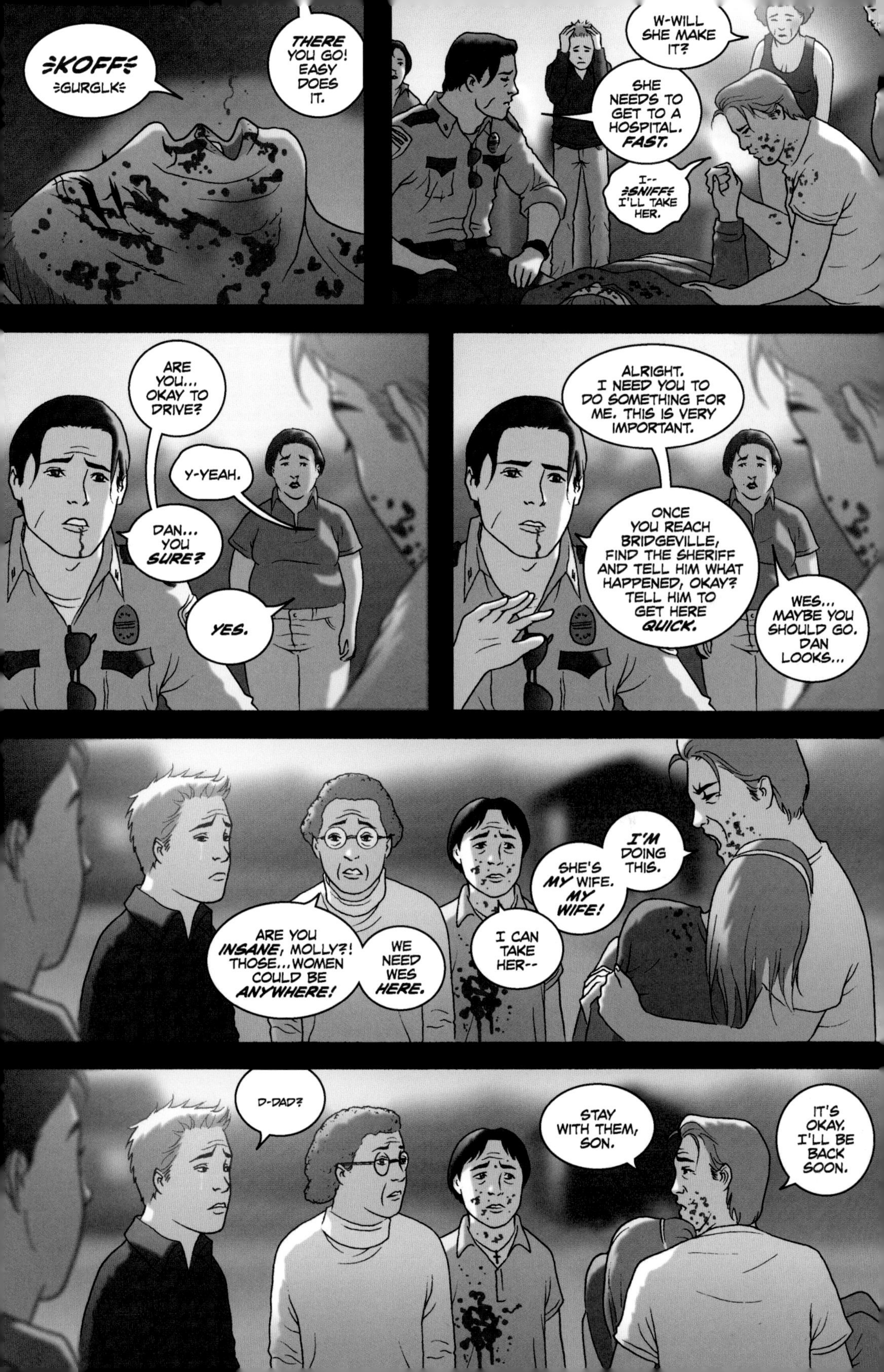

KOFF
GURGLK
THERE YOU GO! EASY DOES IT.
W-WILL SHE MAKE IT?
SHE NEEDS TO GET TO A HOSPITAL. FAST.
I-- *SNIFF* I'LL TAKE HER.
ARE YOU... OKAY TO DRIVE?
Y-YEAH.
DAN... YOU SURE?
YES.
ALRIGHT. I NEED YOU TO DO SOMETHING FOR ME. THIS IS VERY IMPORTANT.
ONCE YOU REACH BRIDGEVILLE, FIND THE SHERIFF AND TELL HIM WHAT HAPPENED, OKAY? TELL HIM TO GET HERE QUICK.
WES... MAYBE YOU SHOULD GO. DAN LOOKS...
ARE YOU INSANE, MOLLY?! THOSE...WOMEN COULD BE ANYWHERE!
WE NEED WES HERE.
I CAN TAKE HER--
SHE'S MY WIFE. MY WIFE!
I'M DOING THIS.
D-DAD?
STAY WITH THEM, SON.
IT'S OKAY. I'LL BE BACK SOON.

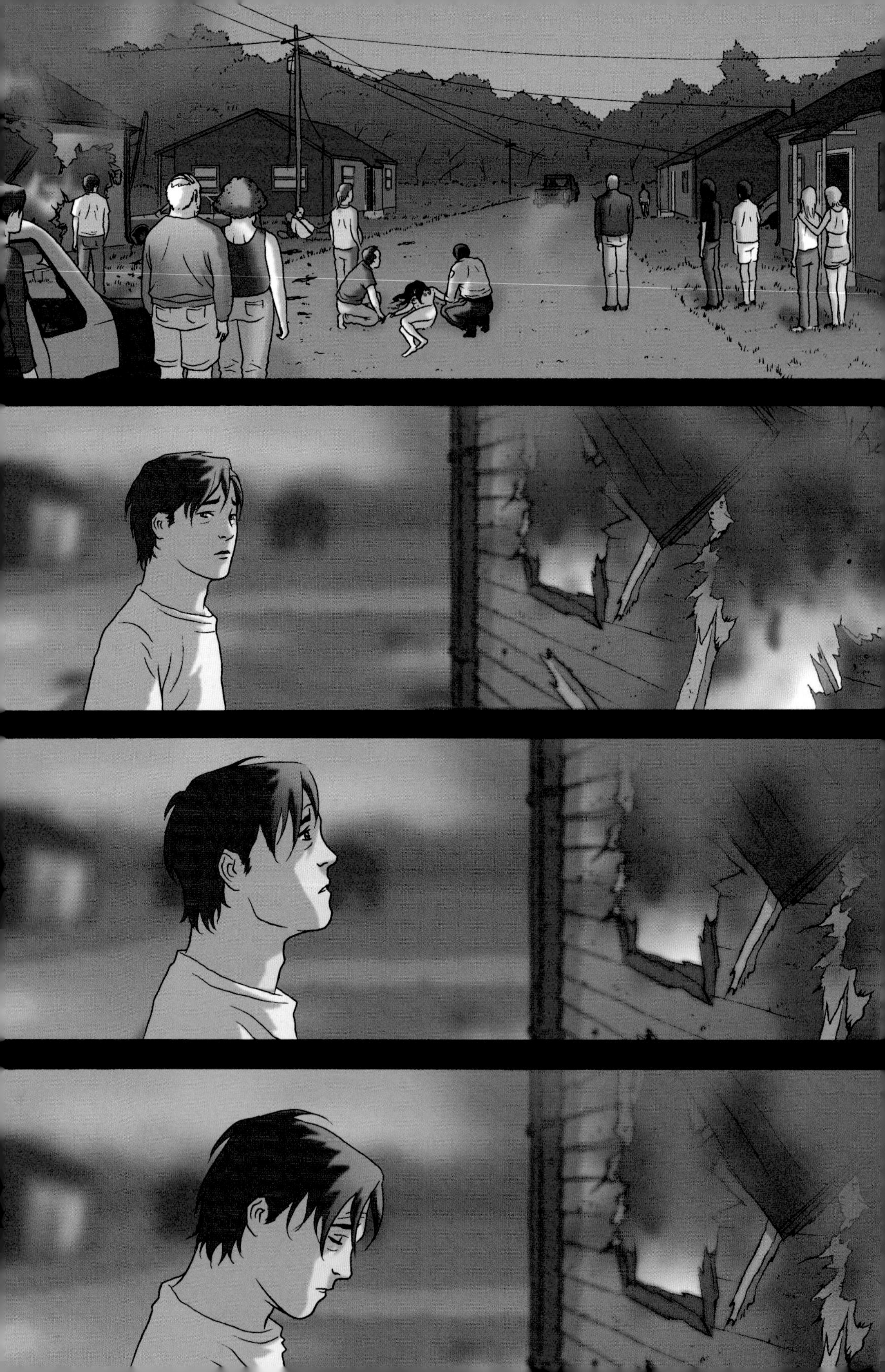

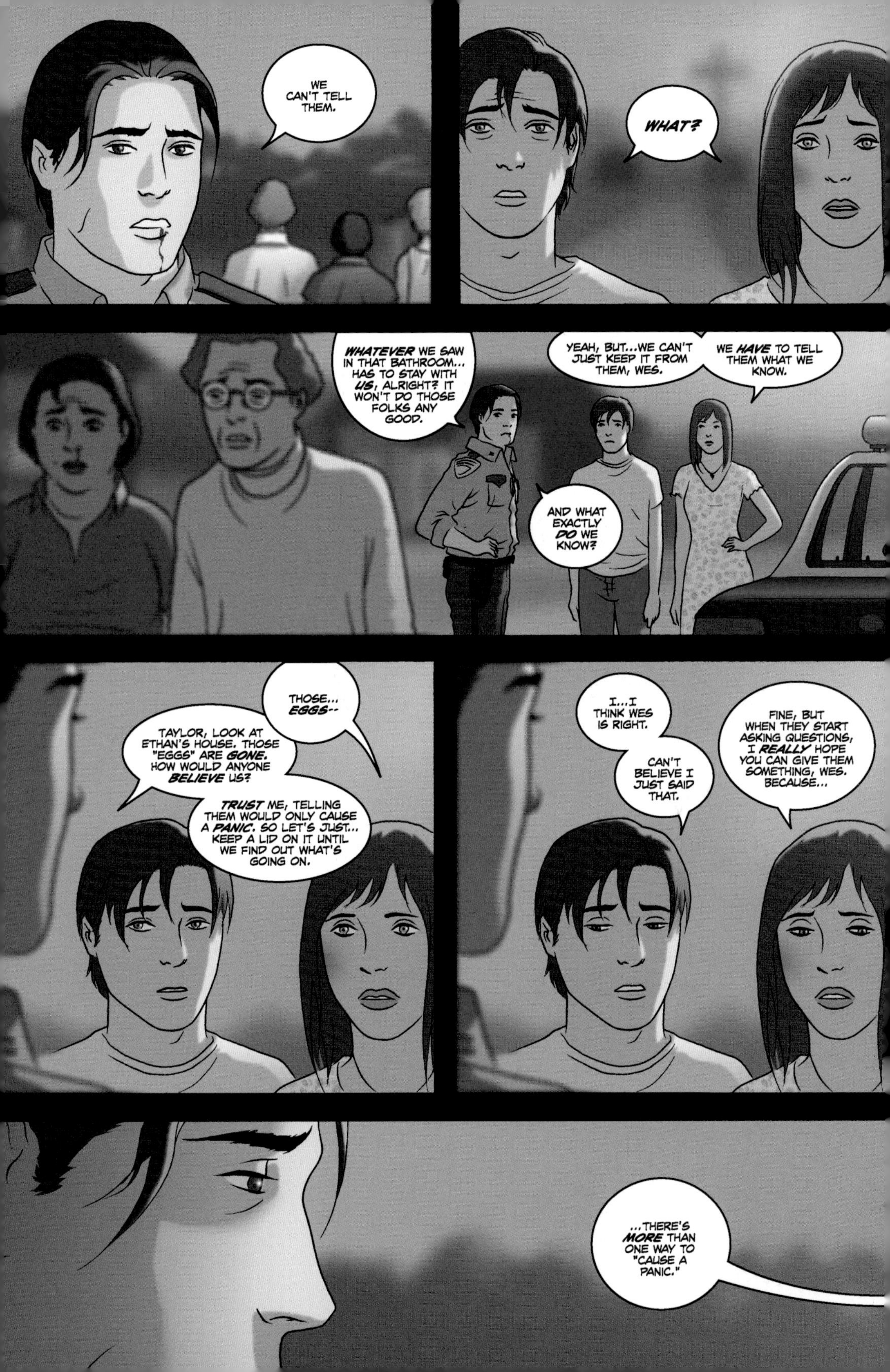
WE CAN'T TELL THEM.
WHAT?
WHATEVER WE SAW IN THAT BATHROOM... HAS TO STAY WITH US, ALRIGHT? IT WON'T DO THOSE FOLKS ANY GOOD.
YEAH, BUT...WE CAN'T JUST KEEP IT FROM THEM, WES.
WE HAVE TO TELL THEM WHAT WE KNOW.
AND WHAT EXACTLY DO WE KNOW?
THOSE... EGGS--
TAYLOR, LOOK AT ETHAN'S HOUSE. THOSE "EGGS" ARE GONE. HOW WOULD ANYONE BELIEVE US?
TRUST ME, TELLING THEM WOULD ONLY CAUSE A PANIC. SO LET'S JUST... KEEP A LID ON IT UNTIL WE FIND OUT WHAT'S GOING ON.
I...I THINK WES IS RIGHT.
CAN'T BELIEVE I JUST SAID THAT.
FINE, BUT WHEN THEY START ASKING QUESTIONS, I REALLY HOPE YOU CAN GIVE THEM SOMETHING, WES. BECAUSE...
...THERE'S MORE THAN ONE WAY TO "CAUSE A PANIC."

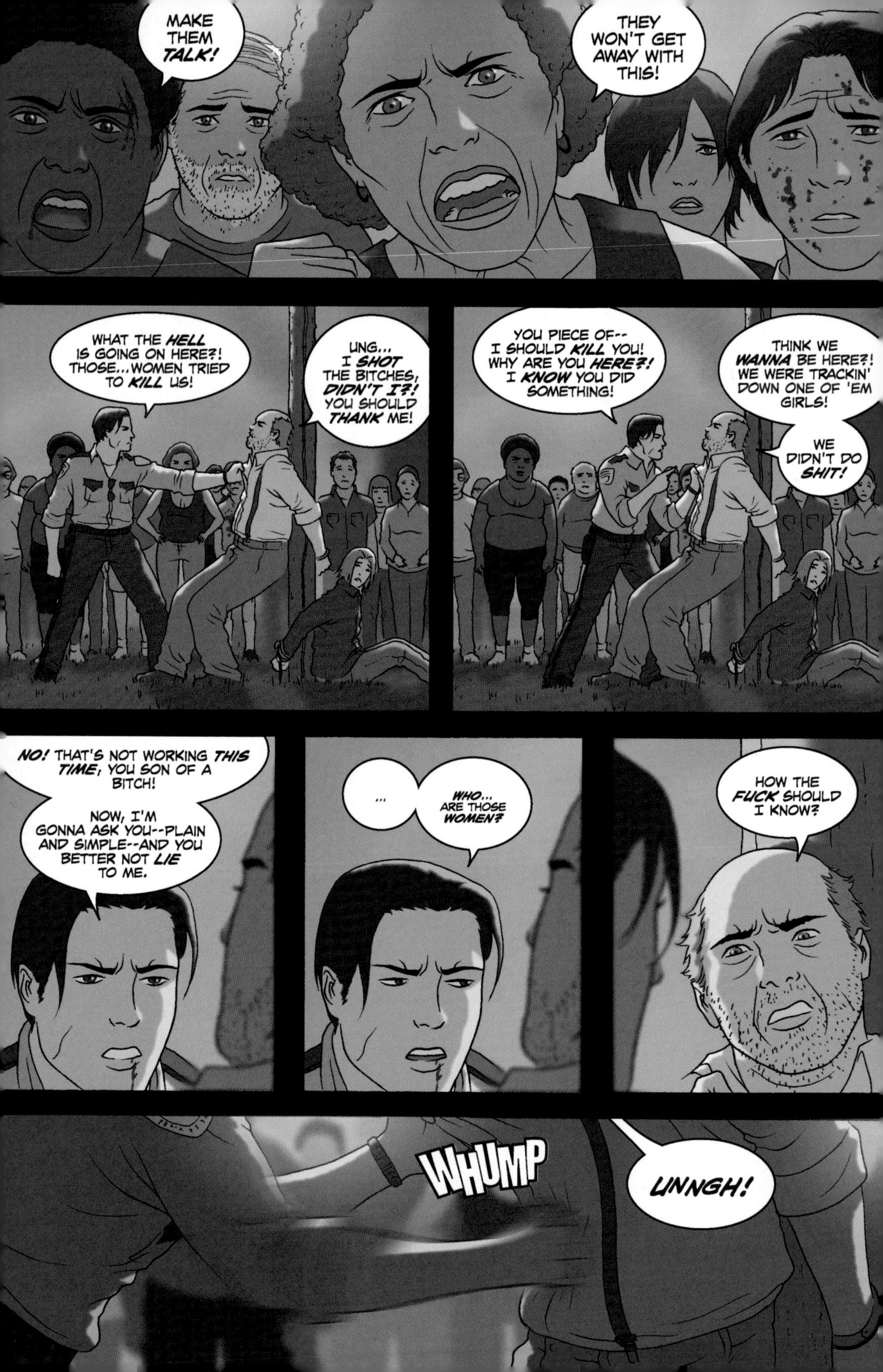

MAKE THEM TALK!
THEY WON'T GET AWAY WITH THIS!
WHAT THE HELL IS GOING ON HERE?! THOSE...WOMEN TRIED TO KILL US!
UNG... I SHOT THE BITCHES, DIDN'T I?! YOU SHOULD THANK ME!
YOU PIECE OF-- I SHOULD KILL YOU! WHY ARE YOU HERE?! I KNOW YOU DID SOMETHING!
THINK WE WANNA BE HERE?! WE WERE TRACKIN' DOWN ONE OF 'EM GIRLS!
WE DIDN'T DO SHIT!
NO! THAT'S NOT WORKING THIS TIME, YOU SON OF A BITCH!
NOW, I'M GONNA ASK YOU--PLAIN AND SIMPLE--AND YOU BETTER NOT LIE TO ME.
...
WHO... ARE THOSE WOMEN?
HOW THE FUCK SHOULD I KNOW?
WHUMP
UNNGH!

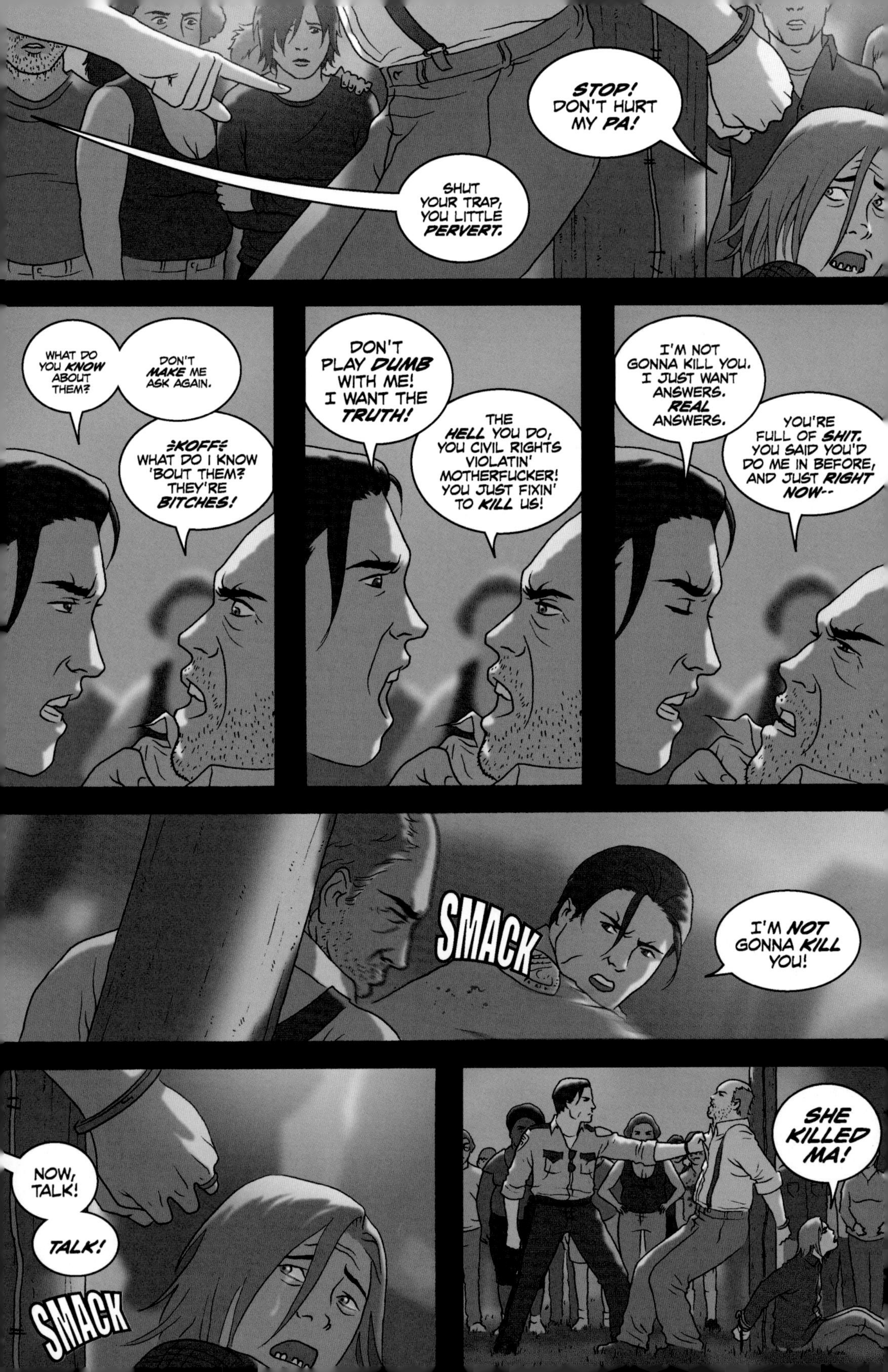
STOP! DON'T HURT MY PA!
SHUT YOUR TRAP, YOU LITTLE PERVERT.
WHAT DO YOU KNOW ABOUT THEM?
DON'T MAKE ME ASK AGAIN.
KOFF WHAT DO I KNOW 'BOUT THEM? THEY'RE BITCHES!
DON'T PLAY DUMB WITH ME! I WANT THE TRUTH!
THE HELL YOU DO, YOU CIVIL RIGHTS VIOLATIN' MOTHERFUCKER! YOU JUST FIXIN' TO KILL US!
I'M NOT GONNA KILL YOU. I JUST WANT ANSWERS. REAL ANSWERS.
YOU'RE FULL OF SHIT. YOU SAID YOU'D DO ME IN BEFORE, AND JUST RIGHT NOW--
SMACK
I'M NOT GONNA KILL YOU!
NOW, TALK!
TALK!
SMACK
SHE KILLED MA!

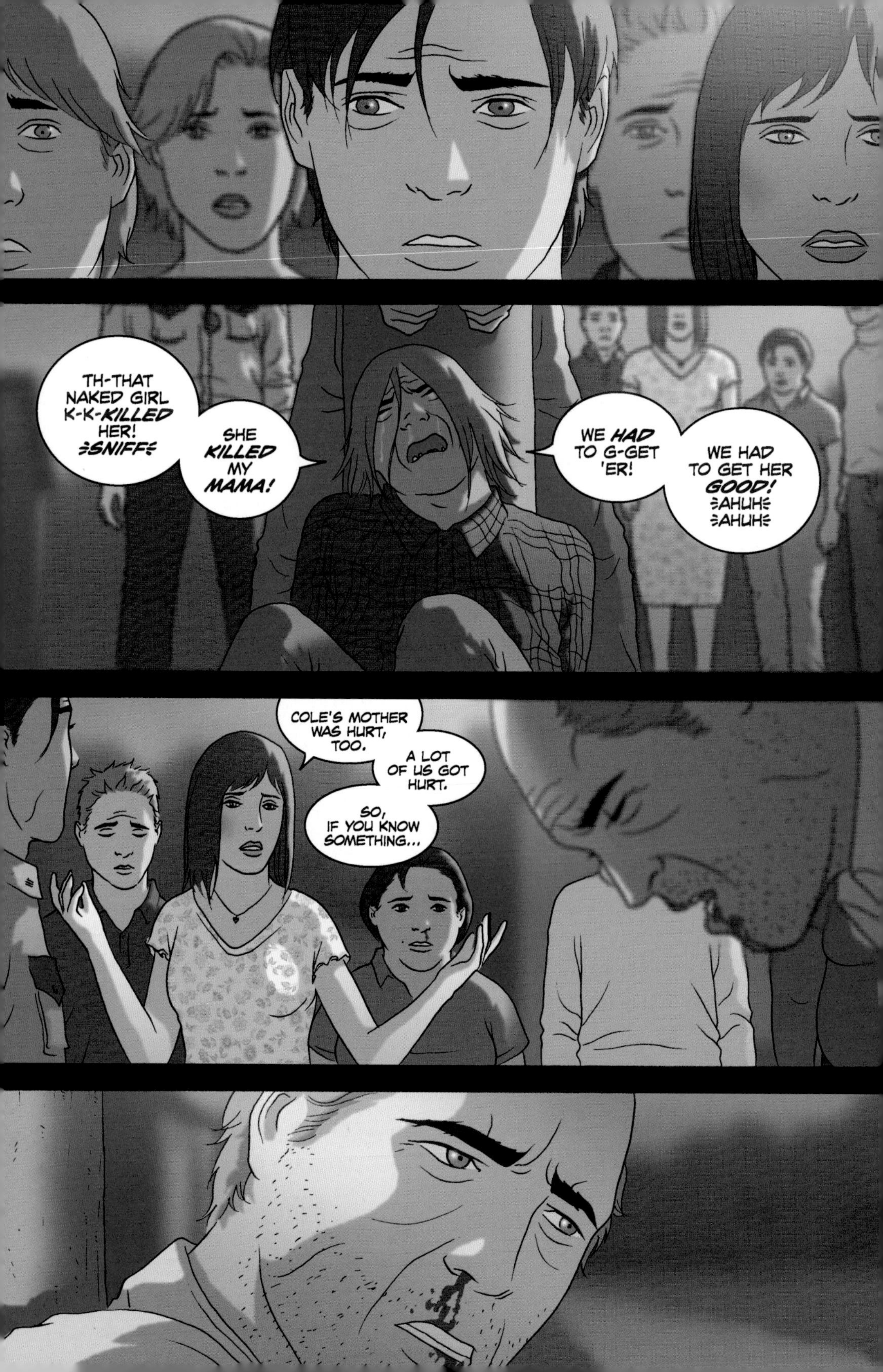
TH-THAT NAKED GIRL K-K-*KILLED* HER! *SNIFF*
SHE *KILLED* MY *MAMA!*
WE *HAD* TO G-GET 'ER!
WE HAD TO GET HER *GOOD!* AHUH AHUH
COLE'S MOTHER WAS HURT, TOO.
A LOT OF US GOT HURT.
SO, IF YOU KNOW SOMETHING...

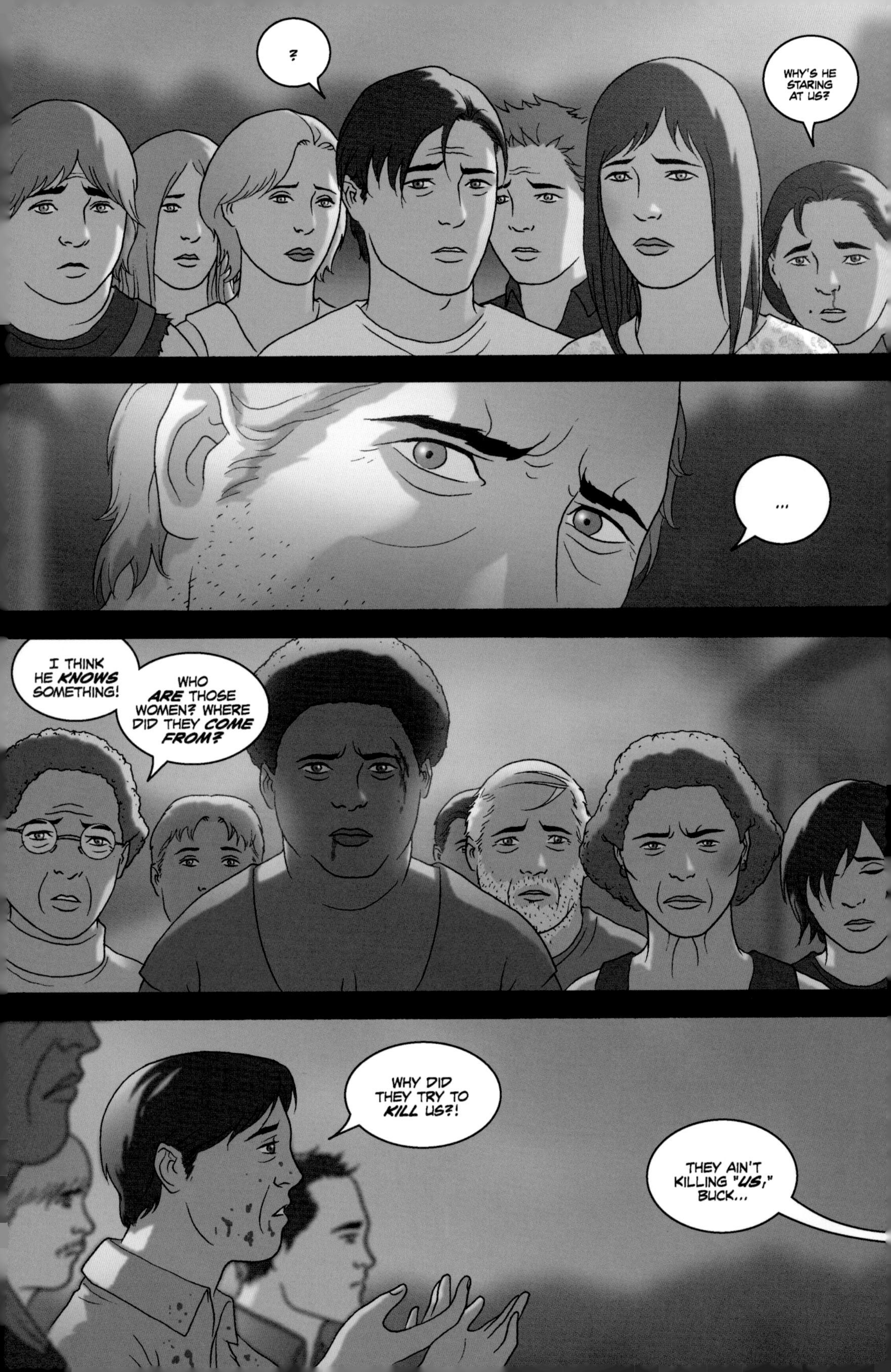
?
WHY'S HE STARING AT US?
...
I THINK HE *KNOWS* SOMETHING!
WHO *ARE* THOSE WOMEN? WHERE DID THEY *COME FROM?*
WHY DID THEY TRY TO *KILL* US?!
THEY AIN'T KILLING "*US,*" BUCK...

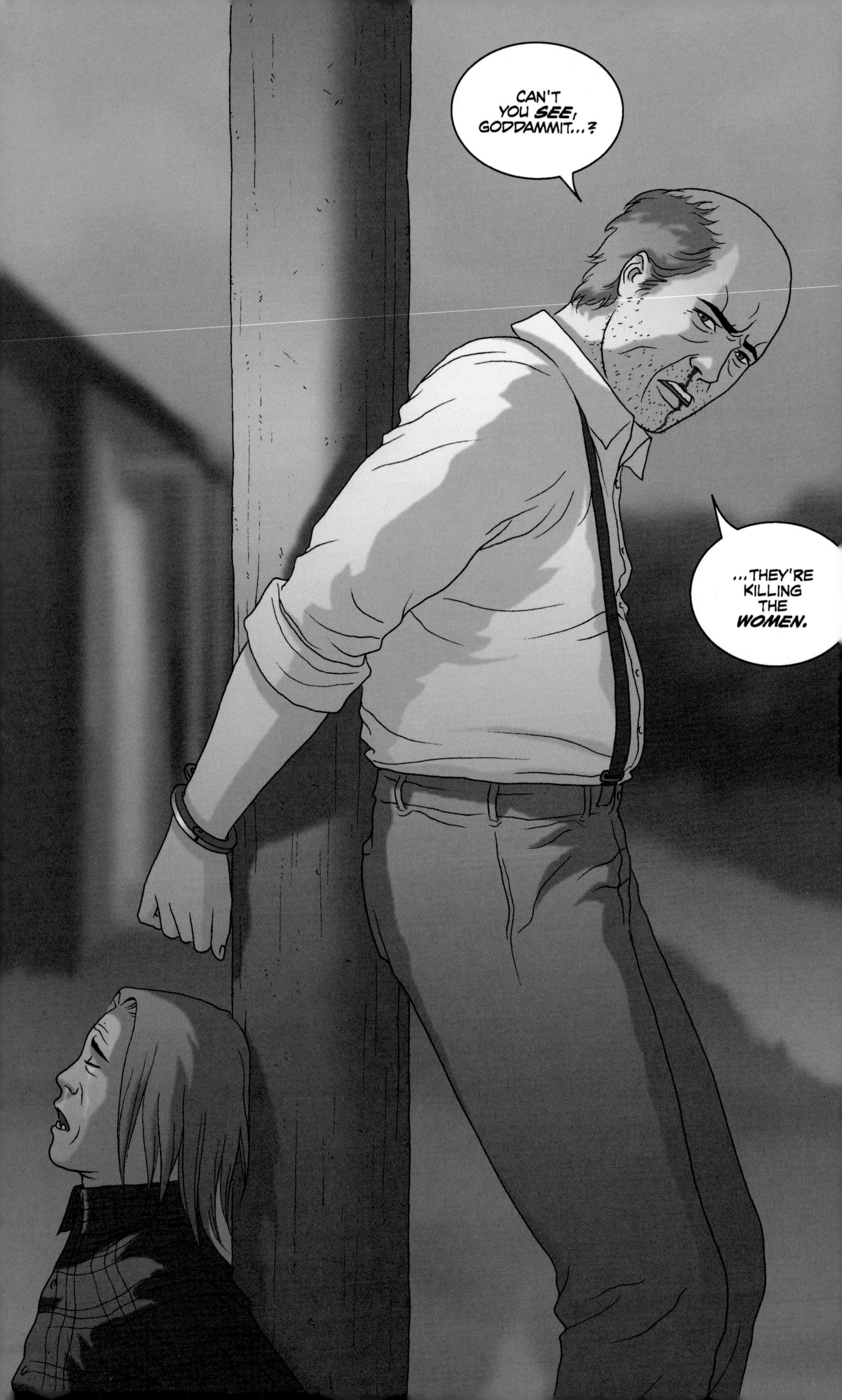
CAN'T YOU SEE, GODDAMMIT...?
...THEY'RE KILLING THE WOMEN.

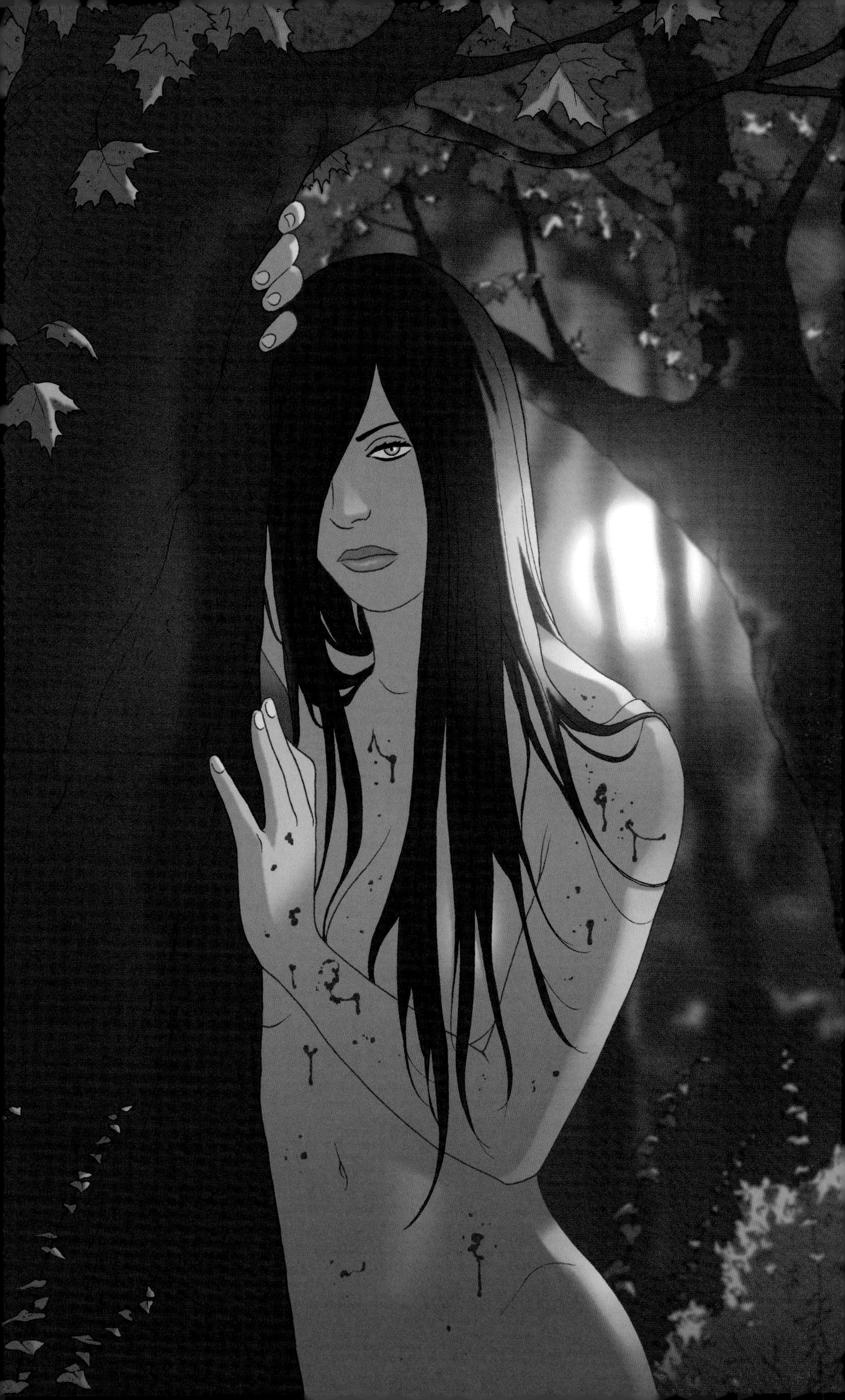

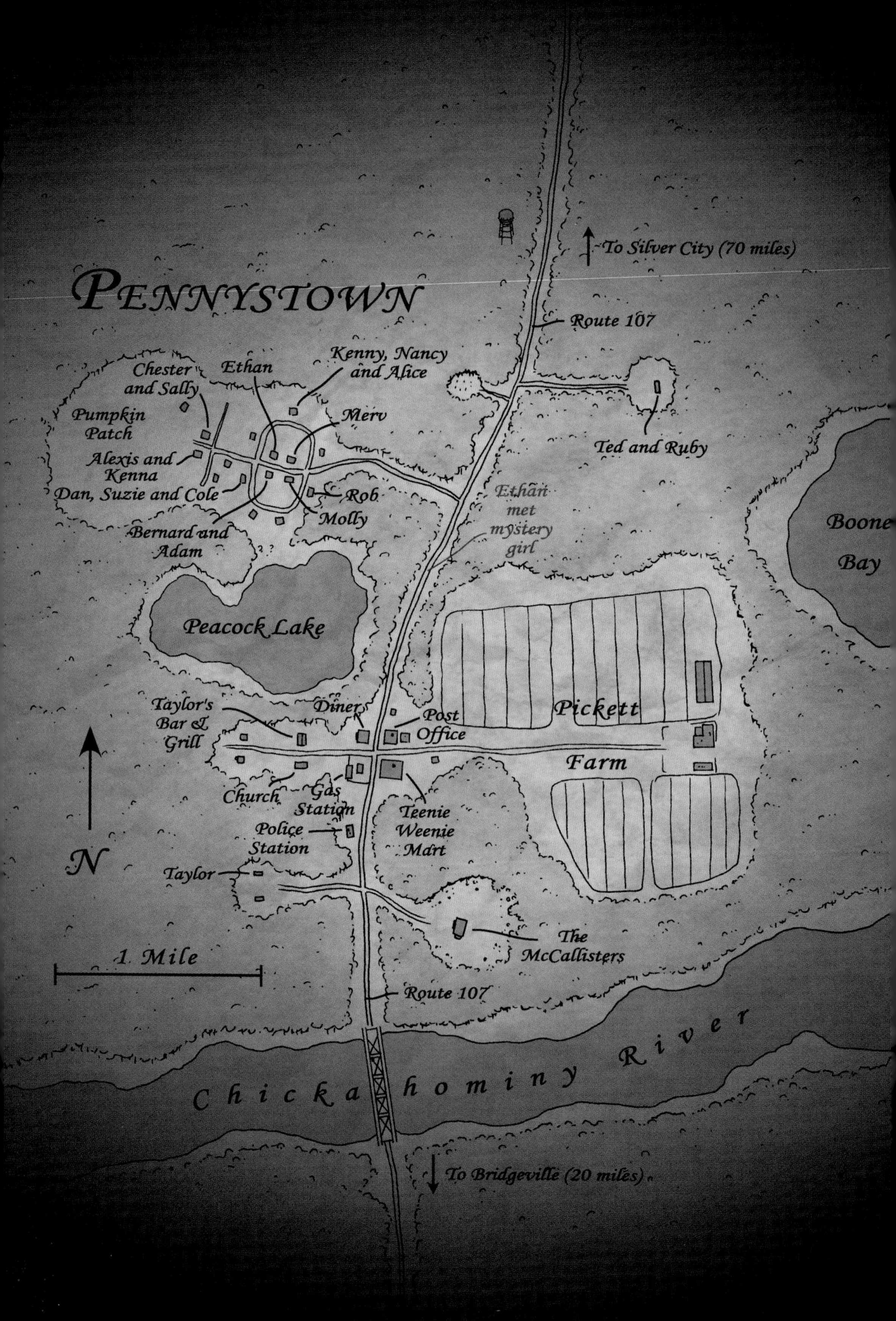
PENNYSTOWN
To Silver City (70 miles)
Route 107
Kenny, Nancy and Alice
Chester and Sally
Ethan
Pumpkin Patch
Merv
Ted and Ruby
Alexis and Kenna
Dan, Suzie and Cole
Rob
Molly
Ethan met mystery girl
Boone Bay
Bernard and Adam
Peacock Lake
Taylor's Bar & Grill
Diner
Post Office
Pickett
Farm
Church
Gas Station
Teenie Weenie Mart
Police Station
N
Taylor
The McCallisters
1 Mile
Route 107
Chickahominy River
To Bridgeville (20 miles)

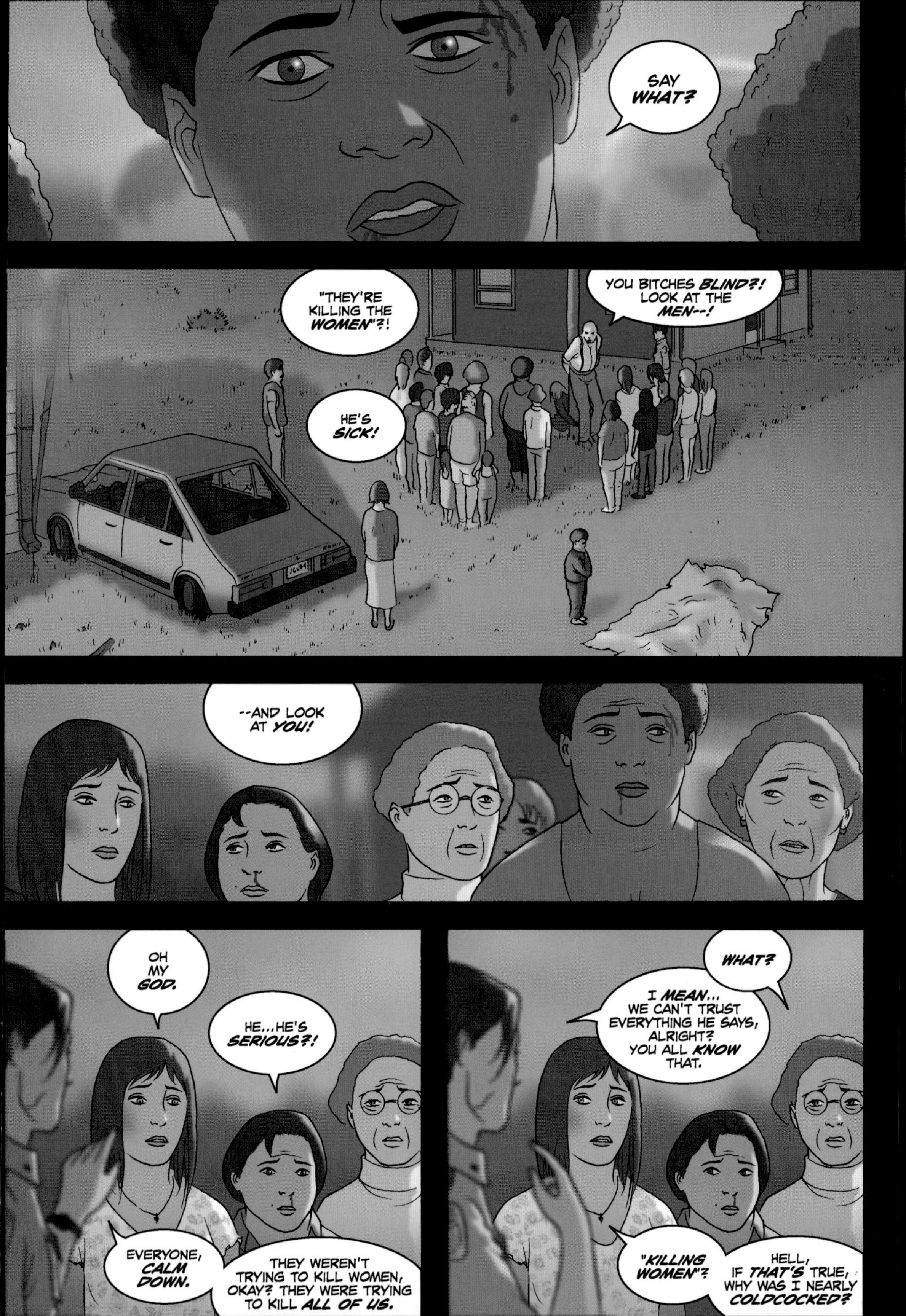
SAY WHAT?
"THEY'RE KILLING THE WOMEN"?!
YOU BITCHES BLIND?! LOOK AT THE MEN--!
HE'S SICK!
--AND LOOK AT YOU!
OH MY GOD.
HE...HE'S SERIOUS?!
EVERYONE, CALM DOWN.
THEY WEREN'T TRYING TO KILL WOMEN, OKAY? THEY WERE TRYING TO KILL ALL OF US.
WHAT?
I MEAN... WE CAN'T TRUST EVERYTHING HE SAYS, ALRIGHT? YOU ALL KNOW THAT.
"KILLING WOMEN"?
HELL, IF THAT'S TRUE, WHY WAS I NEARLY COLDCOCKED?

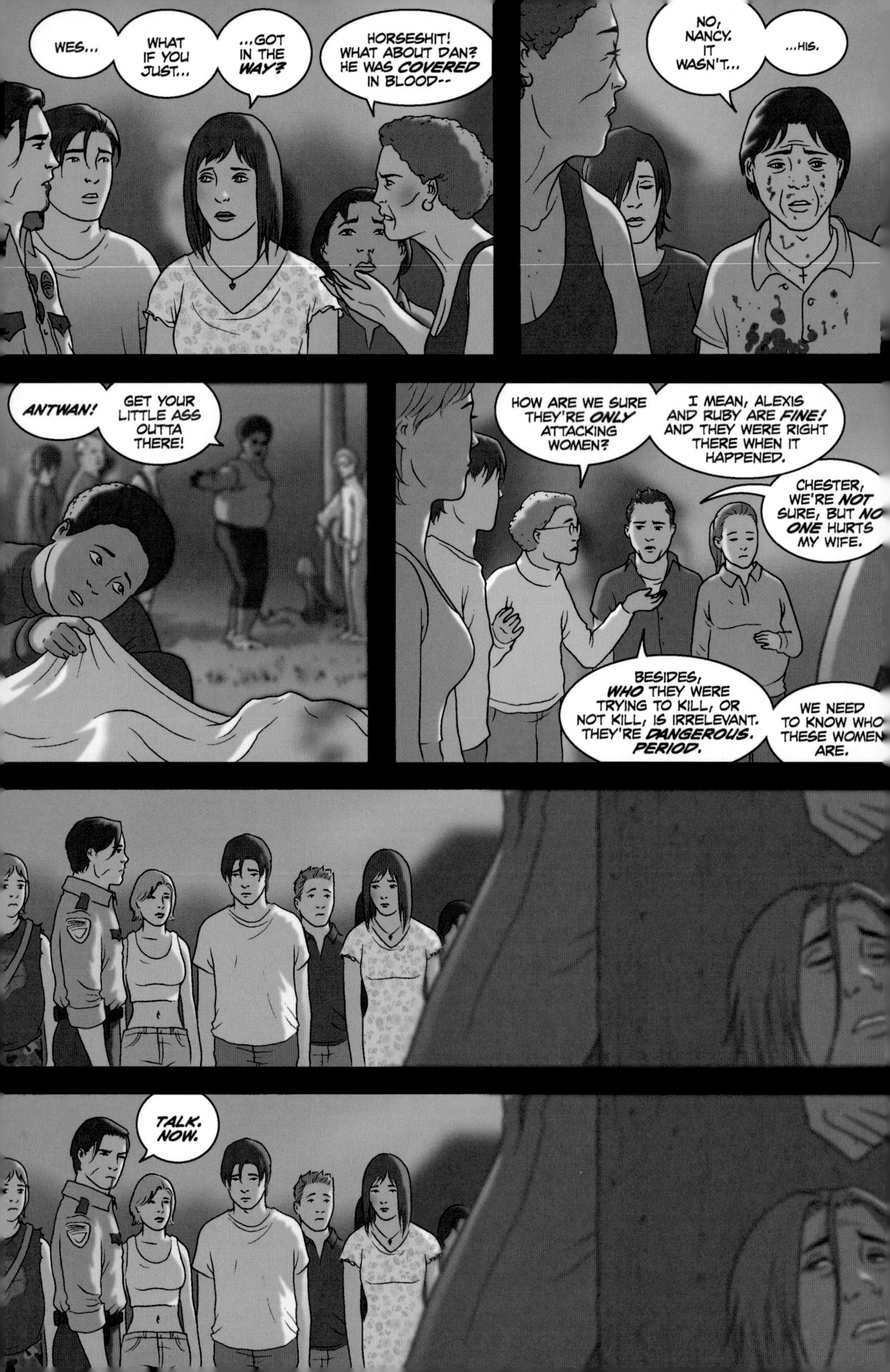
WES...
WHAT IF YOU JUST...
...GOT IN THE WAY?
HORSESHIT! WHAT ABOUT DAN? HE WAS COVERED IN BLOOD--
NO, NANCY. IT WASN'T...
...HIS.
ANTWAN!
GET YOUR LITTLE ASS OUTTA THERE!
HOW ARE WE SURE THEY'RE ONLY ATTACKING WOMEN?
I MEAN, ALEXIS AND RUBY ARE FINE! AND THEY WERE RIGHT THERE WHEN IT HAPPENED.
CHESTER, WE'RE NOT SURE, BUT NO ONE HURTS MY WIFE.
BESIDES, WHO THEY WERE TRYING TO KILL, OR NOT KILL, IS IRRELEVANT. THEY'RE DANGEROUS. PERIOD.
WE NEED TO KNOW WHO THESE WOMEN ARE.
TALK. NOW.

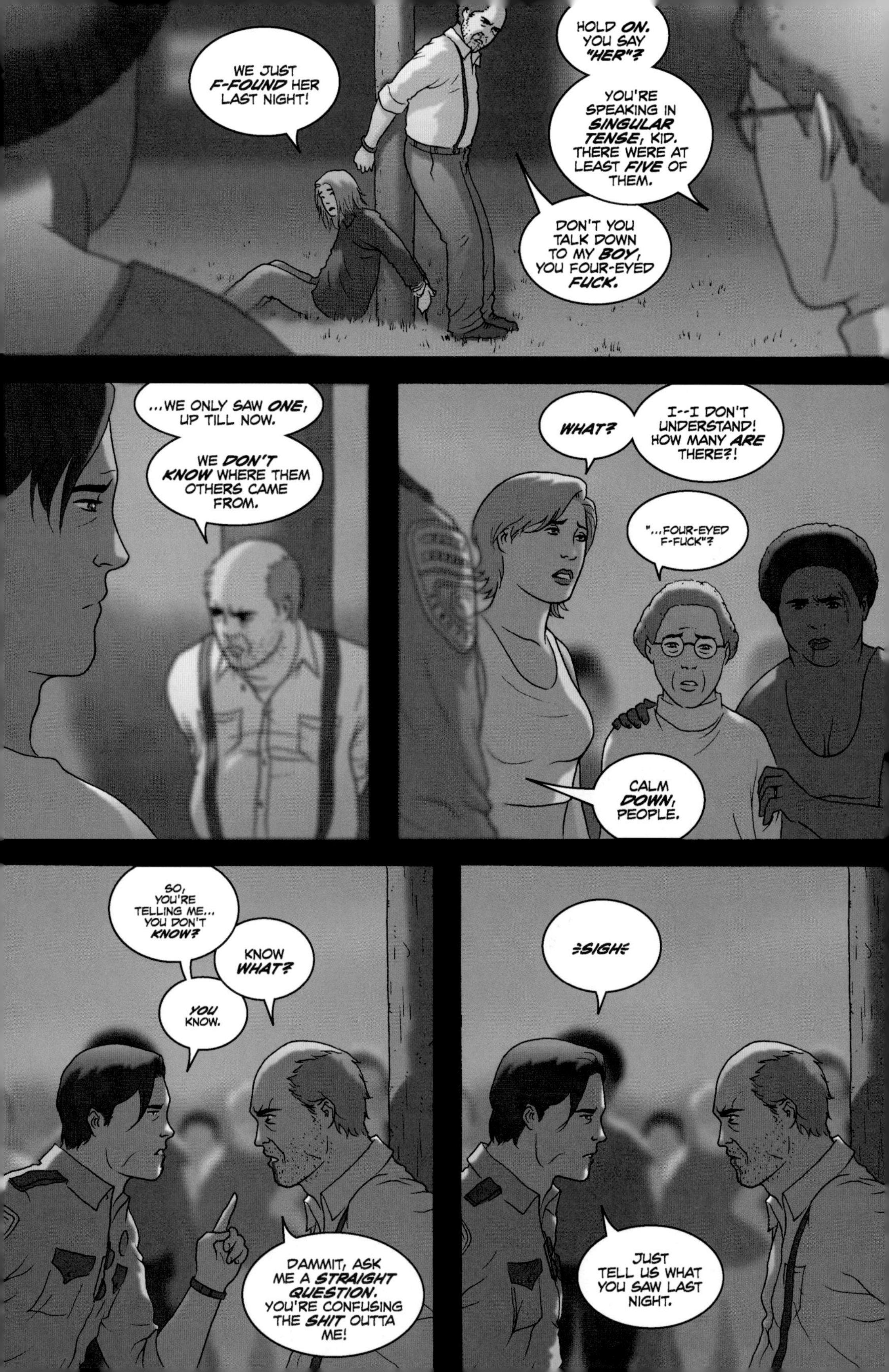
WE JUST F-FOUND HER LAST NIGHT!
HOLD ON. YOU SAY "HER"?
YOU'RE SPEAKING IN SINGULAR TENSE, KID. THERE WERE AT LEAST FIVE OF THEM.
DON'T YOU TALK DOWN TO MY BOY, YOU FOUR-EYED FUCK.
...WE ONLY SAW ONE, UP TILL NOW.
WE DON'T KNOW WHERE THEM OTHERS CAME FROM.
WHAT?
I--I DON'T UNDERSTAND! HOW MANY ARE THERE?!
"...FOUR-EYED F-FUCK"?
CALM DOWN, PEOPLE.
SO, YOU'RE TELLING ME... YOU DON'T KNOW?
KNOW WHAT?
YOU KNOW.
DAMMIT, ASK ME A STRAIGHT QUESTION. YOU'RE CONFUSING THE SHIT OUTTA ME!
≈SIGH≈
JUST TELL US WHAT YOU SAW LAST NIGHT.

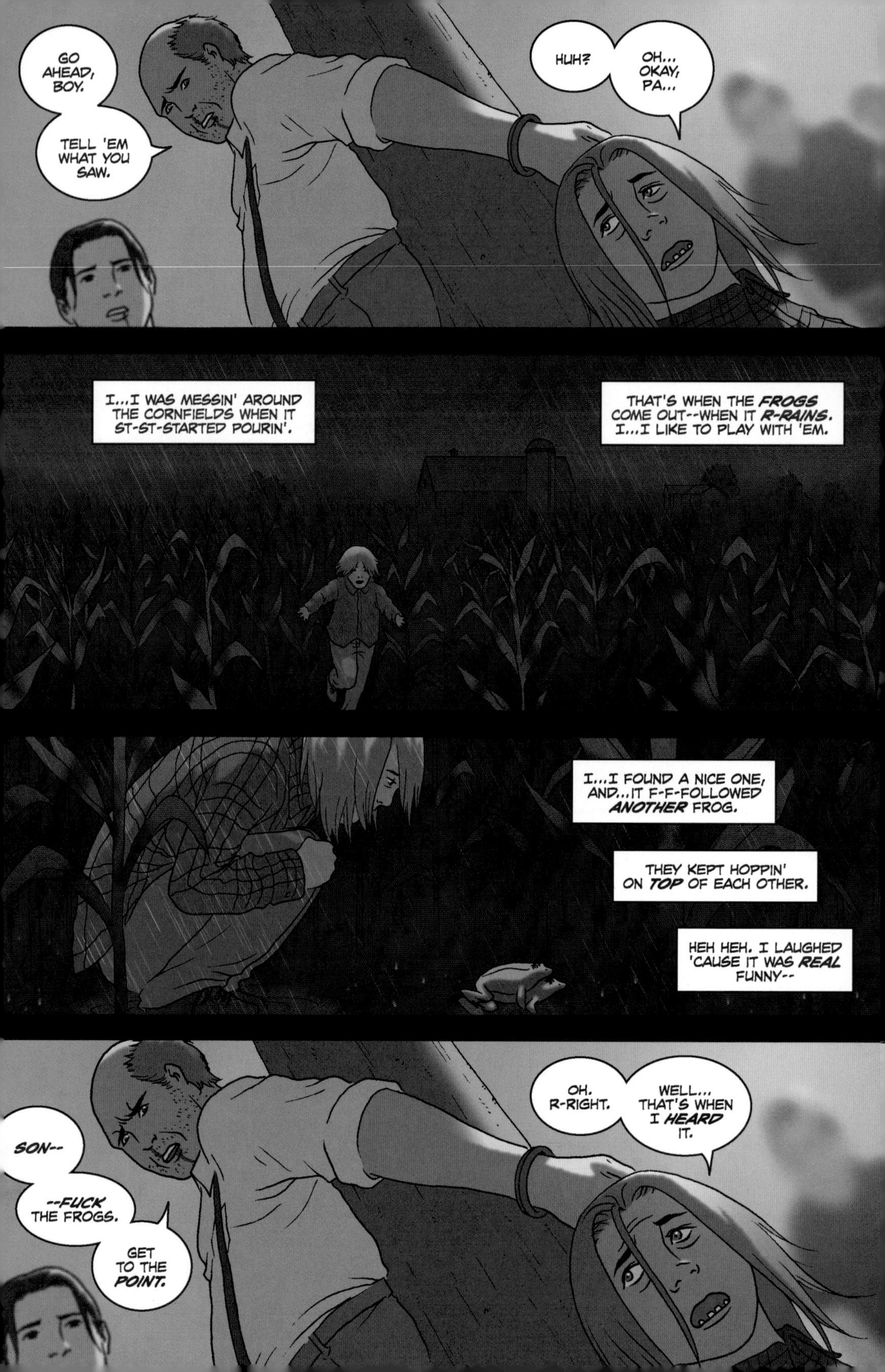
GO AHEAD, BOY.
TELL 'EM WHAT YOU SAW.
HUH?
OH... OKAY, PA...
I...I WAS MESSIN' AROUND THE CORNFIELDS WHEN IT ST-ST-STARTED POURIN'.
THAT'S WHEN THE FROGS COME OUT--WHEN IT R-RAINS. I...I LIKE TO PLAY WITH 'EM.
I...I FOUND A NICE ONE, AND...IT F-F-FOLLOWED ANOTHER FROG.
THEY KEPT HOPPIN' ON TOP OF EACH OTHER.
HEH HEH. I LAUGHED 'CAUSE IT WAS REAL FUNNY--
SON--
--FUCK THE FROGS.
GET TO THE POINT.
OH. R-RIGHT.
WELL... THAT'S WHEN I HEARD IT.

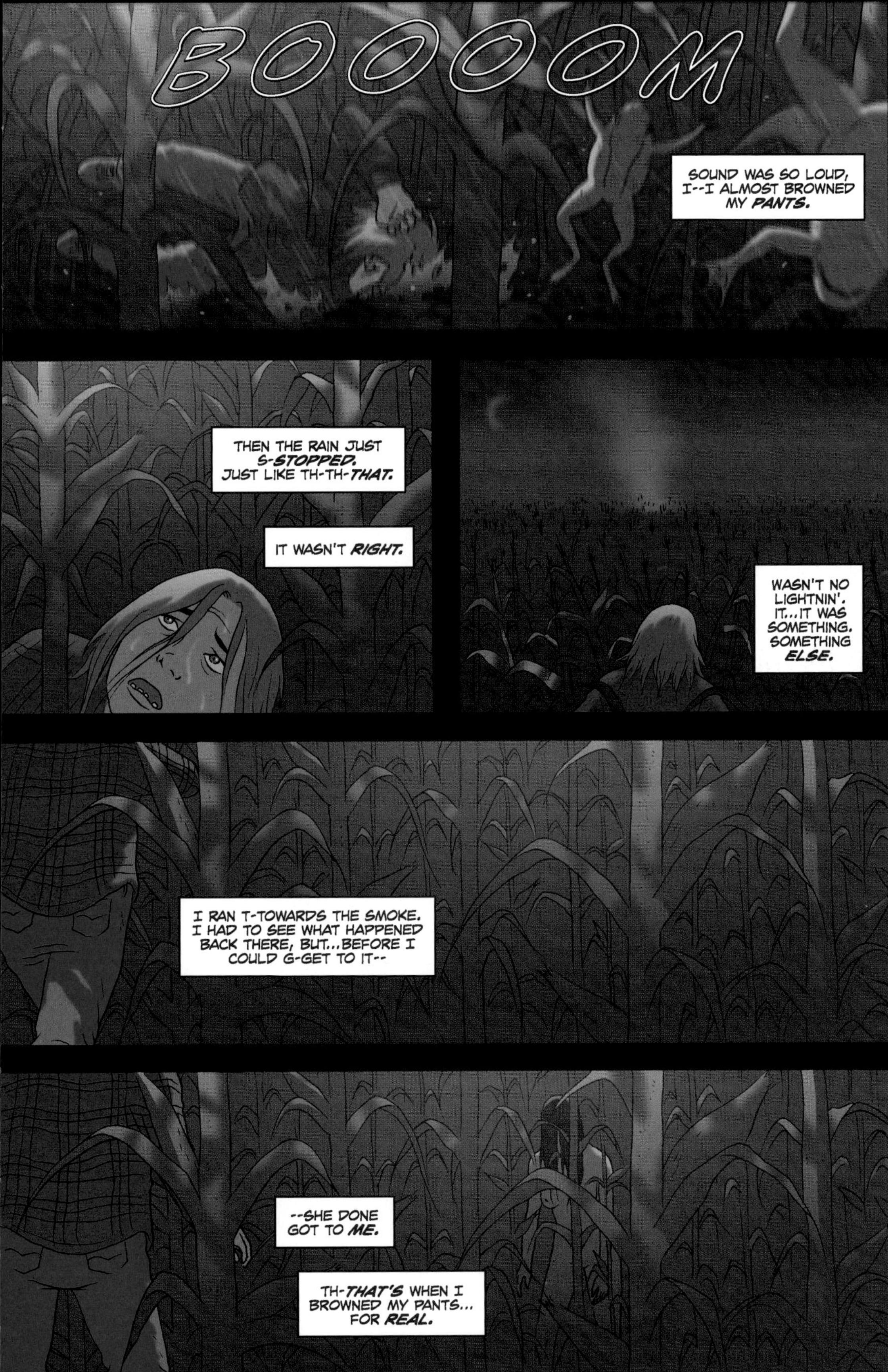
BOOOOM
SOUND WAS SO LOUD, I--I ALMOST BROWNED MY PANTS.
THEN THE RAIN JUST S-STOPPED. JUST LIKE TH-TH-THAT.
IT WASN'T RIGHT.
WASN'T NO LIGHTNIN'. IT...IT WAS SOMETHING. SOMETHING ELSE.
I RAN T-TOWARDS THE SMOKE. I HAD TO SEE WHAT HAPPENED BACK THERE, BUT...BEFORE I COULD G-GET TO IT--
--SHE DONE GOT TO ME.
TH-THAT'S WHEN I BROWNED MY PANTS... FOR REAL.

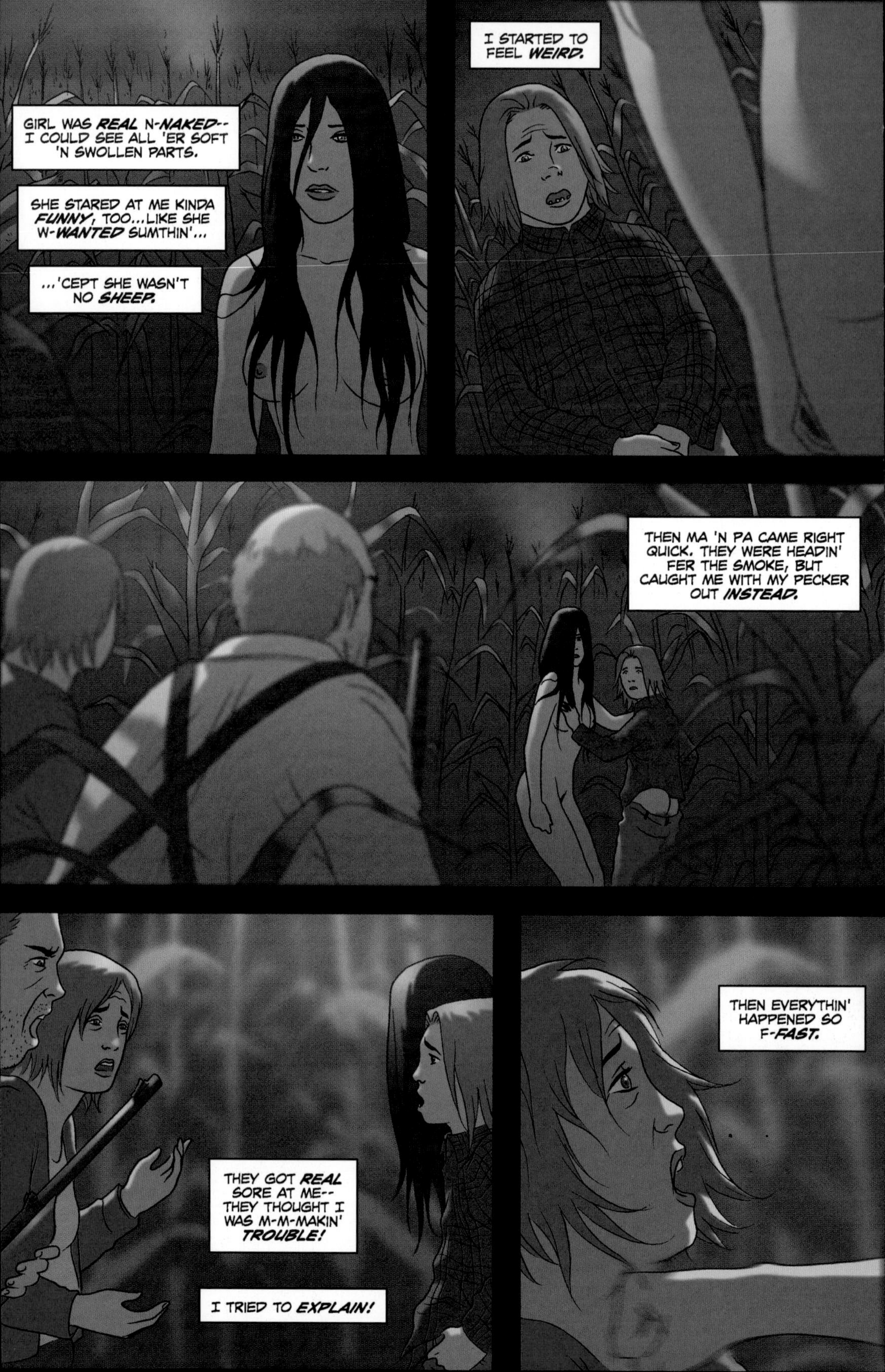
GIRL WAS REAL N-NAKED-- I COULD SEE ALL 'ER SOFT 'N SWOLLEN PARTS.
SHE STARED AT ME KINDA FUNNY, TOO...LIKE SHE W-WANTED SUMTHIN'...
...'CEPT SHE WASN'T NO SHEEP.
I STARTED TO FEEL WEIRD.
THEN MA 'N PA CAME RIGHT QUICK. THEY WERE HEADIN' FER THE SMOKE; BUT CAUGHT ME WITH MY PECKER OUT INSTEAD.
THEY GOT REAL SORE AT ME-- THEY THOUGHT I WAS M-M-MAKIN' TROUBLE!
I TRIED TO EXPLAIN!
THEN EVERYTHIN' HAPPENED SO F-FAST.

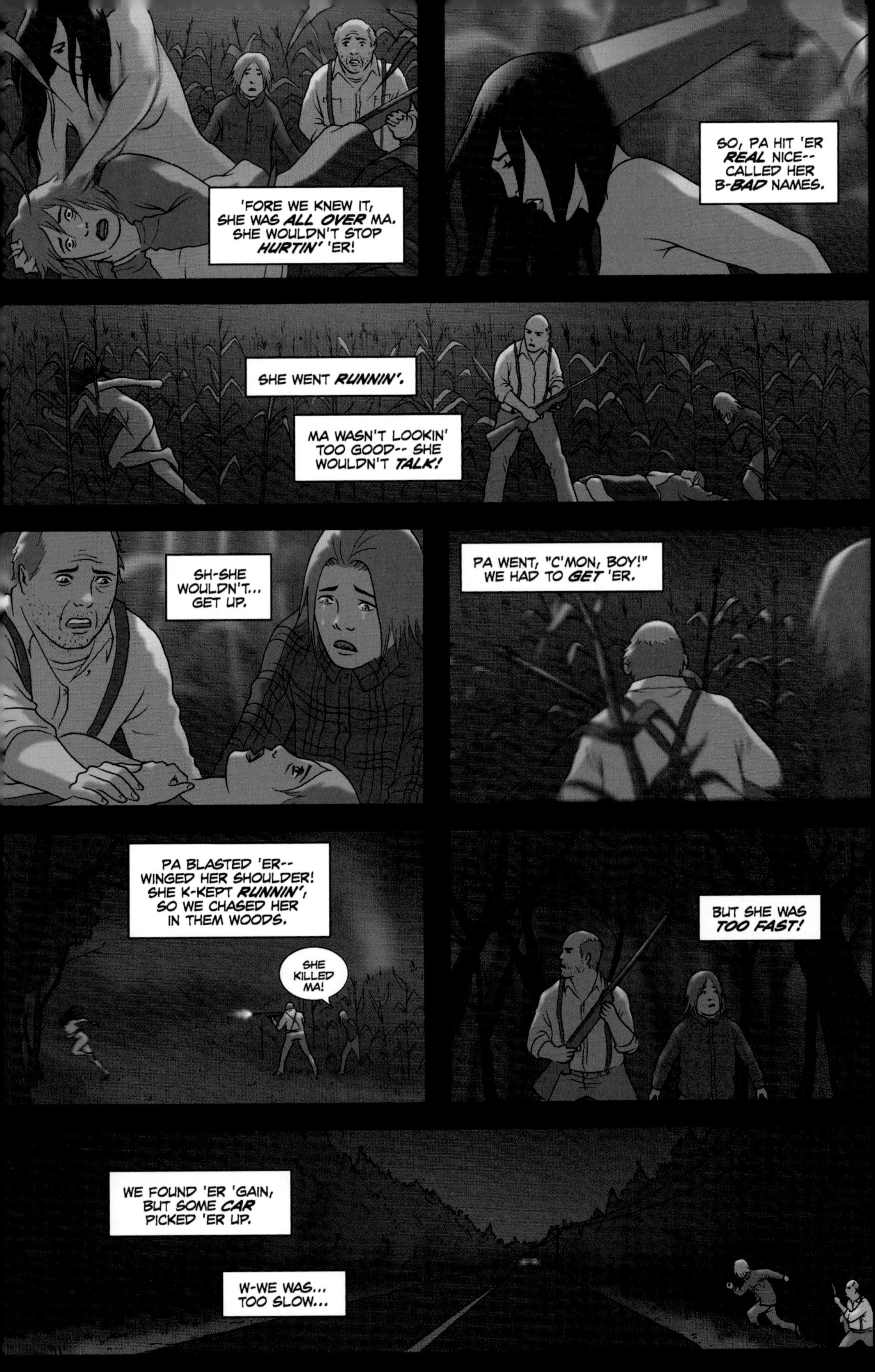
'FORE WE KNEW IT, SHE WAS ALL OVER MA. SHE WOULDN'T STOP HURTIN' 'ER!
SO, PA HIT 'ER REAL NICE-- CALLED HER B-BAD NAMES.
SHE WENT RUNNIN'.
MA WASN'T LOOKIN' TOO GOOD-- SHE WOULDN'T TALK!
SH-SHE WOULDN'T... GET UP.
PA WENT, "C'MON, BOY!" WE HAD TO GET 'ER.
PA BLASTED 'ER-- WINGED HER SHOULDER! SHE K-KEPT RUNNIN', SO WE CHASED HER IN THEM WOODS.
SHE KILLED MA!
BUT SHE WAS TOO FAST!
WE FOUND 'ER 'GAIN, BUT SOME CAR PICKED 'ER UP.
W-WE WAS... TOO SLOW...

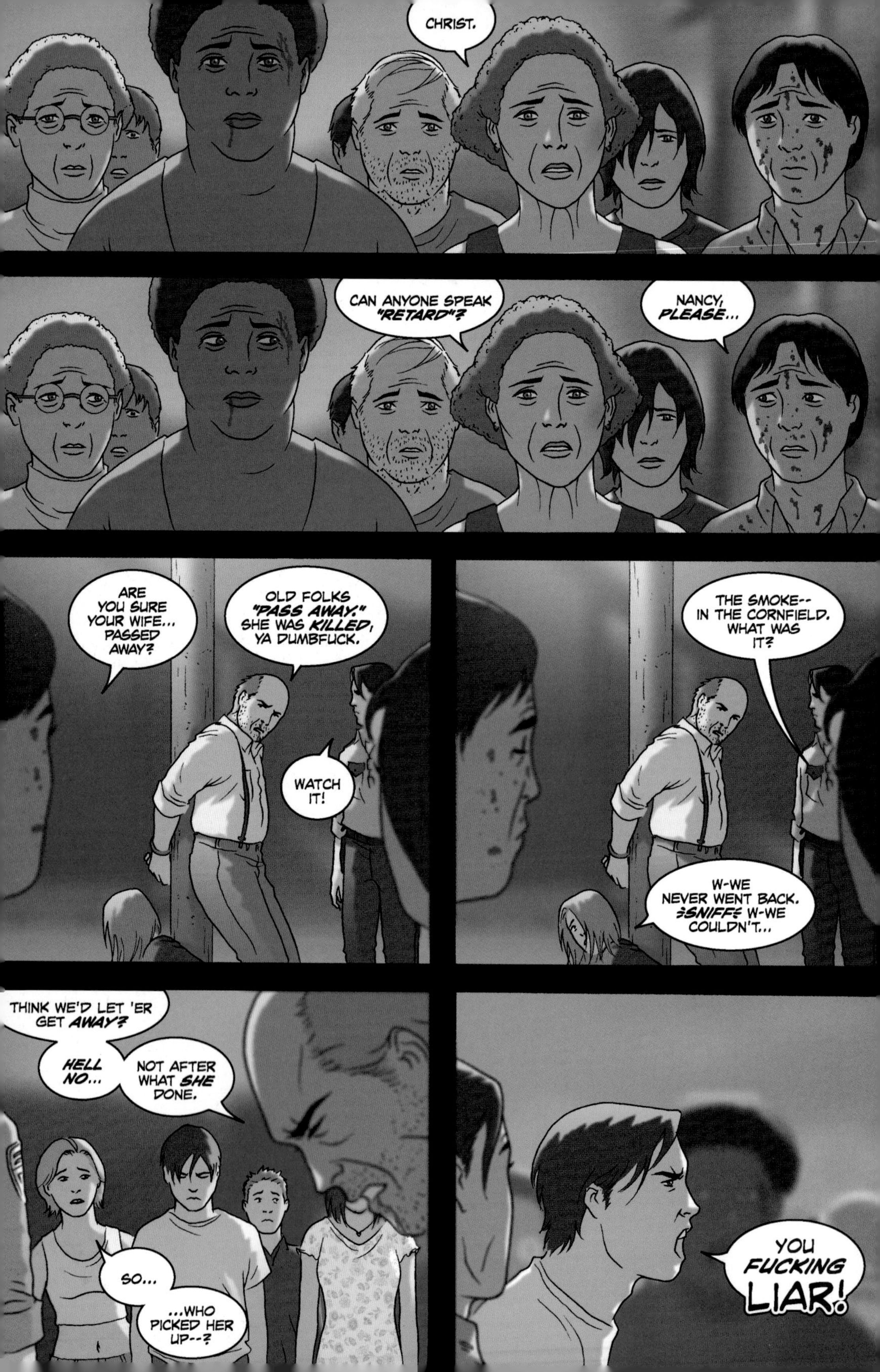
CHRIST.
CAN ANYONE SPEAK "RETARD"?
NANCY, PLEASE...
ARE YOU SURE YOUR WIFE... PASSED AWAY?
OLD FOLKS "PASS AWAY." SHE WAS KILLED, YA DUMBFUCK.
WATCH IT!
THE SMOKE-- IN THE CORNFIELD. WHAT WAS IT?
W-WE NEVER WENT BACK. *SNIFF* W-WE COULDN'T...
THINK WE'D LET 'ER GET AWAY?
HELL NO...
NOT AFTER WHAT SHE DONE.
SO...
...WHO PICKED HER UP--?
YOU FUCKING LIAR!

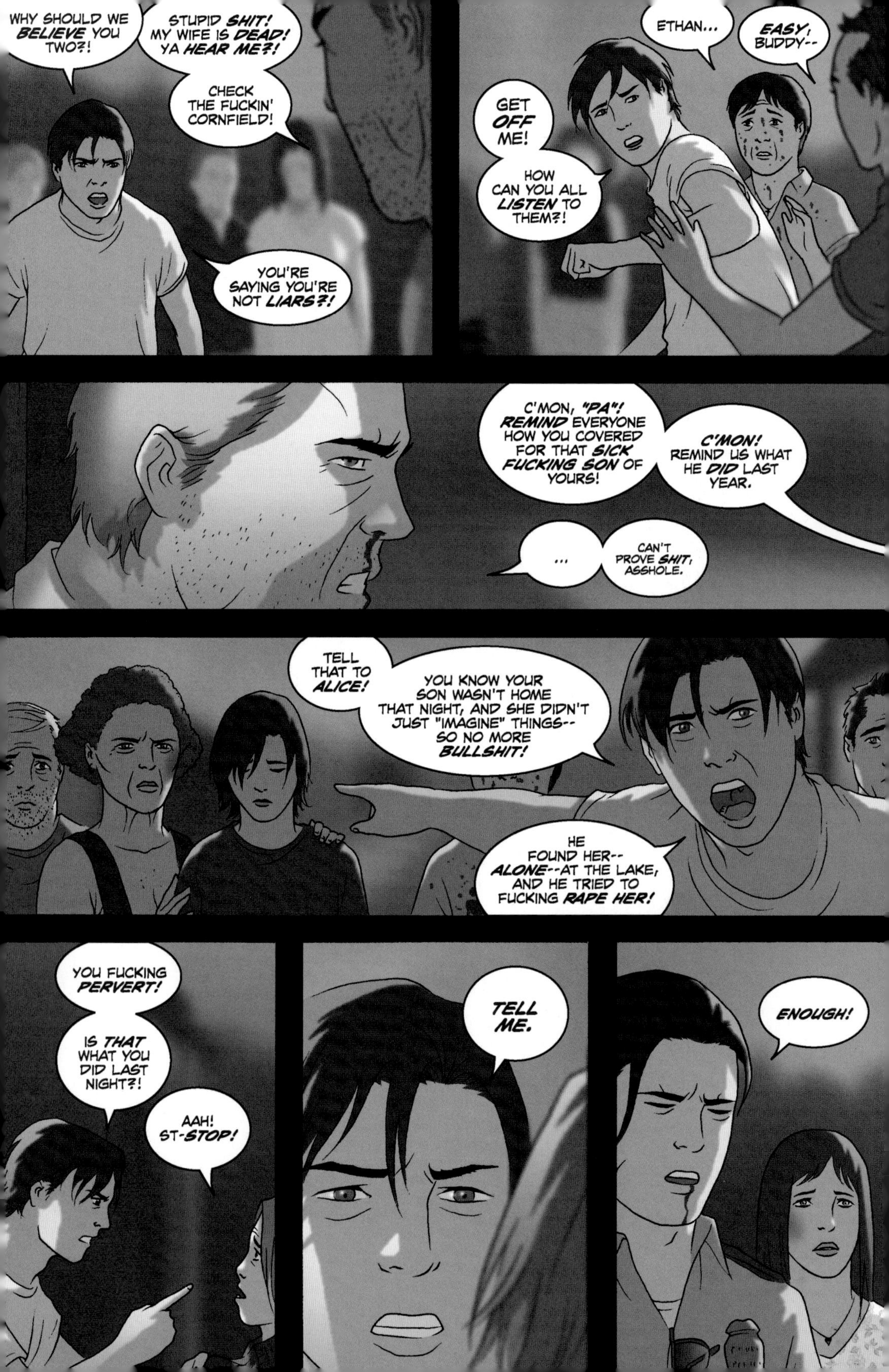
WHY SHOULD WE BELIEVE YOU TWO?!
STUPID SHIT! MY WIFE IS DEAD! YA HEAR ME?!
CHECK THE FUCKIN' CORNFIELD!
YOU'RE SAYING YOU'RE NOT LIARS?!
ETHAN...
EASY, BUDDY--
GET OFF ME!
HOW CAN YOU ALL LISTEN TO THEM?!
C'MON, "PA"! REMIND EVERYONE HOW YOU COVERED FOR THAT SICK FUCKING SON OF YOURS!
C'MON! REMIND US WHAT HE DID LAST YEAR.
...
CAN'T PROVE SHIT, ASSHOLE.
TELL THAT TO ALICE!
YOU KNOW YOUR SON WASN'T HOME THAT NIGHT, AND SHE DIDN'T JUST "IMAGINE" THINGS-- SO NO MORE BULLSHIT!
HE FOUND HER--ALONE--AT THE LAKE, AND HE TRIED TO FUCKING RAPE HER!
YOU FUCKING PERVERT!
IS THAT WHAT YOU DID LAST NIGHT?!
AAH! ST-STOP!
TELL ME.
ENOUGH!

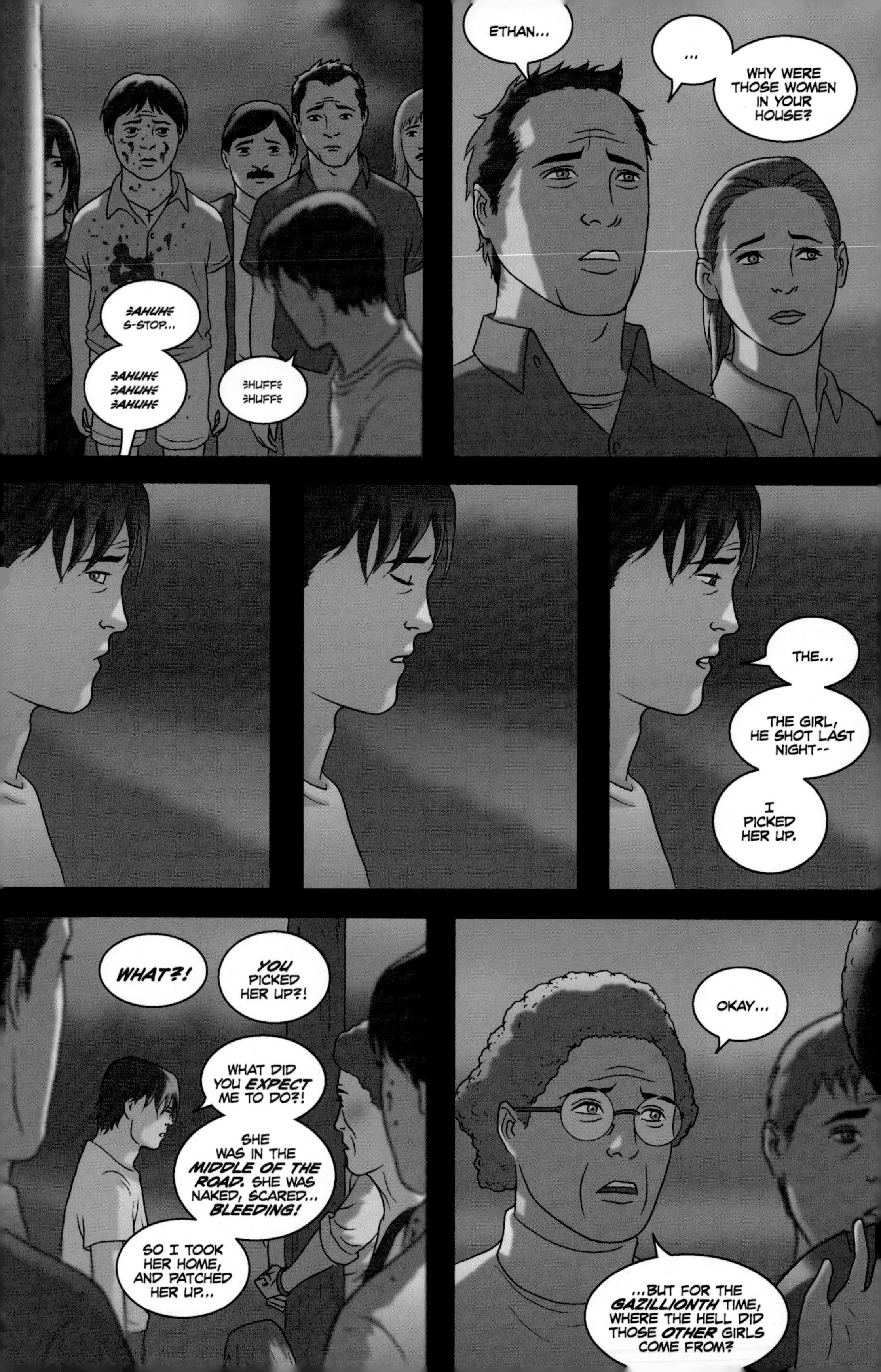

ƎAHUHƐ S-STOP...
ƎAHUHƐ ƎAHUHƐ ƎAHUHƐ
ƎHUFFƐ ƎHUFFƐ
ETHAN...
...
WHY WERE THOSE WOMEN IN YOUR HOUSE?
THE...
THE GIRL, HE SHOT LAST NIGHT--
I PICKED HER UP.
WHAT?!
YOU PICKED HER UP?!
WHAT DID YOU EXPECT ME TO DO?!
SHE WAS IN THE MIDDLE OF THE ROAD. SHE WAS NAKED, SCARED... BLEEDING!
SO I TOOK HER HOME, AND PATCHED HER UP...
OKAY...
...BUT FOR THE GAZILLIONTH TIME, WHERE THE HELL DID THOSE OTHER GIRLS COME FROM?

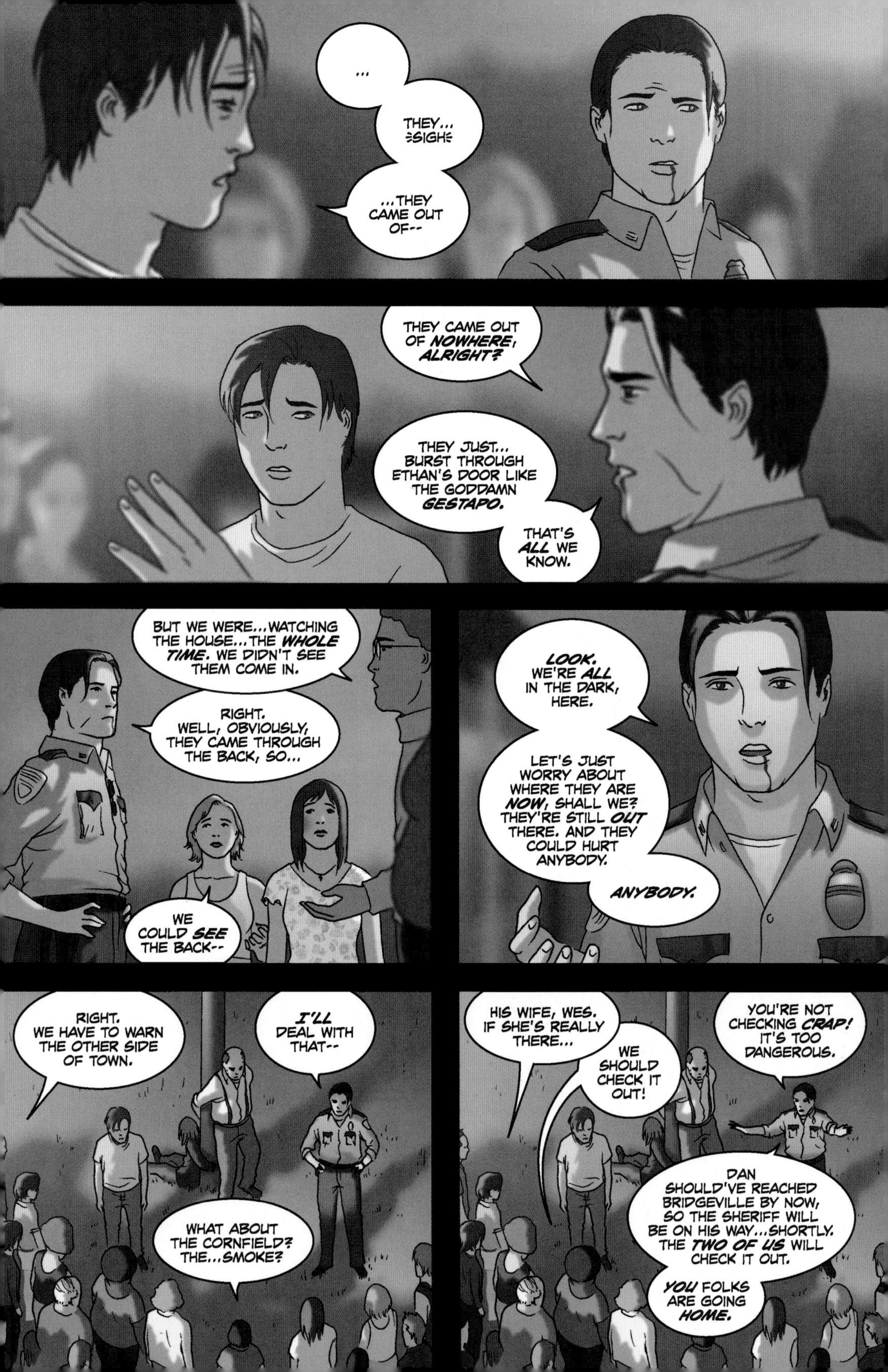
...
THEY... ≡SIGH≡
...THEY CAME OUT OF--
THEY CAME OUT OF NOWHERE, ALRIGHT?
THEY JUST... BURST THROUGH ETHAN'S DOOR LIKE THE GODDAMN GESTAPO.
THAT'S ALL WE KNOW.
BUT WE WERE...WATCHING THE HOUSE...THE WHOLE TIME. WE DIDN'T SEE THEM COME IN.
RIGHT. WELL, OBVIOUSLY, THEY CAME THROUGH THE BACK, SO...
WE COULD SEE THE BACK--
LOOK. WE'RE ALL IN THE DARK, HERE.
LET'S JUST WORRY ABOUT WHERE THEY ARE NOW, SHALL WE? THEY'RE STILL OUT THERE. AND THEY COULD HURT ANYBODY.
ANYBODY.
RIGHT. WE HAVE TO WARN THE OTHER SIDE OF TOWN.
I'LL DEAL WITH THAT--
WHAT ABOUT THE CORNFIELD? THE...SMOKE?
HIS WIFE, WES. IF SHE'S REALLY THERE...
WE SHOULD CHECK IT OUT!
YOU'RE NOT CHECKING CRAP! IT'S TOO DANGEROUS.
DAN SHOULD'VE REACHED BRIDGEVILLE BY NOW, SO THE SHERIFF WILL BE ON HIS WAY...SHORTLY. THE TWO OF US WILL CHECK IT OUT.
YOU FOLKS ARE GOING HOME.

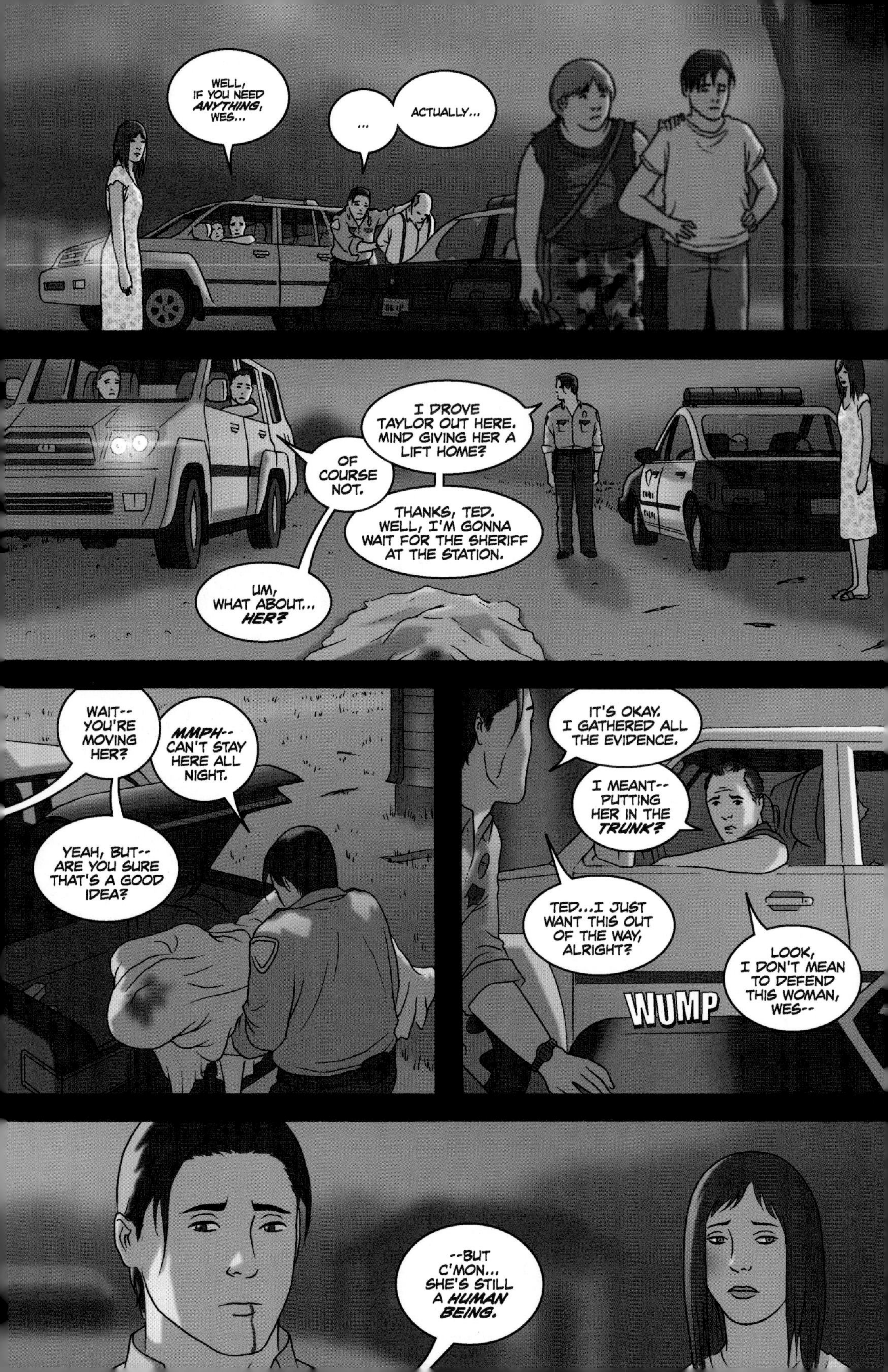
WELL, IF YOU NEED *ANYTHING*, WES...
...
ACTUALLY...
I DROVE TAYLOR OUT HERE. MIND GIVING HER A LIFT HOME?
OF COURSE NOT.
THANKS, TED. WELL, I'M GONNA WAIT FOR THE SHERIFF AT THE STATION.
UM, WHAT ABOUT... *HER?*
WAIT-- YOU'RE MOVING HER?
MMPH-- CAN'T STAY HERE ALL NIGHT.
YEAH, BUT-- ARE YOU SURE THAT'S A GOOD IDEA?
IT'S OKAY. I GATHERED ALL THE EVIDENCE.
I MEANT-- PUTTING HER IN THE *TRUNK?*
TED...I JUST WANT THIS OUT OF THE WAY, ALRIGHT?
WUMP
LOOK, I DON'T MEAN TO DEFEND THIS WOMAN, WES--
--BUT C'MON... SHE'S STILL A *HUMAN BEING.*

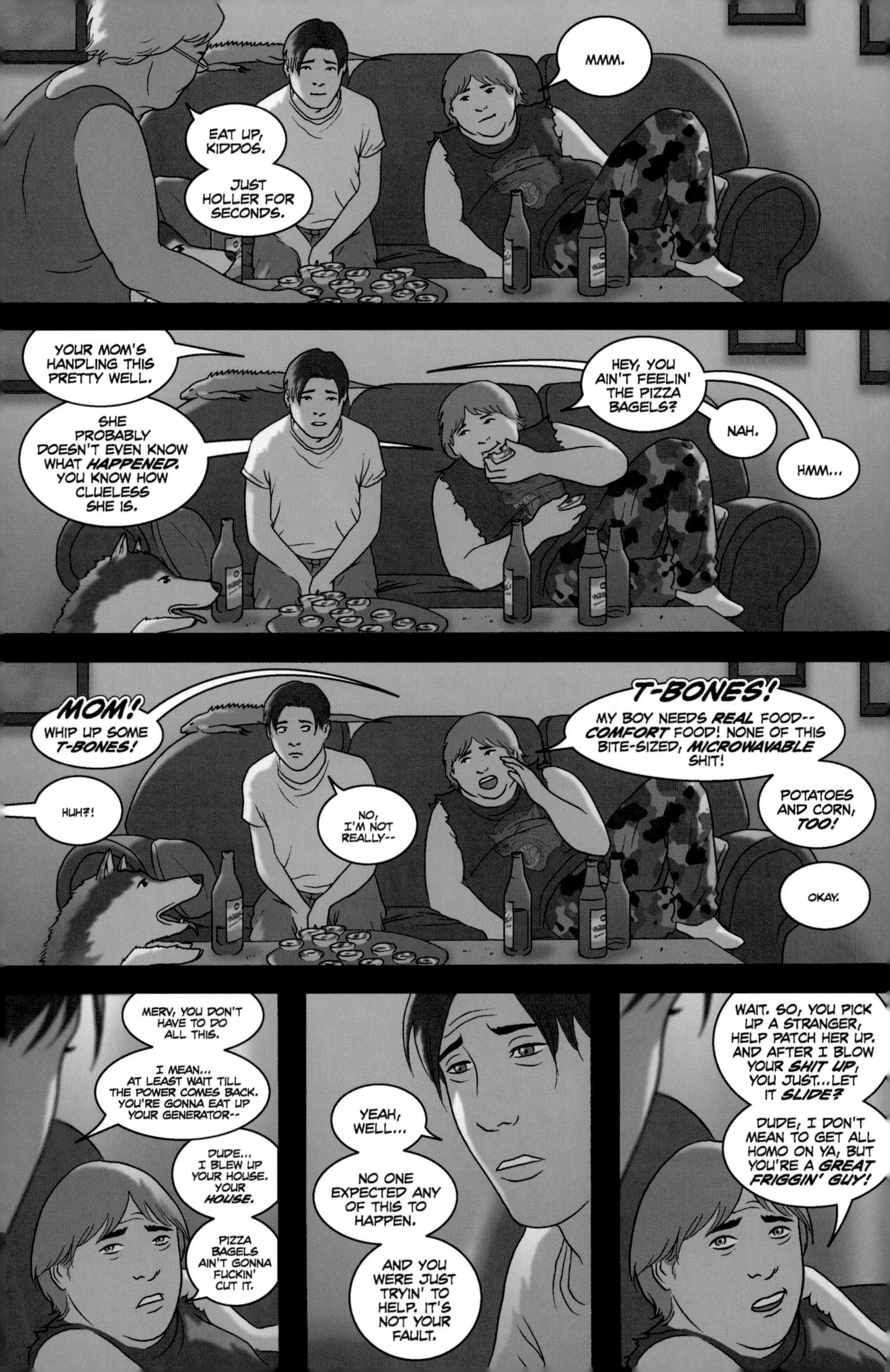
EAT UP, KIDDOS.
JUST HOLLER FOR SECONDS.
MMM.
YOUR MOM'S HANDLING THIS PRETTY WELL.
SHE PROBABLY DOESN'T EVEN KNOW WHAT HAPPENED. YOU KNOW HOW CLUELESS SHE IS.
HEY, YOU AIN'T FEELIN' THE PIZZA BAGELS?
NAH.
HMM...
MOM! WHIP UP SOME T-BONES!
HUH?!
NO, I'M NOT REALLY--
T-BONES! MY BOY NEEDS REAL FOOD-- COMFORT FOOD! NONE OF THIS BITE-SIZED, MICROWAVABLE SHIT!
POTATOES AND CORN, TOO!
OKAY.
MERV, YOU DON'T HAVE TO DO ALL THIS.
I MEAN... AT LEAST WAIT TILL THE POWER COMES BACK. YOU'RE GONNA EAT UP YOUR GENERATOR--
DUDE... I BLEW UP YOUR HOUSE. YOUR HOUSE.
PIZZA BAGELS AIN'T GONNA FUCKIN' CUT IT.
YEAH, WELL...
NO ONE EXPECTED ANY OF THIS TO HAPPEN.
AND YOU WERE JUST TRYIN' TO HELP. IT'S NOT YOUR FAULT.
WAIT. SO, YOU PICK UP A STRANGER, HELP PATCH HER UP. AND AFTER I BLOW YOUR SHIT UP, YOU JUST...LET IT SLIDE?
DUDE, I DON'T MEAN TO GET ALL HOMO ON YA, BUT YOU'RE A GREAT FRIGGIN' GUY!

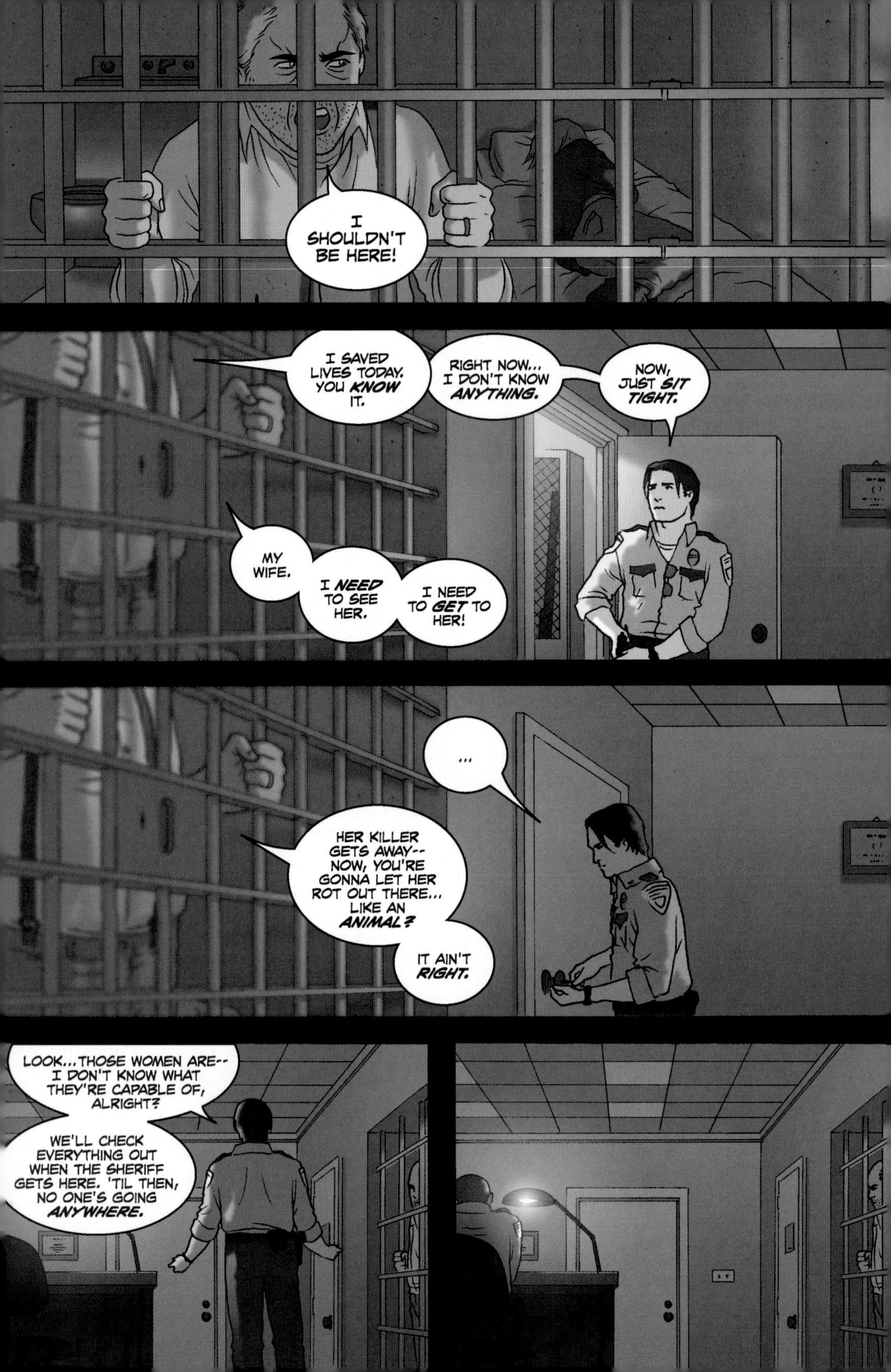
I SHOULDN'T BE HERE!
I SAVED LIVES TODAY. YOU KNOW IT.
RIGHT NOW... I DON'T KNOW ANYTHING.
NOW, JUST SIT TIGHT.
MY WIFE.
I NEED TO SEE HER.
I NEED TO GET TO HER!
...
HER KILLER GETS AWAY-- NOW, YOU'RE GONNA LET HER ROT OUT THERE... LIKE AN ANIMAL?
IT AIN'T RIGHT.
LOOK... THOSE WOMEN ARE-- I DON'T KNOW WHAT THEY'RE CAPABLE OF, ALRIGHT?
WE'LL CHECK EVERYTHING OUT WHEN THE SHERIFF GETS HERE. 'TIL THEN, NO ONE'S GOING ANYWHERE.

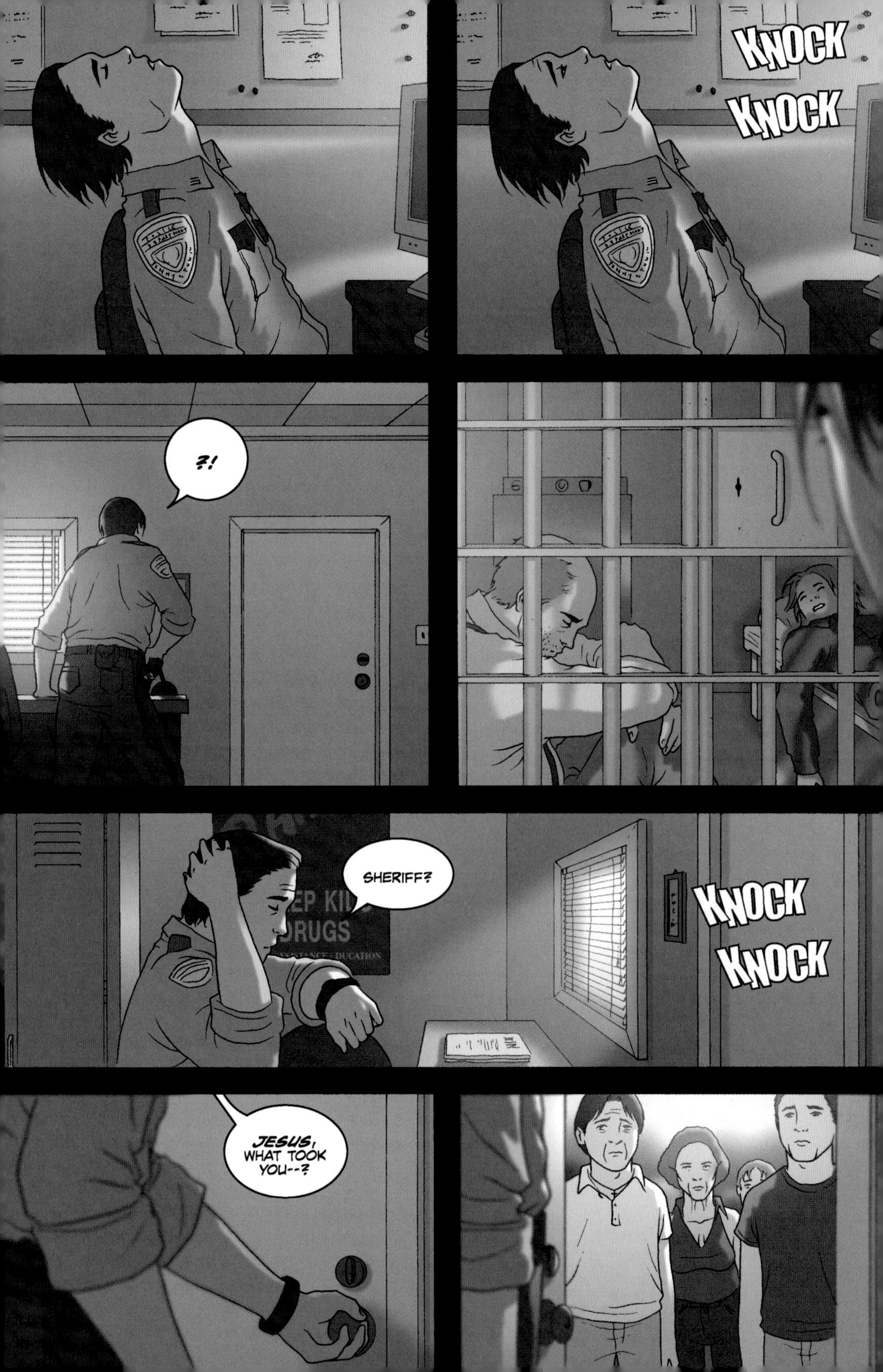
KNOCK
KNOCK
?!
SHERIFF?
KNOCK
KNOCK
JESUS, WHAT TOOK YOU--?

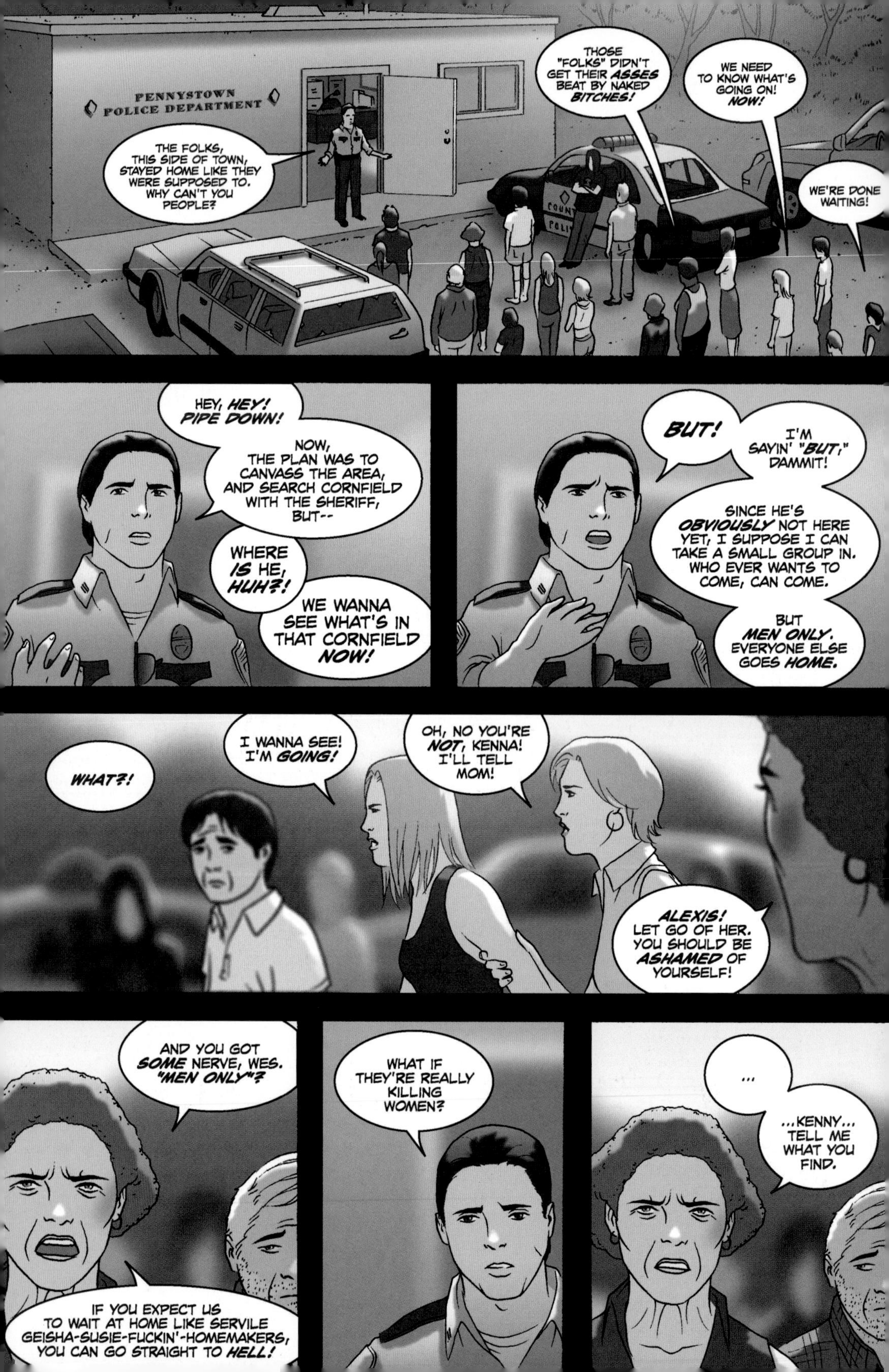
PENNYSTOWN POLICE DEPARTMENT
THE FOLKS, THIS SIDE OF TOWN, STAYED HOME LIKE THEY WERE SUPPOSED TO. WHY CAN'T YOU PEOPLE?
THOSE "FOLKS" DIDN'T GET THEIR ASSES BEAT BY NAKED BITCHES!
WE NEED TO KNOW WHAT'S GOING ON! NOW!
WE'RE DONE WAITING!
HEY, HEY! PIPE DOWN!
NOW, THE PLAN WAS TO CANVASS THE AREA, AND SEARCH CORNFIELD WITH THE SHERIFF, BUT--
WHERE IS HE, HUH?!
WE WANNA SEE WHAT'S IN THAT CORNFIELD NOW!
BUT!
I'M SAYIN' "BUT," DAMMIT!
SINCE HE'S OBVIOUSLY NOT HERE YET, I SUPPOSE I CAN TAKE A SMALL GROUP IN. WHO EVER WANTS TO COME, CAN COME.
BUT MEN ONLY. EVERYONE ELSE GOES HOME.
WHAT?!
I WANNA SEE! I'M GOING!
OH, NO YOU'RE NOT, KENNA! I'LL TELL MOM!
ALEXIS! LET GO OF HER. YOU SHOULD BE ASHAMED OF YOURSELF!
AND YOU GOT SOME NERVE, WES. "MEN ONLY"?
IF YOU EXPECT US TO WAIT AT HOME LIKE SERVILE GEISHA-SUSIE-FUCKIN'-HOMEMAKERS, YOU CAN GO STRAIGHT TO HELL!
WHAT IF THEY'RE REALLY KILLING WOMEN?
...
...KENNY... TELL ME WHAT YOU FIND.

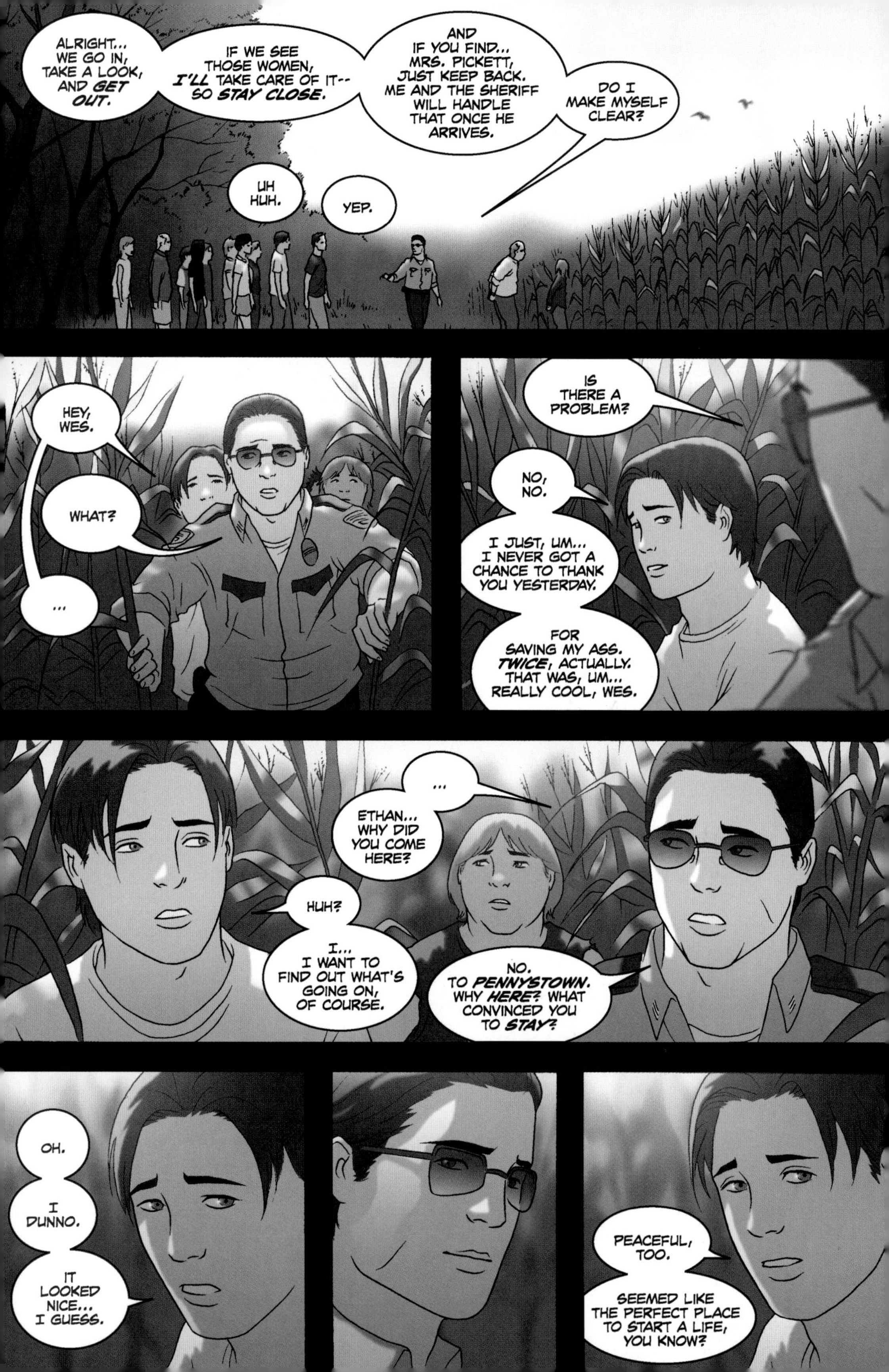

ALRIGHT... WE GO IN, TAKE A LOOK, AND *GET OUT*.
IF WE SEE THOSE WOMEN, *I'LL* TAKE CARE OF IT-- SO *STAY CLOSE*.
AND IF YOU FIND... MRS. PICKETT, JUST KEEP BACK. ME AND THE SHERIFF WILL HANDLE THAT ONCE HE ARRIVES.
DO I MAKE MYSELF CLEAR?
UH HUH.
YEP.
HEY, WES.
WHAT?
...
IS THERE A PROBLEM?
NO, NO.
I JUST, UM... I NEVER GOT A CHANCE TO THANK YOU YESTERDAY.
FOR SAVING MY ASS. *TWICE*, ACTUALLY. THAT WAS, UM... REALLY COOL, WES.
...
ETHAN... WHY DID YOU COME HERE?
HUH?
I... I WANT TO FIND OUT WHAT'S GOING ON, OF COURSE.
NO. TO *PENNYSTOWN*. WHY *HERE*? WHAT CONVINCED YOU TO *STAY*?
OH.
I DUNNO.
IT LOOKED NICE... I GUESS.
PEACEFUL, TOO.
SEEMED LIKE THE PERFECT PLACE TO START A LIFE, YOU KNOW?

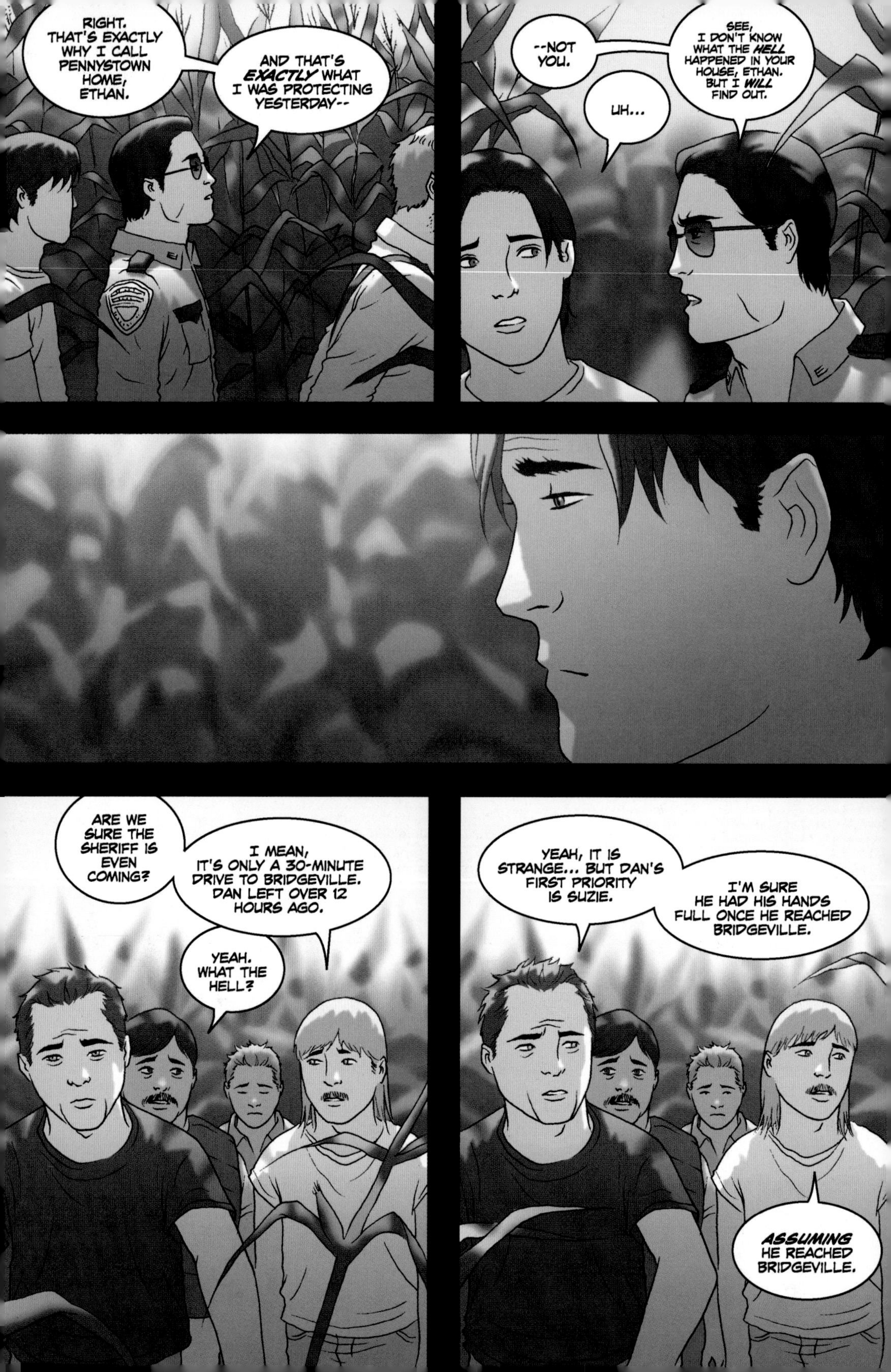
RIGHT. THAT'S EXACTLY WHY I CALL PENNYSTOWN HOME, ETHAN.
AND THAT'S EXACTLY WHAT I WAS PROTECTING YESTERDAY--
--NOT YOU.
SEE, I DON'T KNOW WHAT THE HELL HAPPENED IN YOUR HOUSE, ETHAN. BUT I WILL FIND OUT.
UH...
ARE WE SURE THE SHERIFF IS EVEN COMING?
I MEAN, IT'S ONLY A 30-MINUTE DRIVE TO BRIDGEVILLE. DAN LEFT OVER 12 HOURS AGO.
YEAH. WHAT THE HELL?
YEAH, IT IS STRANGE... BUT DAN'S FIRST PRIORITY IS SUZIE.
I'M SURE HE HAD HIS HANDS FULL ONCE HE REACHED BRIDGEVILLE.
ASSUMING HE REACHED BRIDGEVILLE.

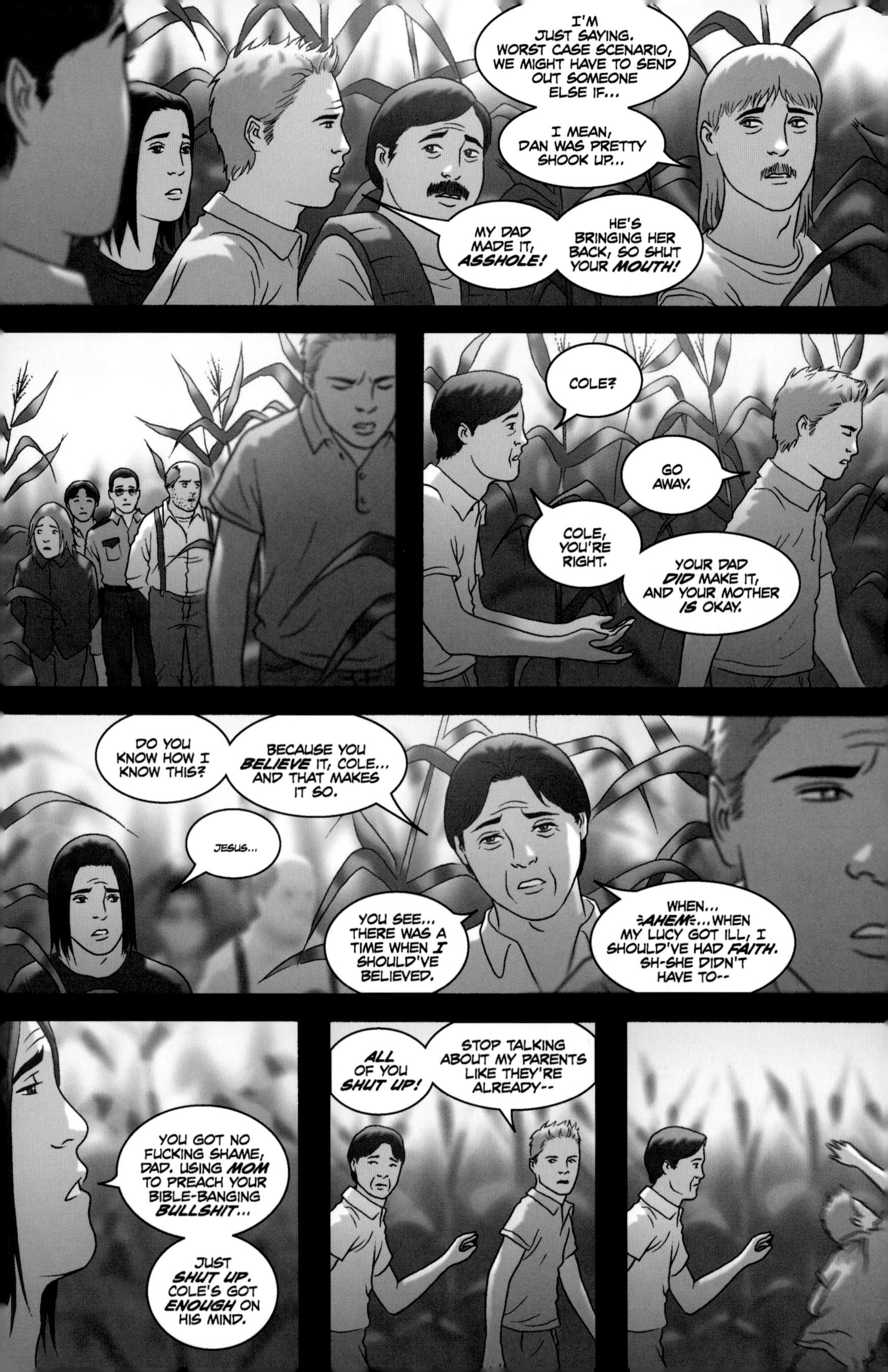
I'M JUST SAYING. WORST CASE SCENARIO, WE MIGHT HAVE TO SEND OUT SOMEONE ELSE IF...
I MEAN, DAN WAS PRETTY SHOOK UP...
MY DAD MADE IT, ASSHOLE!
HE'S BRINGING HER BACK, SO SHUT YOUR MOUTH!
COLE?
GO AWAY.
COLE, YOU'RE RIGHT.
YOUR DAD DID MAKE IT, AND YOUR MOTHER IS OKAY.
DO YOU KNOW HOW I KNOW THIS?
BECAUSE YOU BELIEVE IT, COLE... AND THAT MAKES IT SO.
JESUS...
YOU SEE... THERE WAS A TIME WHEN I SHOULD'VE BELIEVED.
WHEN... AHEM... WHEN MY LUCY GOT ILL, I SHOULD'VE HAD FAITH. SH-SHE DIDN'T HAVE TO--
YOU GOT NO FUCKING SHAME, DAD. USING MOM TO PREACH YOUR BIBLE-BANGING BULLSHIT...
JUST SHUT UP. COLE'S GOT ENOUGH ON HIS MIND.
ALL OF YOU SHUT UP!
STOP TALKING ABOUT MY PARENTS LIKE THEY'RE ALREADY--

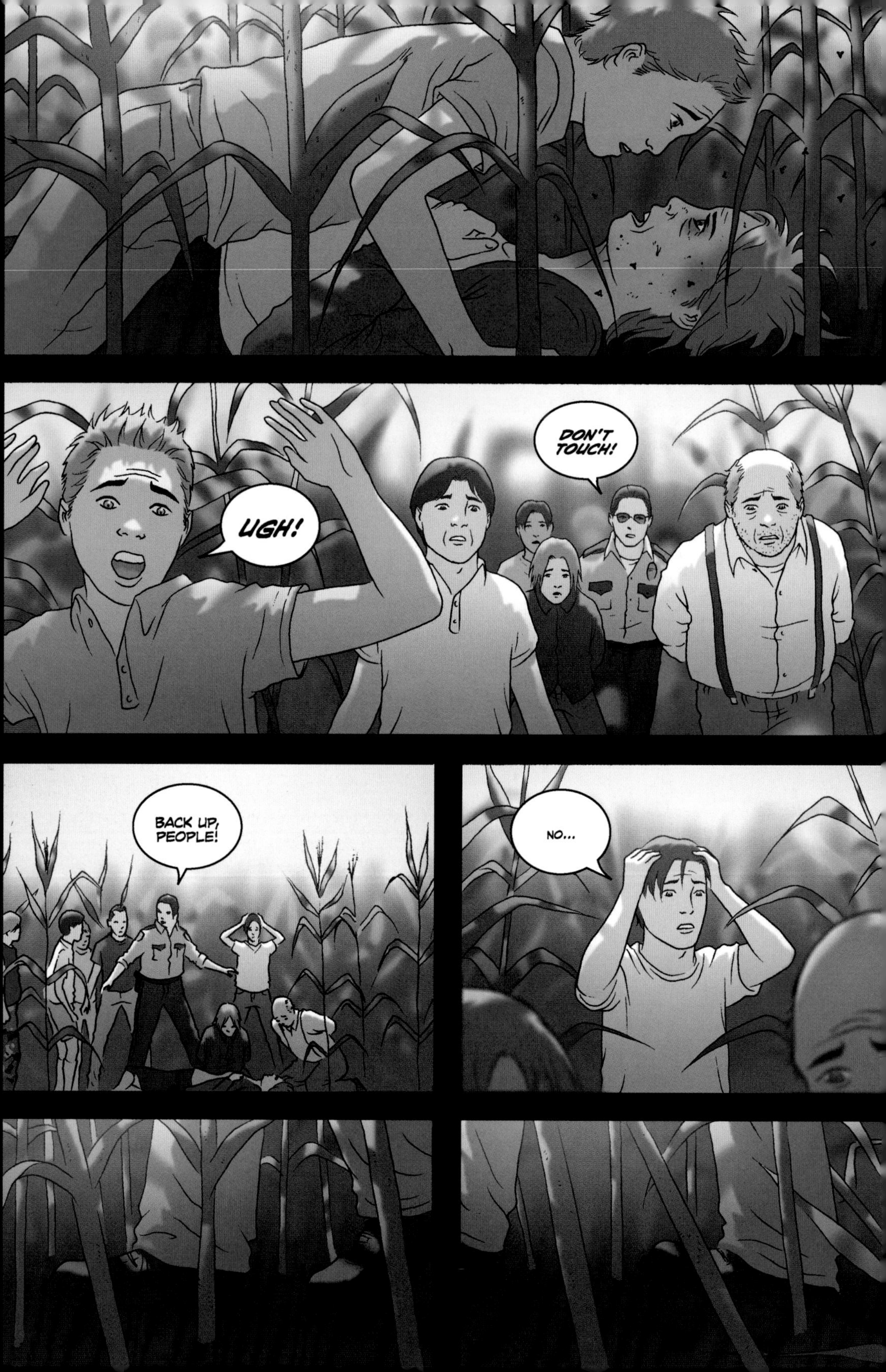
UGH!
DON'T TOUCH!
BACK UP, PEOPLE!
NO...

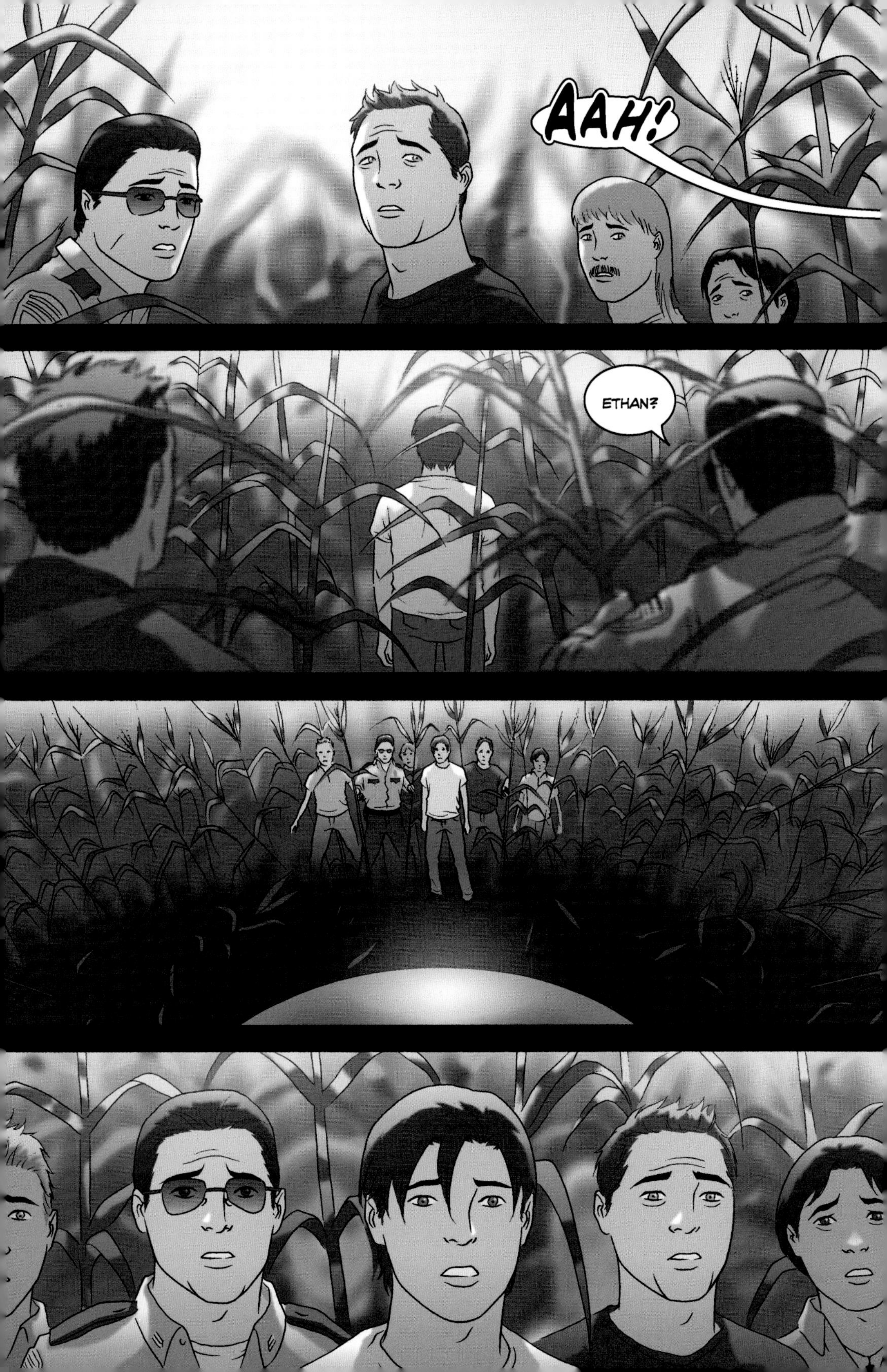
AAH!
ETHAN?

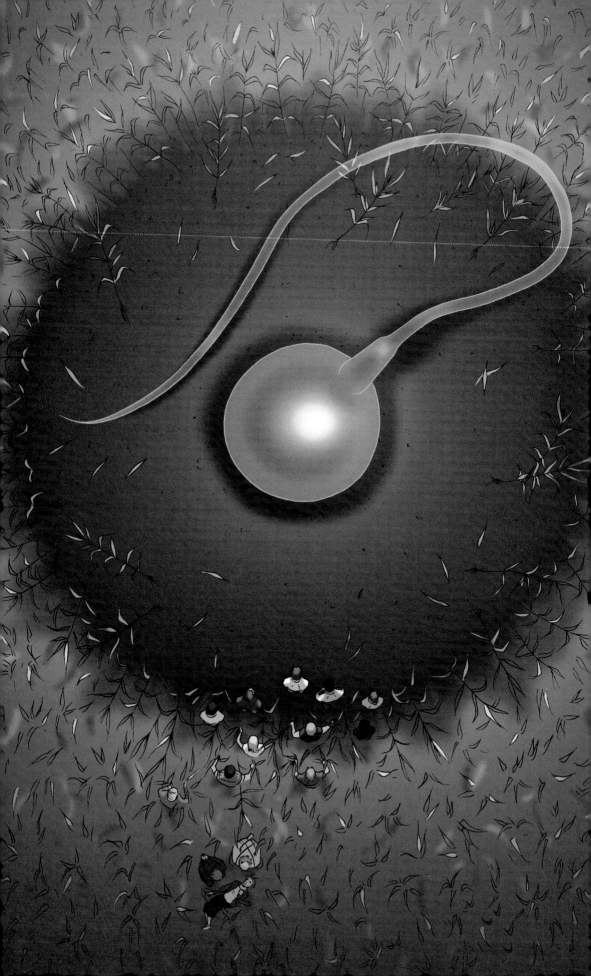

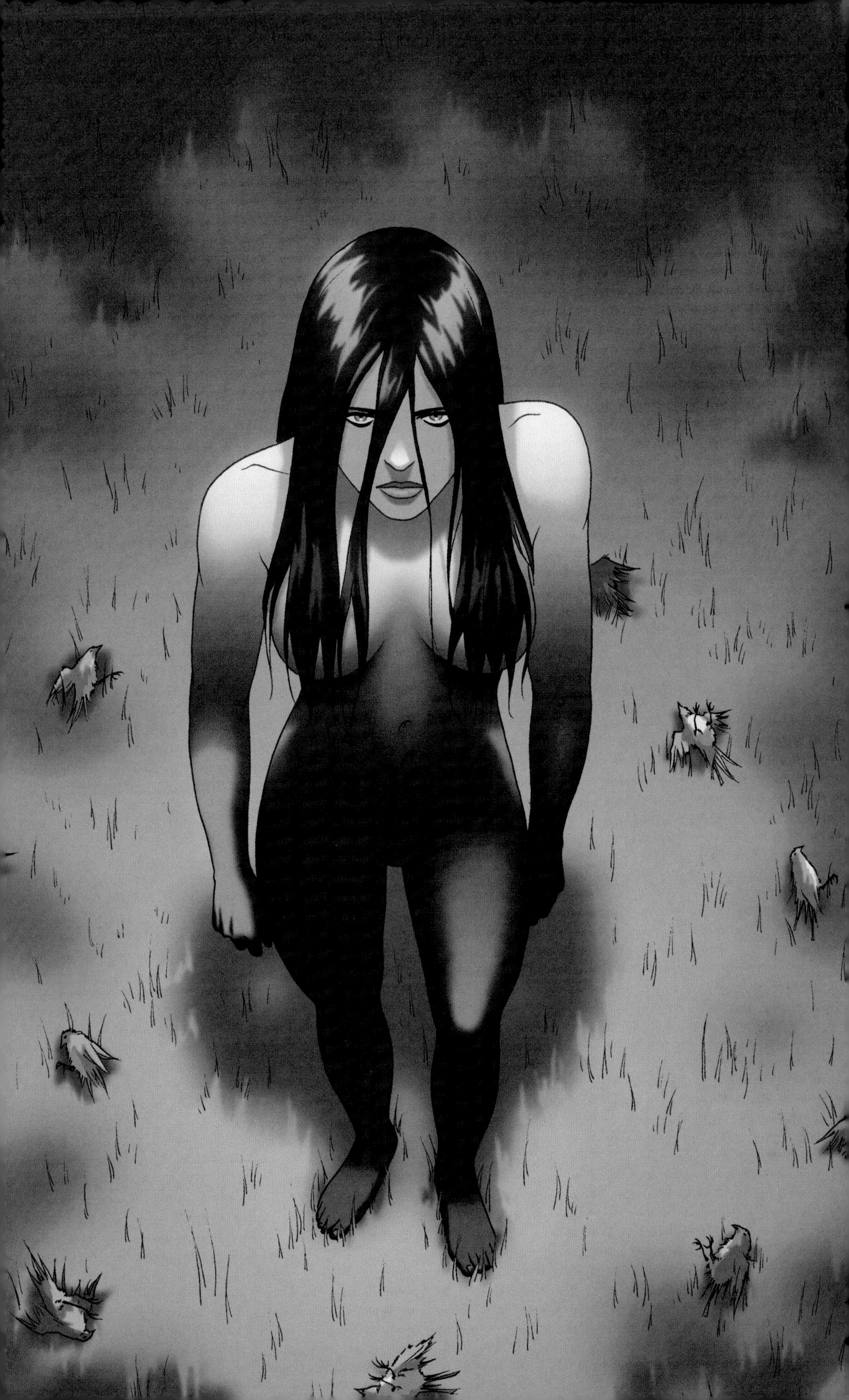

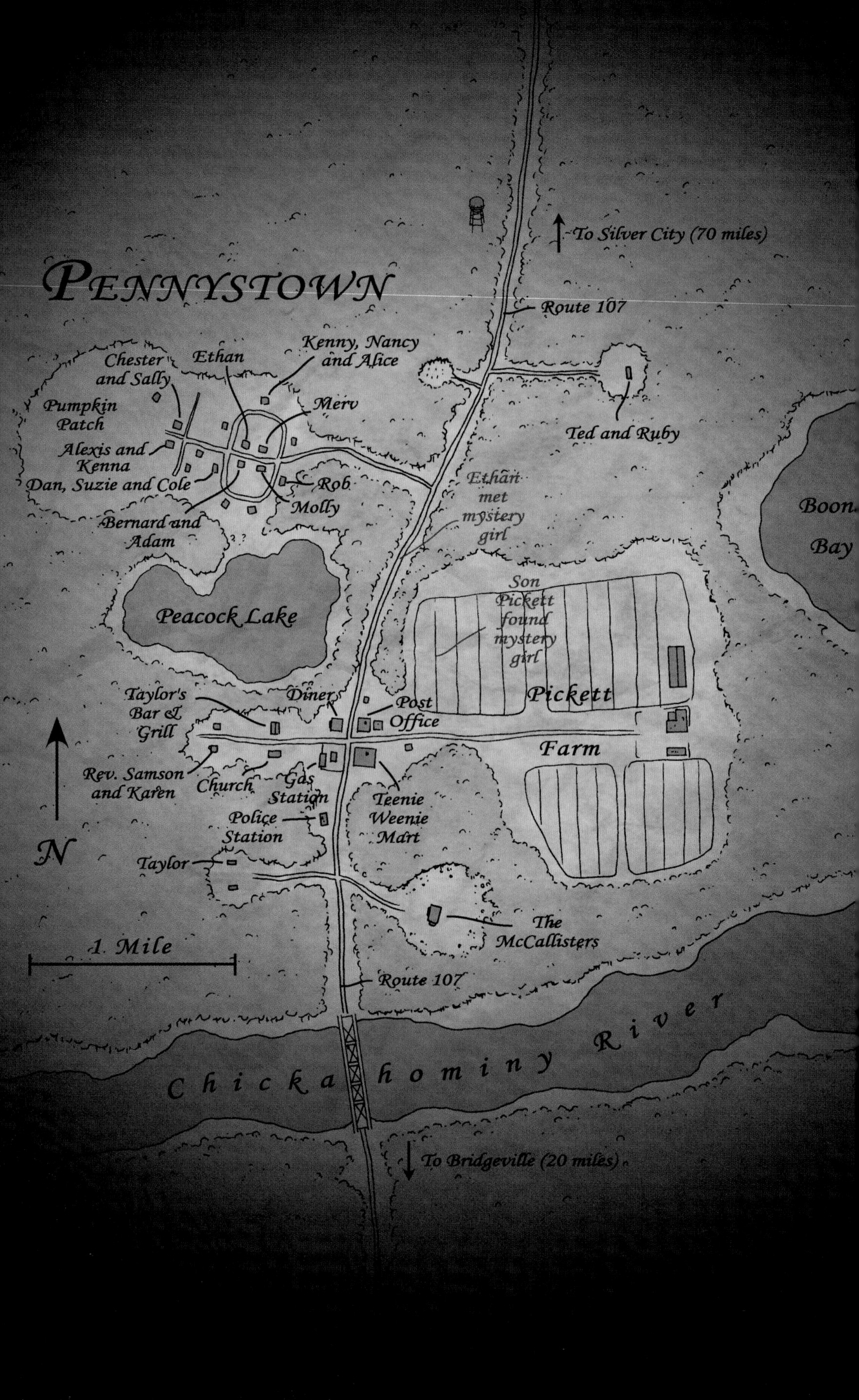
To Silver City (70 miles)
Pennystown
Route 107
Kenny, Nancy and Alice
Chester and Sally
Ethan
Pumpkin Patch
Merv
Ted and Ruby
Alexis and Kenna
Dan, Suzie and Cole
Rob
Molly
Bernard and Adam
Ethan met mystery girl
Boon Bay
Peacock Lake
Son Pickett found mystery girl
Taylor's Bar & Grill
Diner
Post Office
Pickett Farm
Rev. Samson and Karen
Church
Gas Station
Teenie Weenie Mart
Police Station
N
Taylor
The McCallisters
1 Mile
Route 107
Chickahominy River
To Bridgeville (20 miles)

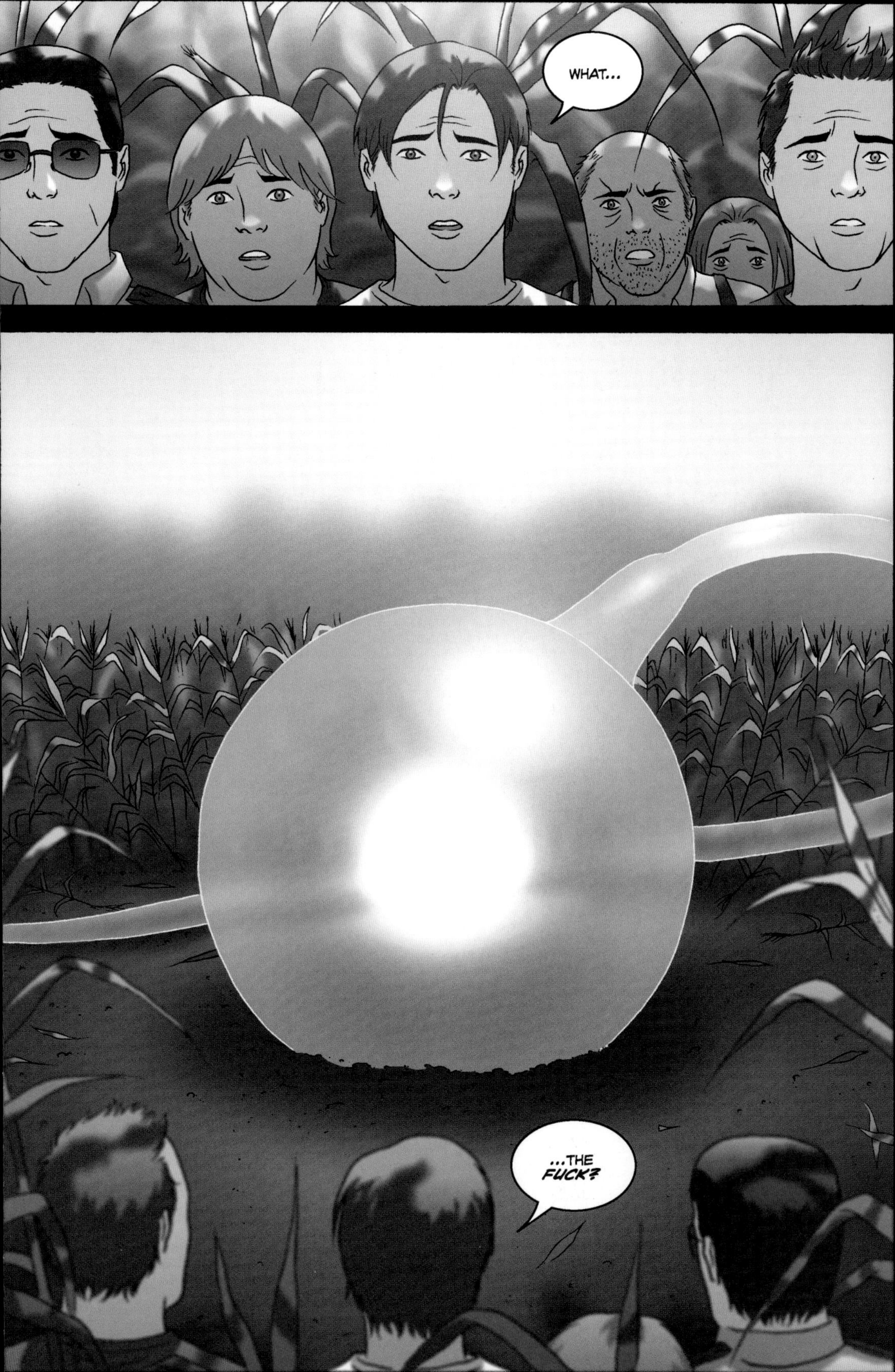
WHAT...
...THE FUCK?

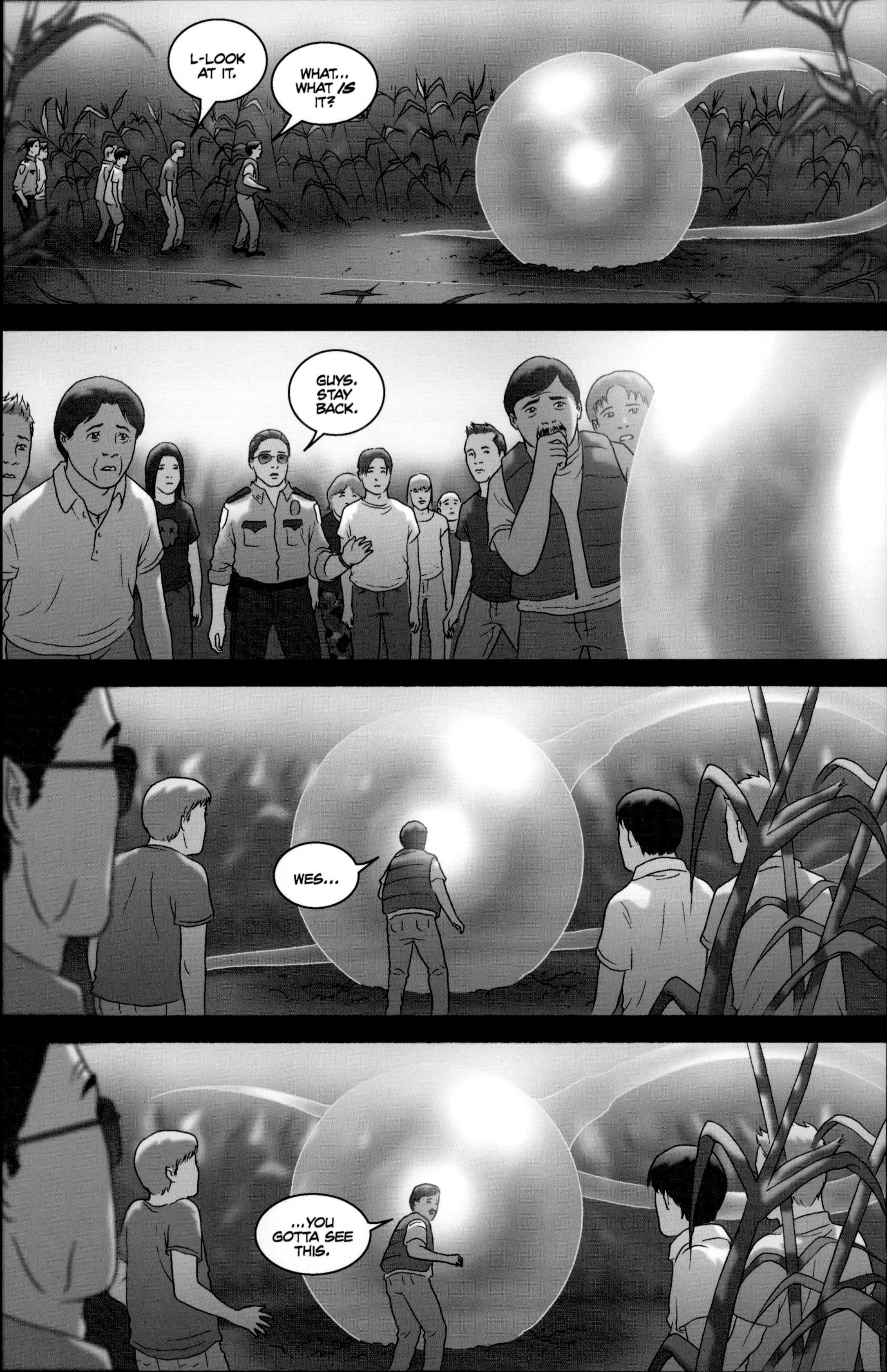
L-LOOK AT IT.
WHAT... WHAT *IS* IT?
GUYS. STAY BACK.
WES...
...YOU GOTTA SEE THIS.

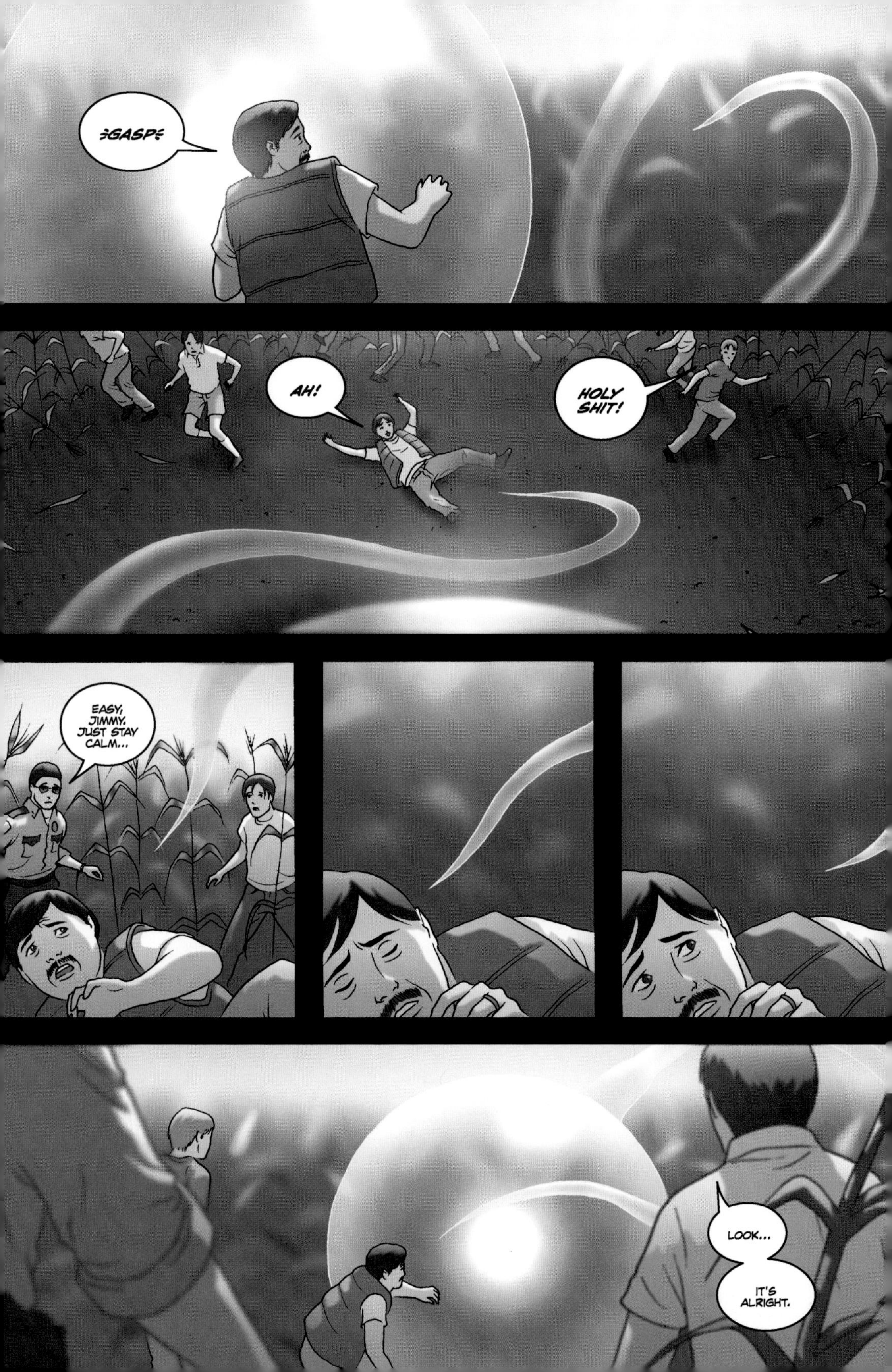

GASP
AH!
HOLY SHIT!
EASY, JIMMY. JUST STAY CALM...
LOOK...
IT'S ALRIGHT.

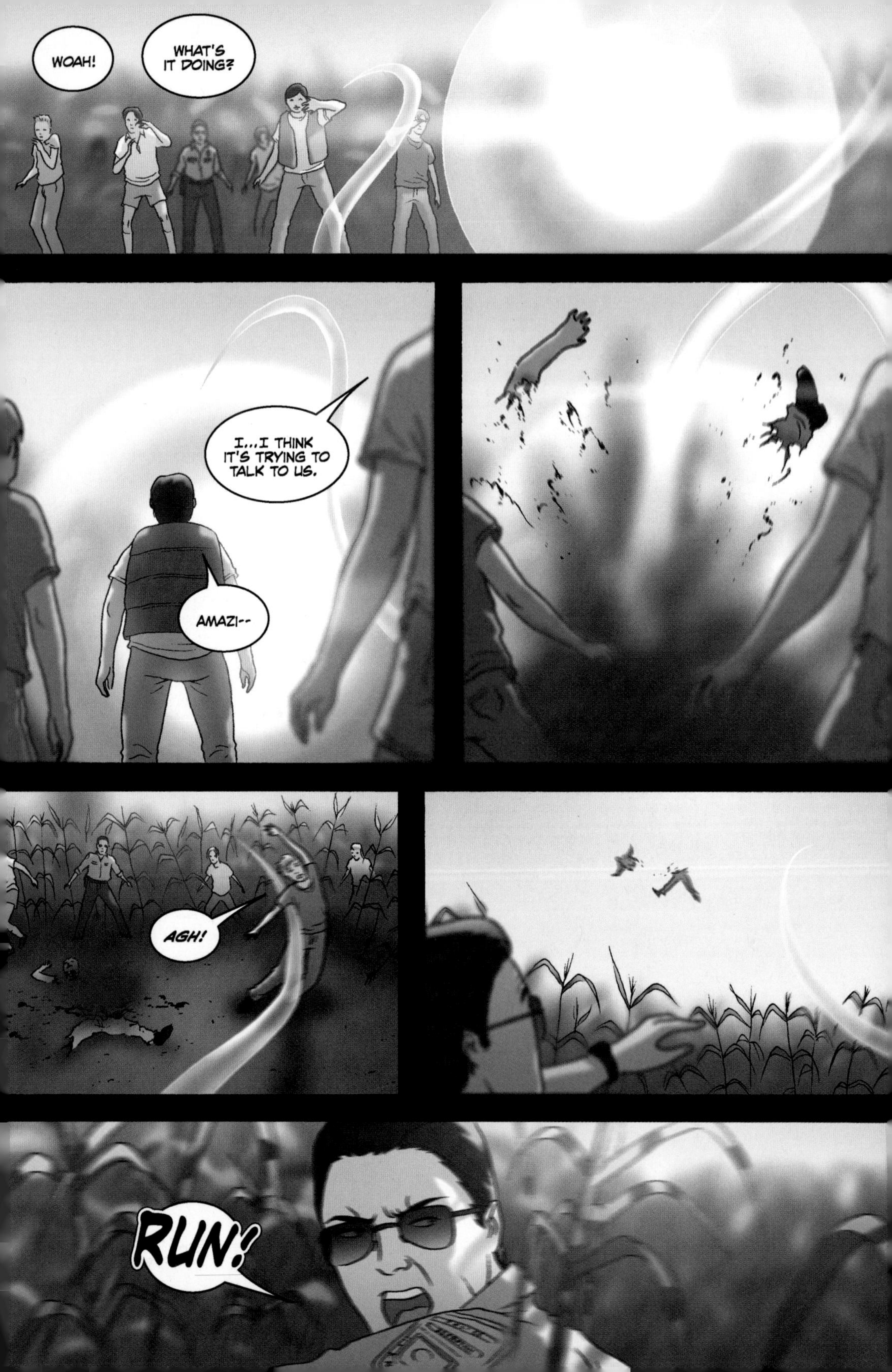
WOAH!
WHAT'S IT DOING?
I...I THINK IT'S TRYING TO TALK TO US.
AMAZI--
AGH!
RUN!

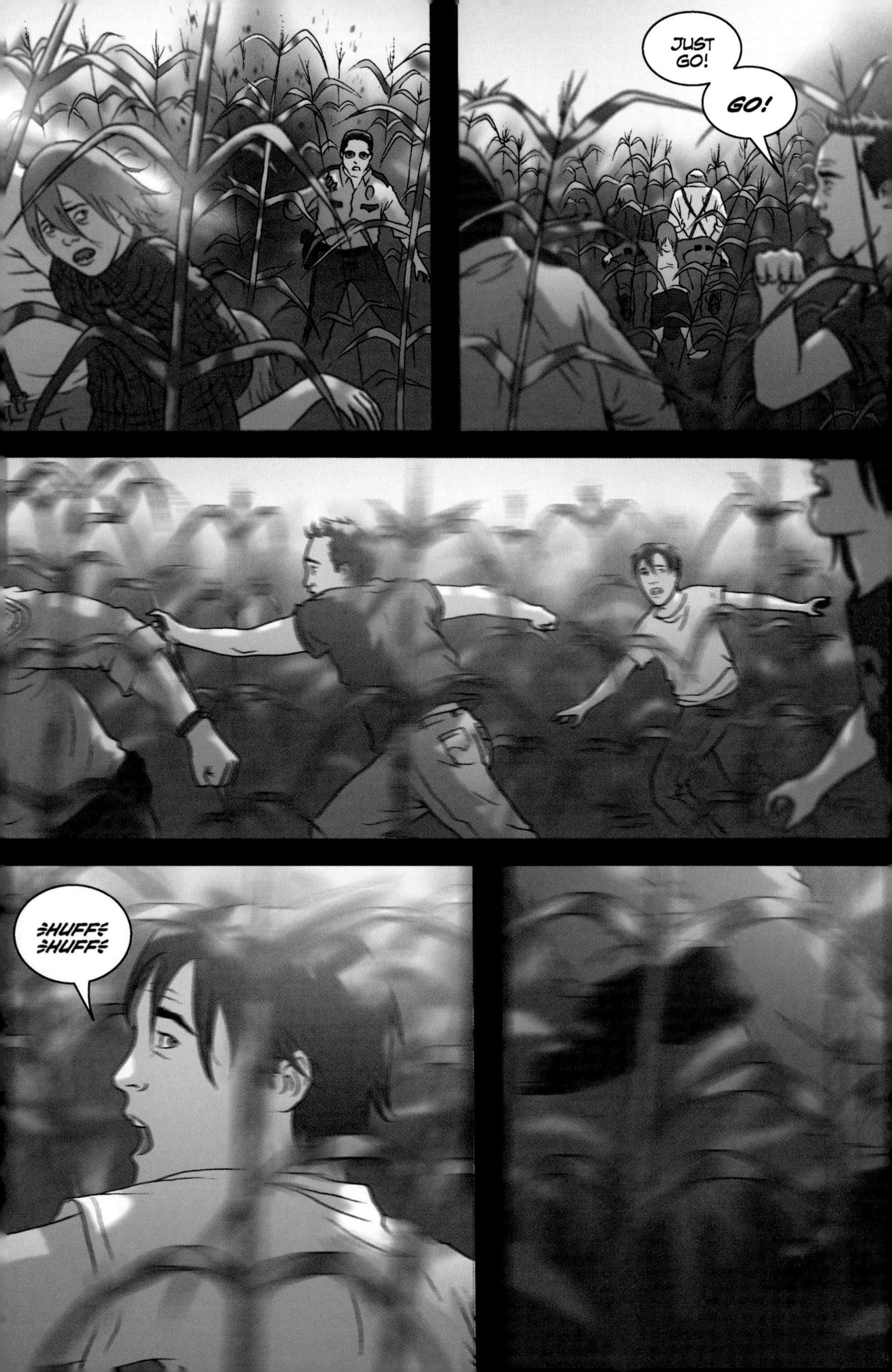
JUST GO!
GO!
≡HUFF≡ ≡HUFF≡

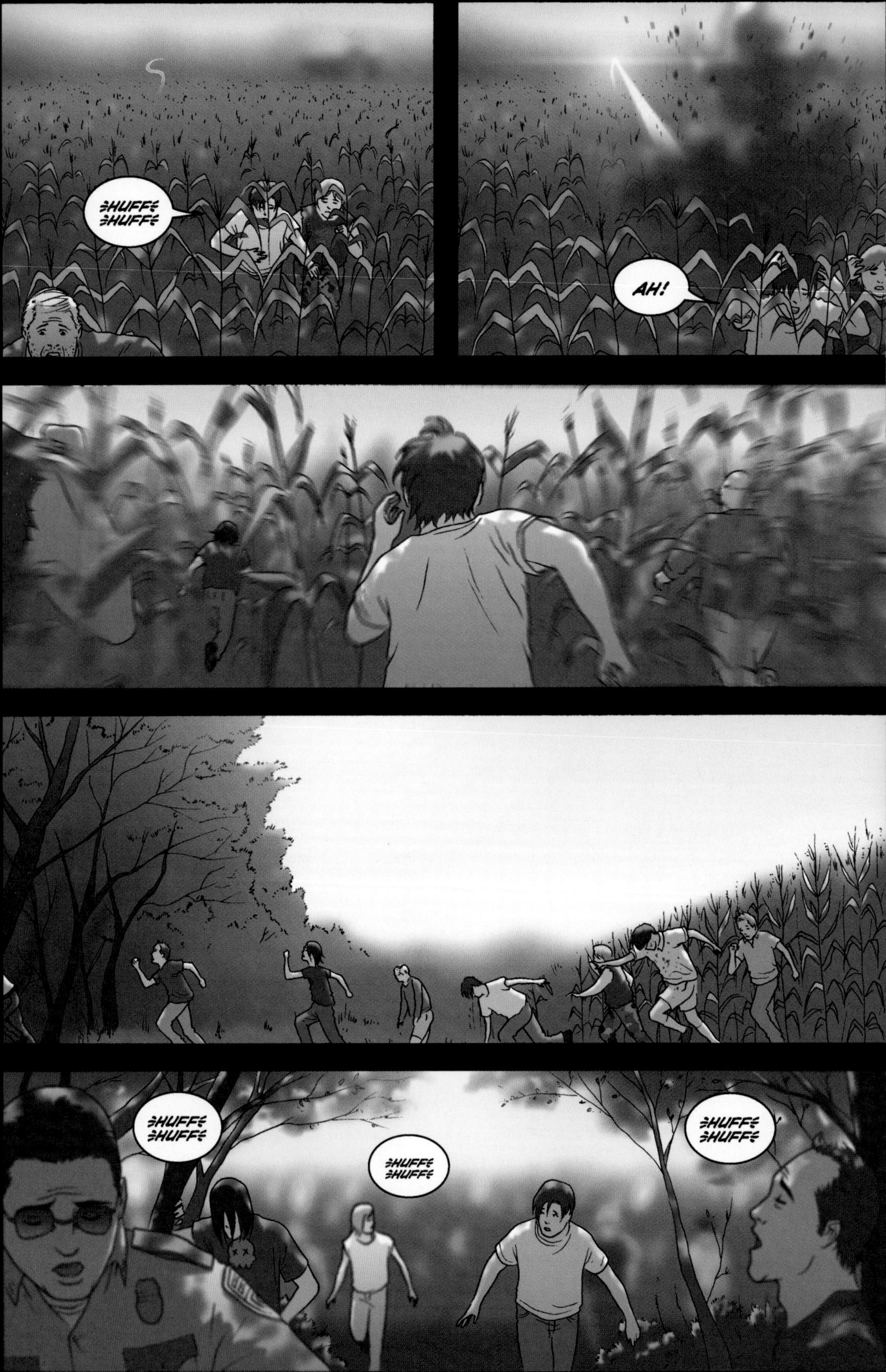
HUFF HUFF
AH!
HUFF HUFF
HUFF HUFF
HUFF HUFF

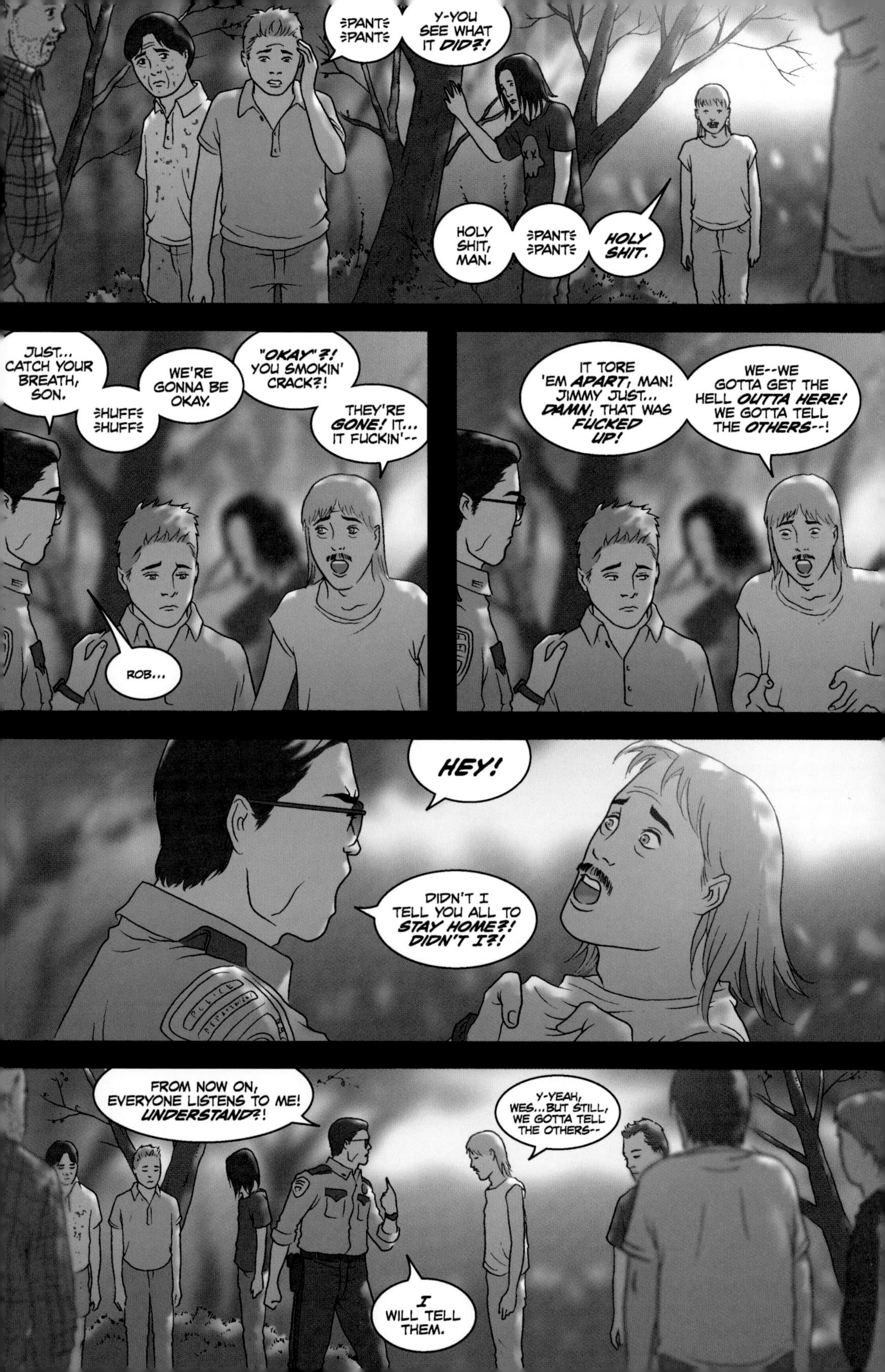

PANT PANT
Y-YOU SEE WHAT IT DID?!
HOLY SHIT, MAN.
PANT PANT
HOLY SHIT.
JUST... CATCH YOUR BREATH, SON.
HUFF HUFF
WE'RE GONNA BE OKAY.
"OKAY"?! YOU SMOKIN' CRACK?!
THEY'RE GONE! IT... IT FUCKIN'--
ROB...
IT TORE 'EM APART, MAN! JIMMY JUST... DAMN, THAT WAS FUCKED UP!
WE--WE GOTTA GET THE HELL OUTTA HERE! WE GOTTA TELL THE OTHERS--!
HEY!
DIDN'T I TELL YOU ALL TO STAY HOME?! DIDN'T I?!
FROM NOW ON, EVERYONE LISTENS TO ME! UNDERSTAND?!
Y-YEAH, WES...BUT STILL, WE GOTTA TELL THE OTHERS--
I WILL TELL THEM.

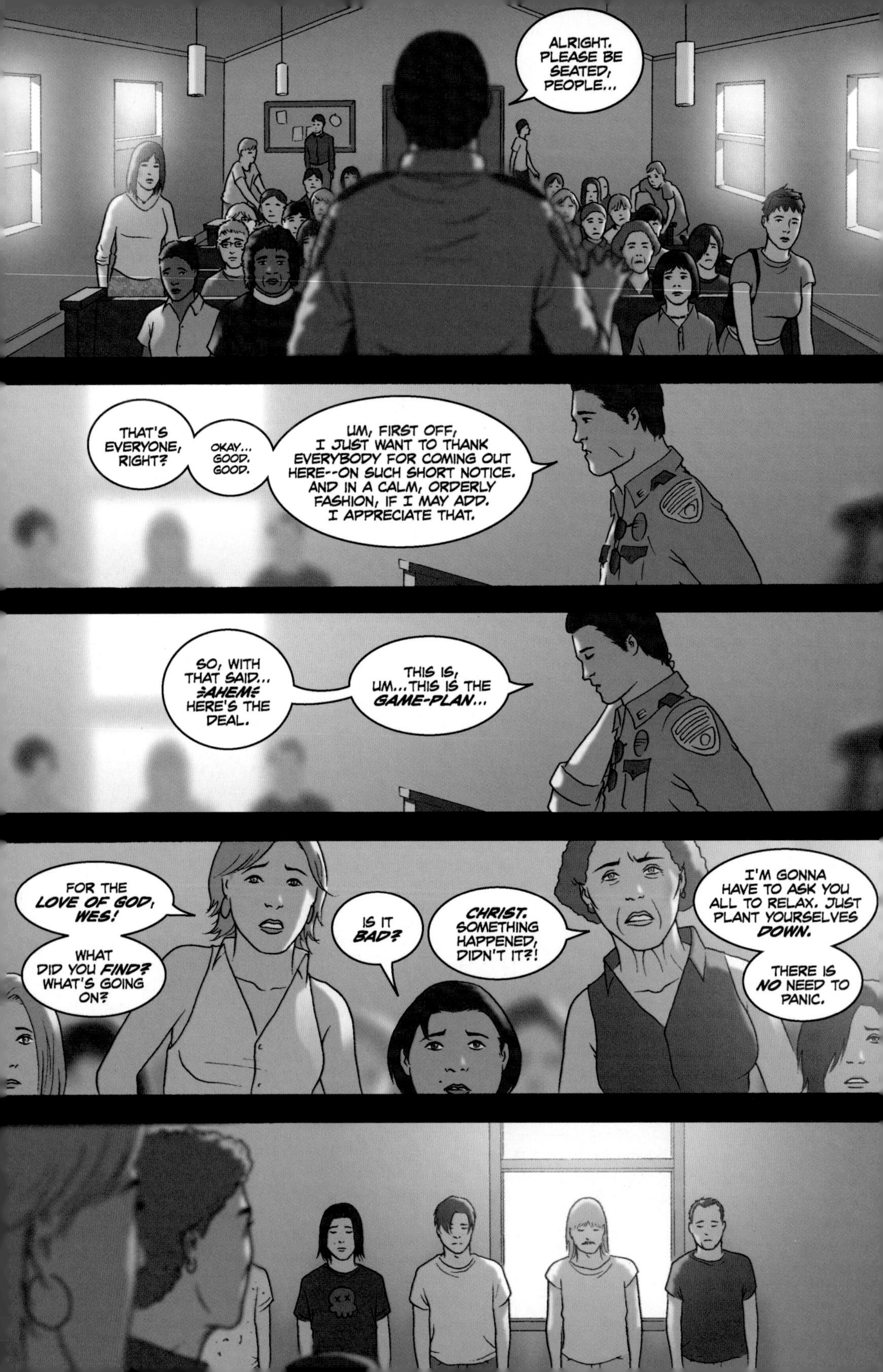
ALRIGHT. PLEASE BE SEATED, PEOPLE...
THAT'S EVERYONE, RIGHT?
OKAY... GOOD. GOOD.
UM, FIRST OFF, I JUST WANT TO THANK EVERYBODY FOR COMING OUT HERE--ON SUCH SHORT NOTICE. AND IN A CALM, ORDERLY FASHION, IF I MAY ADD. I APPRECIATE THAT.
SO, WITH THAT SAID... *AHEM* HERE'S THE DEAL.
THIS IS, UM... THIS IS THE *GAME-PLAN*...
FOR THE *LOVE OF GOD, WES!*
WHAT DID YOU *FIND?* WHAT'S GOING ON?
IS IT *BAD?*
CHRIST. SOMETHING HAPPENED, DIDN'T IT?!
I'M GONNA HAVE TO ASK YOU ALL TO RELAX. JUST PLANT YOURSELVES *DOWN.*
THERE IS *NO* NEED TO PANIC.

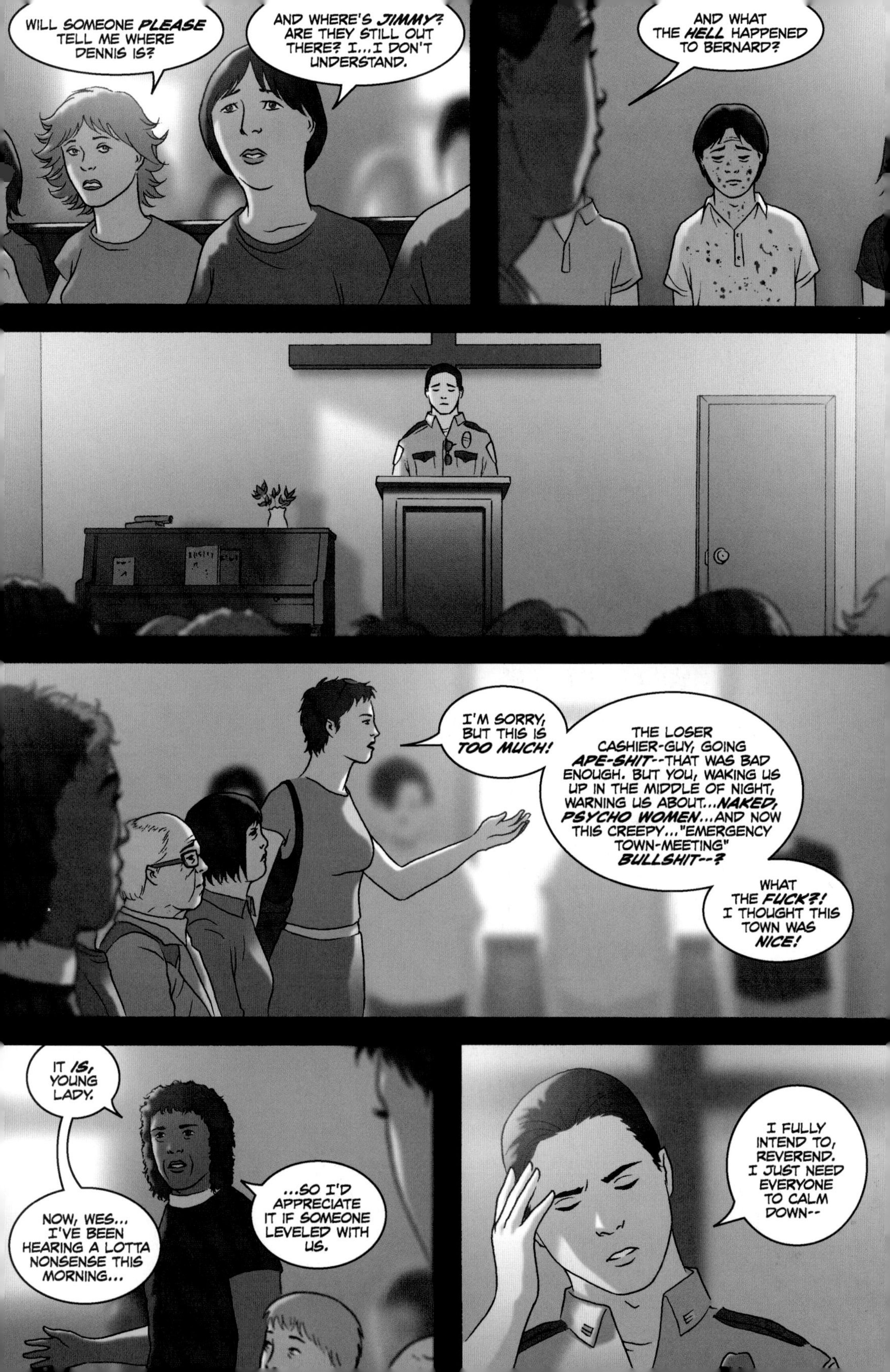
WILL SOMEONE PLEASE TELL ME WHERE DENNIS IS?
AND WHERE'S JIMMY? ARE THEY STILL OUT THERE? I...I DON'T UNDERSTAND.
AND WHAT THE HELL HAPPENED TO BERNARD?
I'M SORRY, BUT THIS IS TOO MUCH!
THE LOSER CASHIER-GUY, GOING APE-SHIT--THAT WAS BAD ENOUGH. BUT YOU, WAKING US UP IN THE MIDDLE OF NIGHT, WARNING US ABOUT...NAKED, PSYCHO WOMEN...AND NOW THIS CREEPY..."EMERGENCY TOWN-MEETING" BULLSHIT--?
WHAT THE FUCK?! I THOUGHT THIS TOWN WAS NICE!
IT IS, YOUNG LADY.
NOW, WES... I'VE BEEN HEARING A LOTTA NONSENSE THIS MORNING...
...SO I'D APPRECIATE IT IF SOMEONE LEVELED WITH US.
I FULLY INTEND TO, REVEREND. I JUST NEED EVERYONE TO CALM DOWN--

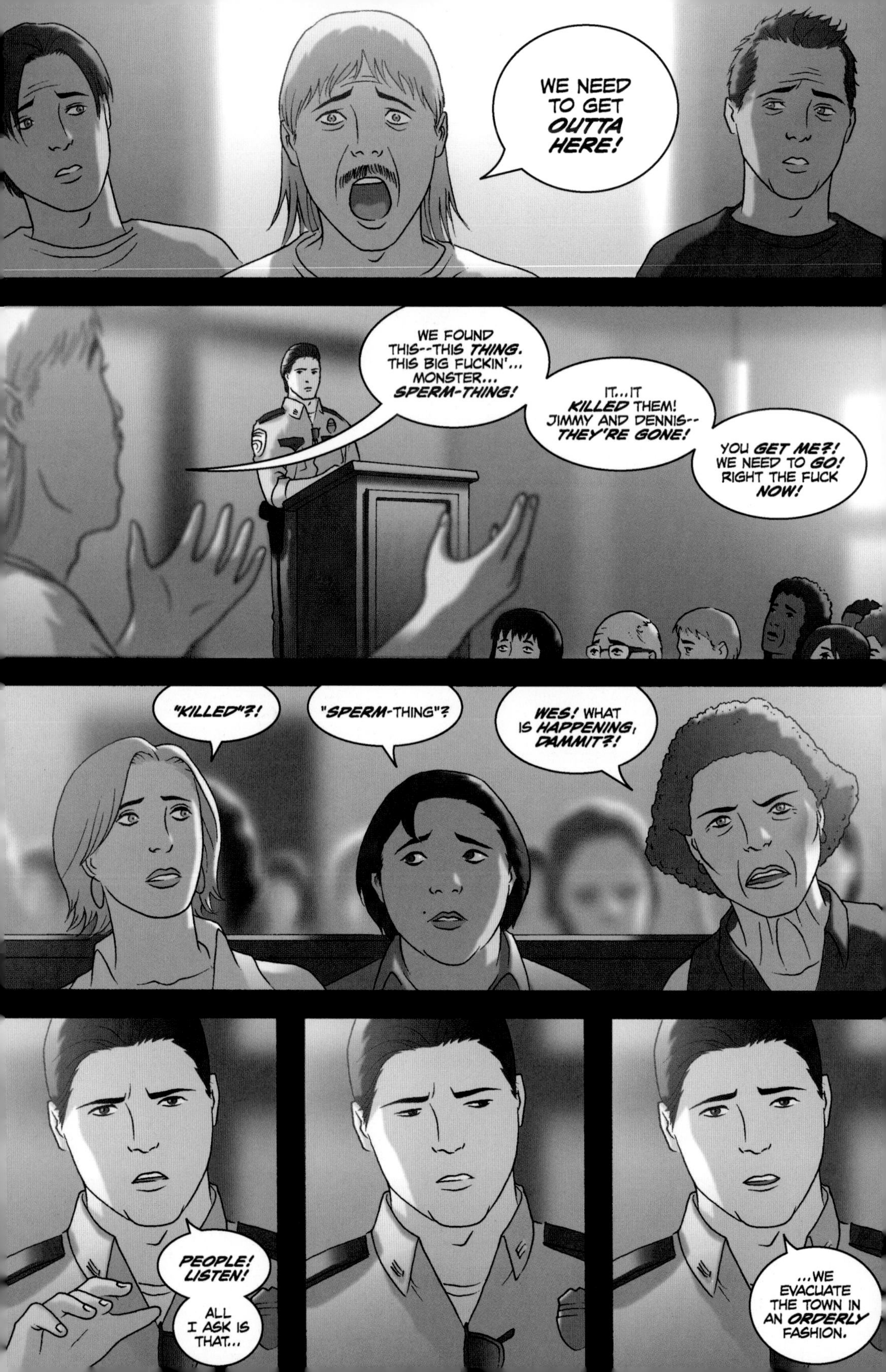
WE NEED TO GET OUTTA HERE!
WE FOUND THIS--THIS THING. THIS BIG FUCKIN'... MONSTER... SPERM-THING!
IT...IT KILLED THEM! JIMMY AND DENNIS--THEY'RE GONE!
YOU GET ME?! WE NEED TO GO! RIGHT THE FUCK NOW!
"KILLED"?!
"SPERM-THING"?
WES! WHAT IS HAPPENING, DAMMIT?!
PEOPLE! LISTEN!
ALL I ASK IS THAT...
...WE EVACUATE THE TOWN IN AN ORDERLY FASHION.

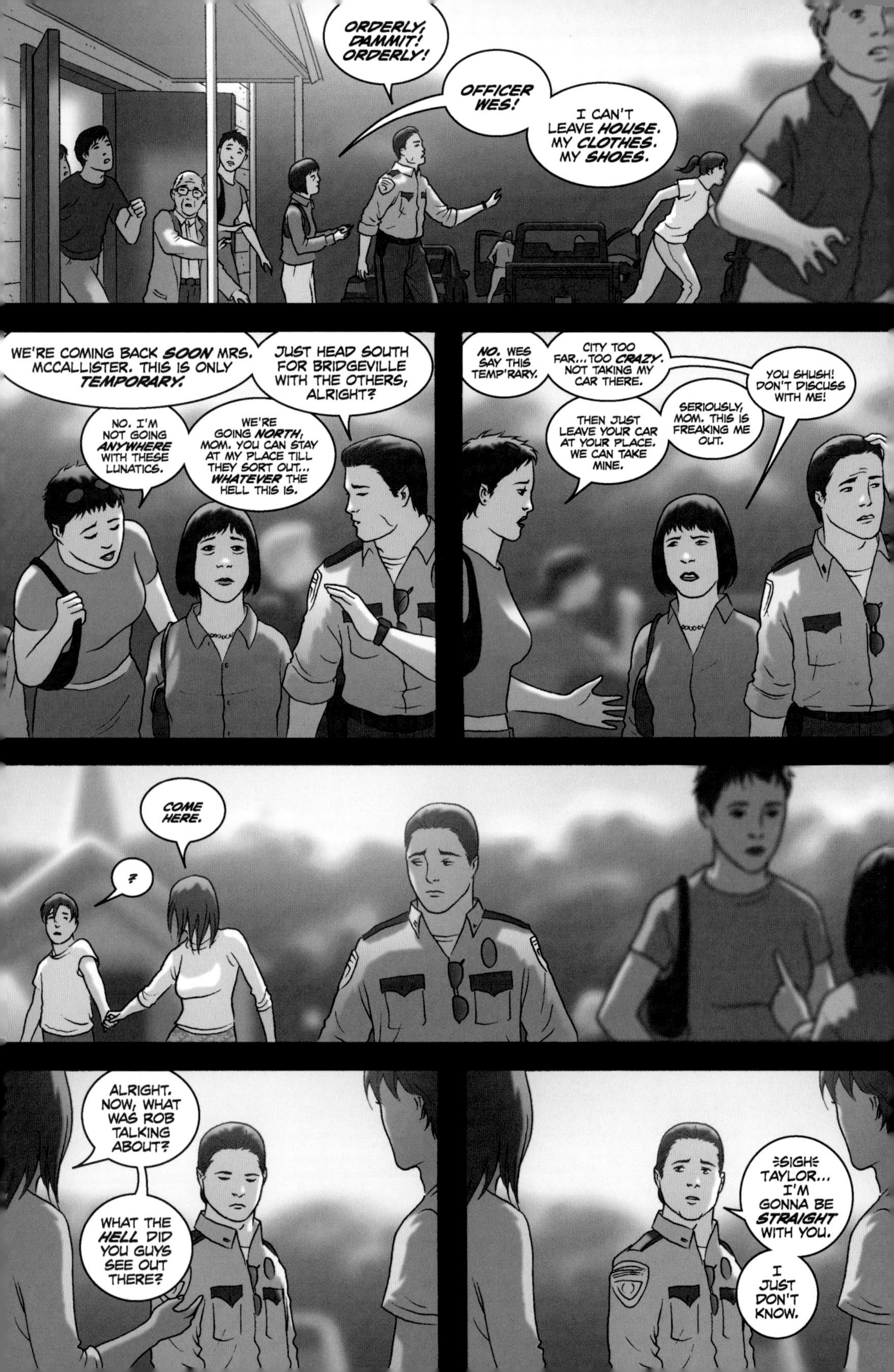
ORDERLY, DAMMIT! ORDERLY!
OFFICER WES!
I CAN'T LEAVE HOUSE. MY CLOTHES. MY SHOES.
WE'RE COMING BACK SOON MRS. MCCALLISTER. THIS IS ONLY TEMPORARY.
JUST HEAD SOUTH FOR BRIDGEVILLE WITH THE OTHERS, ALRIGHT?
NO. I'M NOT GOING ANYWHERE WITH THESE LUNATICS.
WE'RE GOING NORTH, MOM. YOU CAN STAY AT MY PLACE TILL THEY SORT OUT... WHATEVER THE HELL THIS IS.
NO. WES SAY THIS TEMP'RARY.
CITY TOO FAR...TOO CRAZY. NOT TAKING MY CAR THERE.
THEN JUST LEAVE YOUR CAR AT YOUR PLACE. WE CAN TAKE MINE.
SERIOUSLY, MOM. THIS IS FREAKING ME OUT.
YOU SHUSH! DON'T DISCUSS WITH ME!
COME HERE.
?
ALRIGHT. NOW, WHAT WAS ROB TALKING ABOUT?
WHAT THE HELL DID YOU GUYS SEE OUT THERE?
SIGH TAYLOR... I'M GONNA BE STRAIGHT WITH YOU.
I JUST DON'T KNOW.

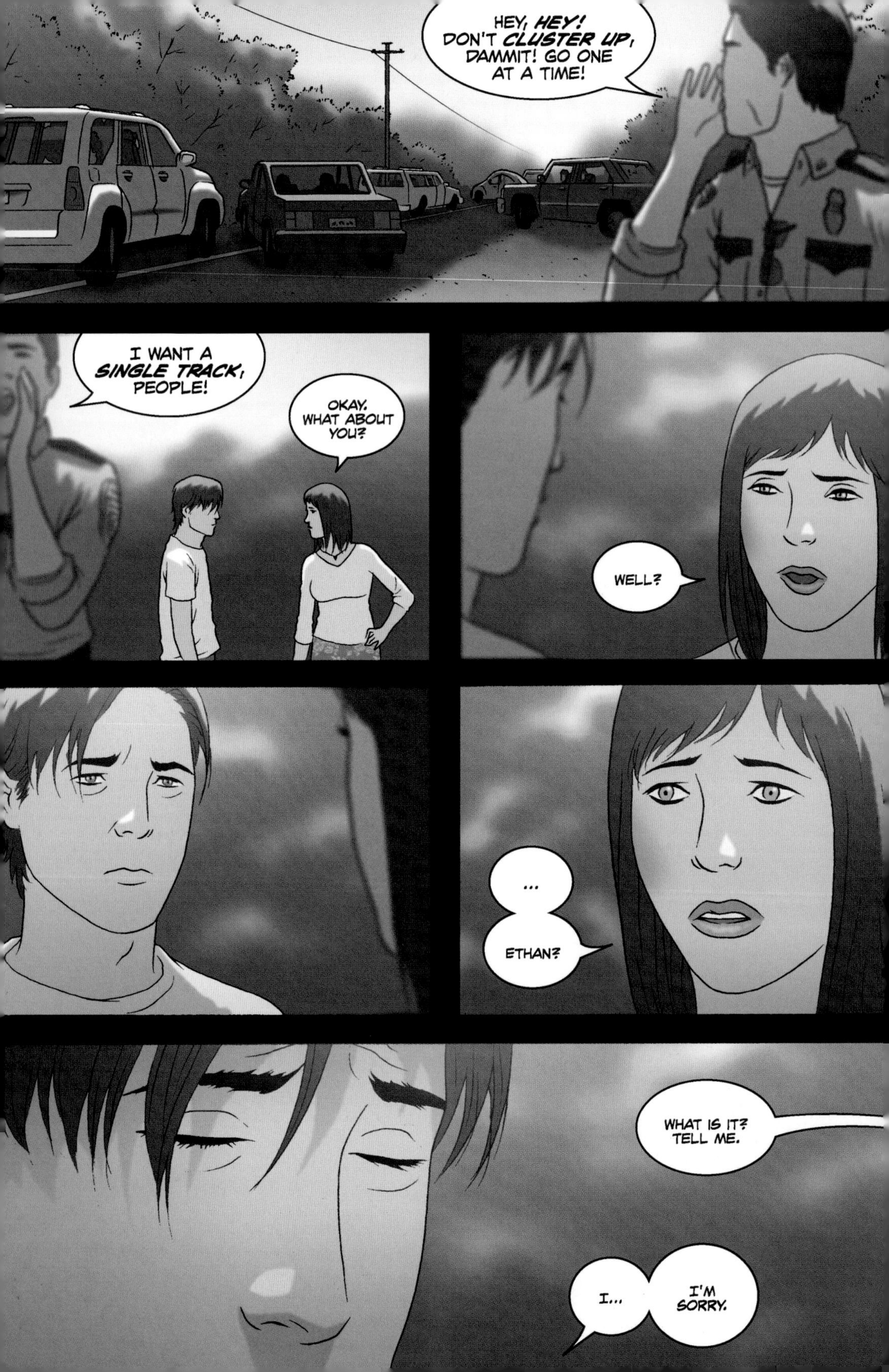
HEY, HEY! DON'T CLUSTER UP, DAMMIT! GO ONE AT A TIME!
I WANT A SINGLE TRACK, PEOPLE!
OKAY. WHAT ABOUT YOU?
WELL?
...
ETHAN?
WHAT IS IT? TELL ME.
I...
I'M SORRY.

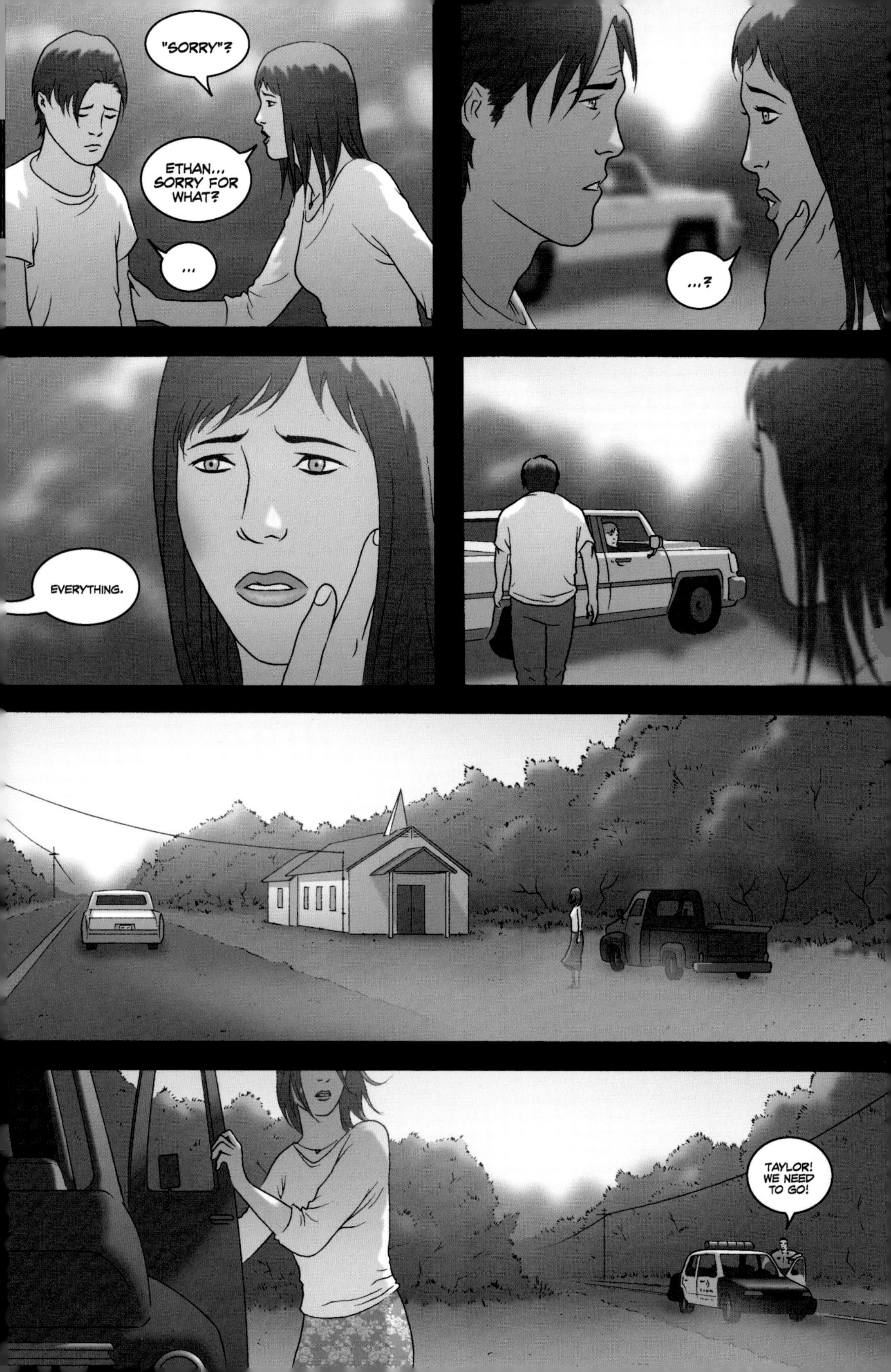
"SORRY"?
ETHAN... SORRY FOR WHAT?
...
...?
EVERYTHING.
TAYLOR! WE NEED TO GO!

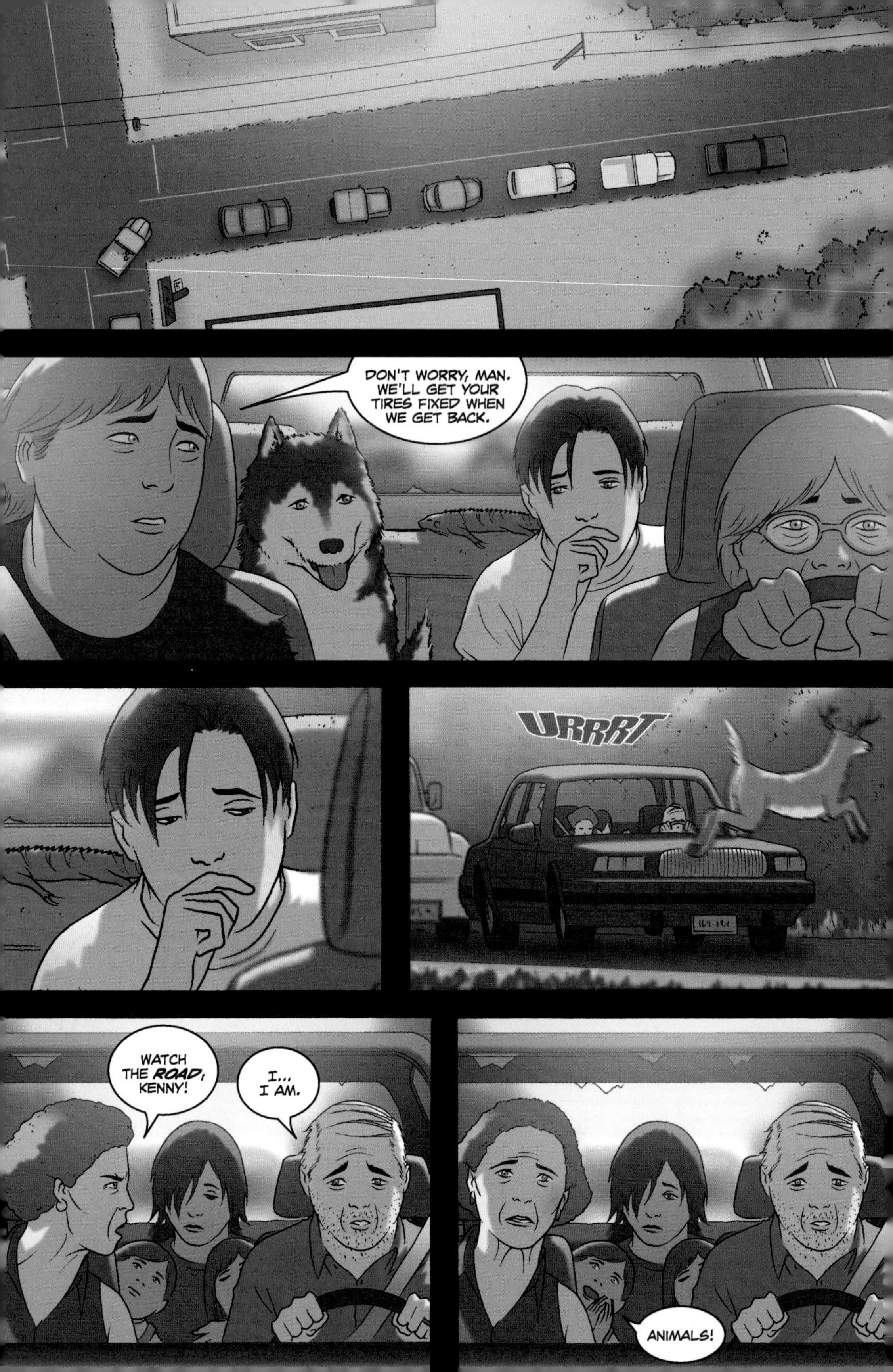
DON'T WORRY, MAN. WE'LL GET YOUR TIRES FIXED WHEN WE GET BACK.
URRRT
WATCH THE *ROAD*, KENNY!
I... I AM.
ANIMALS!

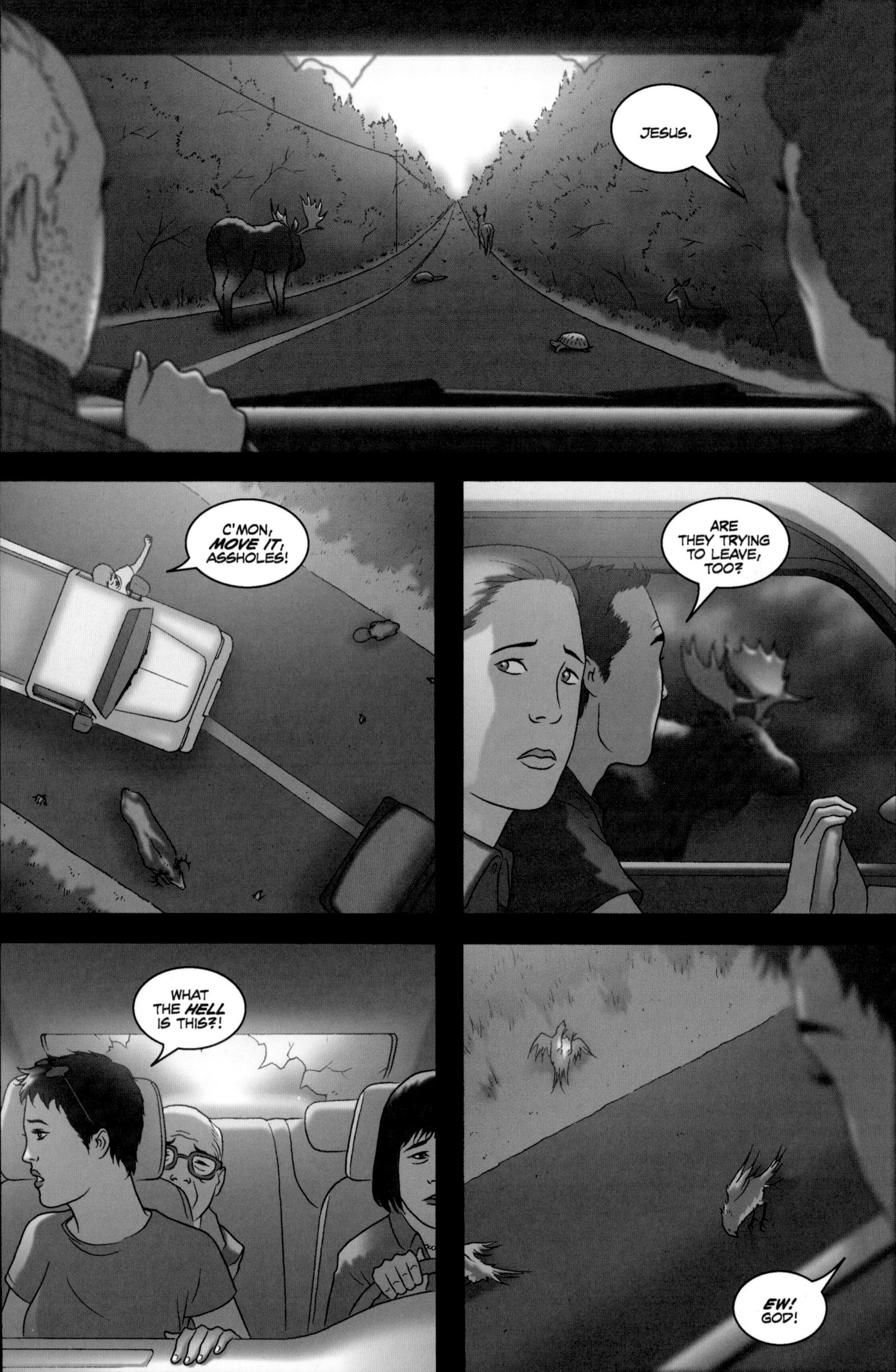
JESUS.
C'MON, *MOVE IT*, ASSHOLES!
ARE THEY TRYING TO LEAVE, TOO?
WHAT THE *HELL* IS THIS?!
EW! GOD!

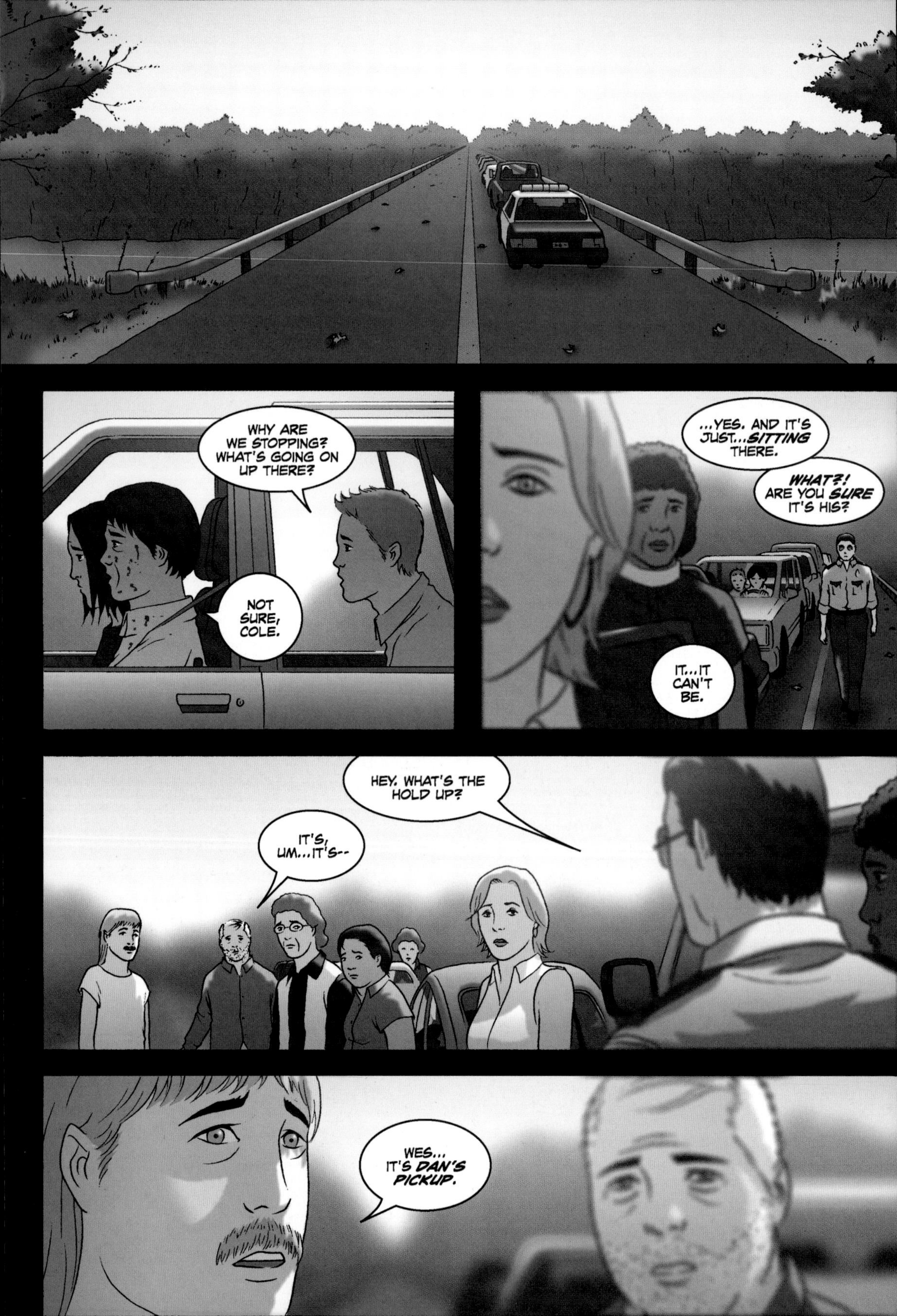
WHY ARE WE STOPPING? WHAT'S GOING ON UP THERE?
NOT SURE, COLE.
...YES. AND IT'S JUST...SITTING THERE.
WHAT?! ARE YOU SURE IT'S HIS?
IT...IT CAN'T BE.
HEY. WHAT'S THE HOLD UP?
IT'S, UM...IT'S--
WES... IT'S DAN'S PICKUP.

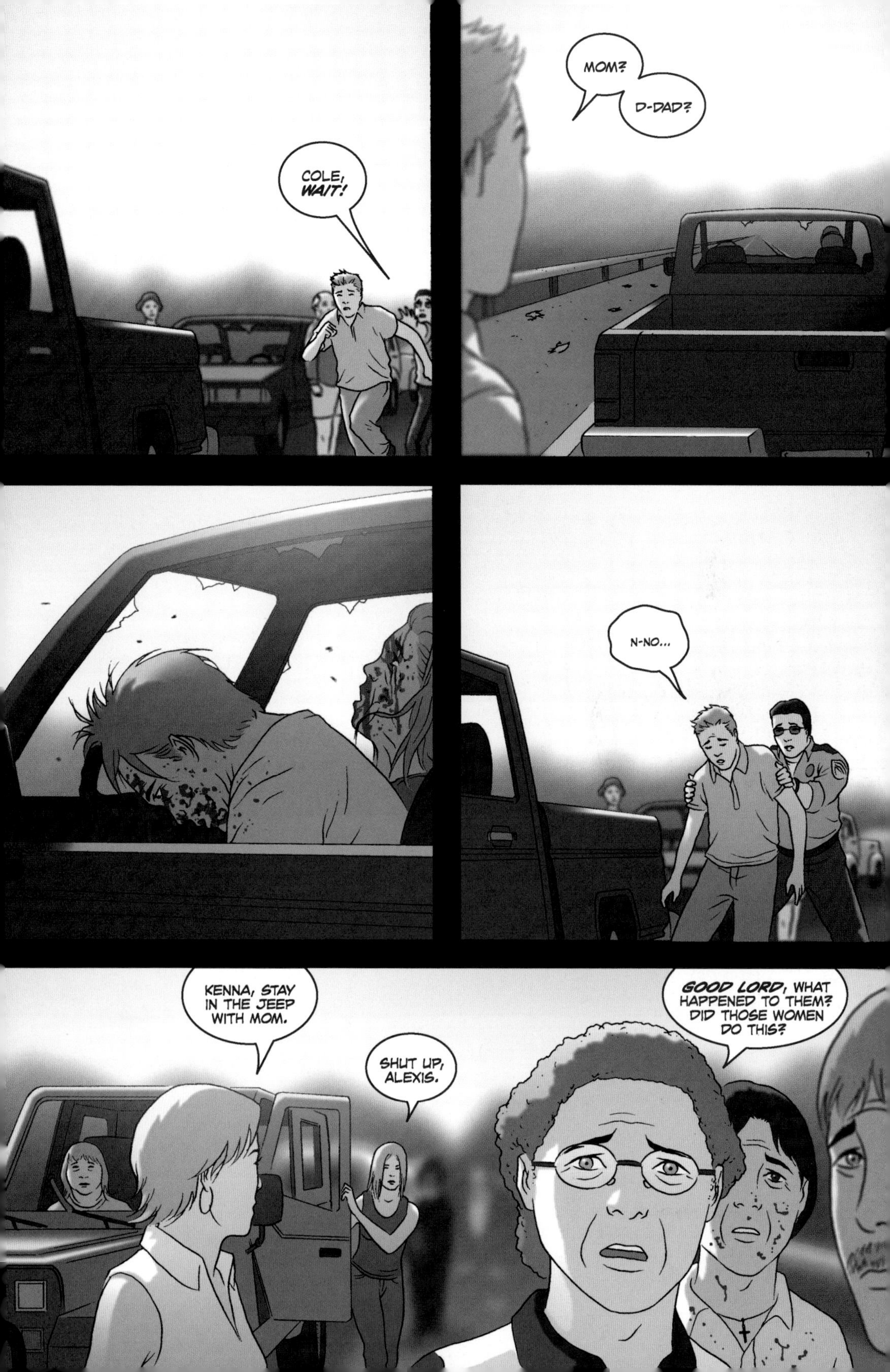
COLE, *WAIT!*
MOM?
D-DAD?
N-NO...
KENNA, STAY IN THE JEEP WITH MOM.
SHUT UP, ALEXIS.
GOOD LORD, WHAT HAPPENED TO THEM? DID THOSE WOMEN DO THIS?

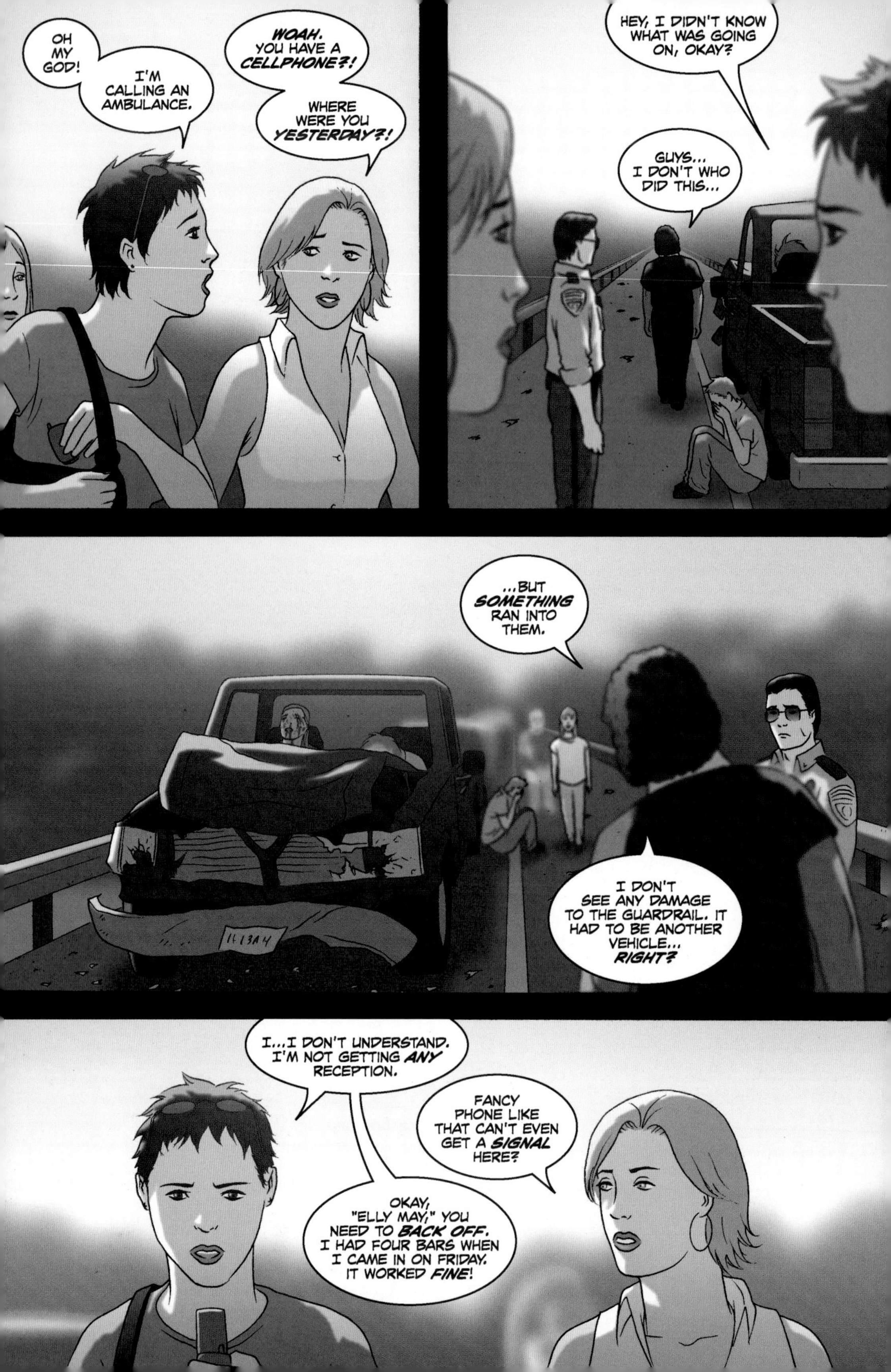

OH MY GOD!
I'M CALLING AN AMBULANCE.
WOAH. YOU HAVE A CELLPHONE?!
WHERE WERE YOU YESTERDAY?!
HEY, I DIDN'T KNOW WHAT WAS GOING ON, OKAY?
GUYS... I DON'T WHO DID THIS...
...BUT SOMETHING RAN INTO THEM.
I DON'T SEE ANY DAMAGE TO THE GUARDRAIL. IT HAD TO BE ANOTHER VEHICLE... RIGHT?
I...I DON'T UNDERSTAND. I'M NOT GETTING ANY RECEPTION.
FANCY PHONE LIKE THAT CAN'T EVEN GET A SIGNAL HERE?
OKAY, "ELLY MAY," YOU NEED TO BACK OFF. I HAD FOUR BARS WHEN I CAME IN ON FRIDAY. IT WORKED FINE!

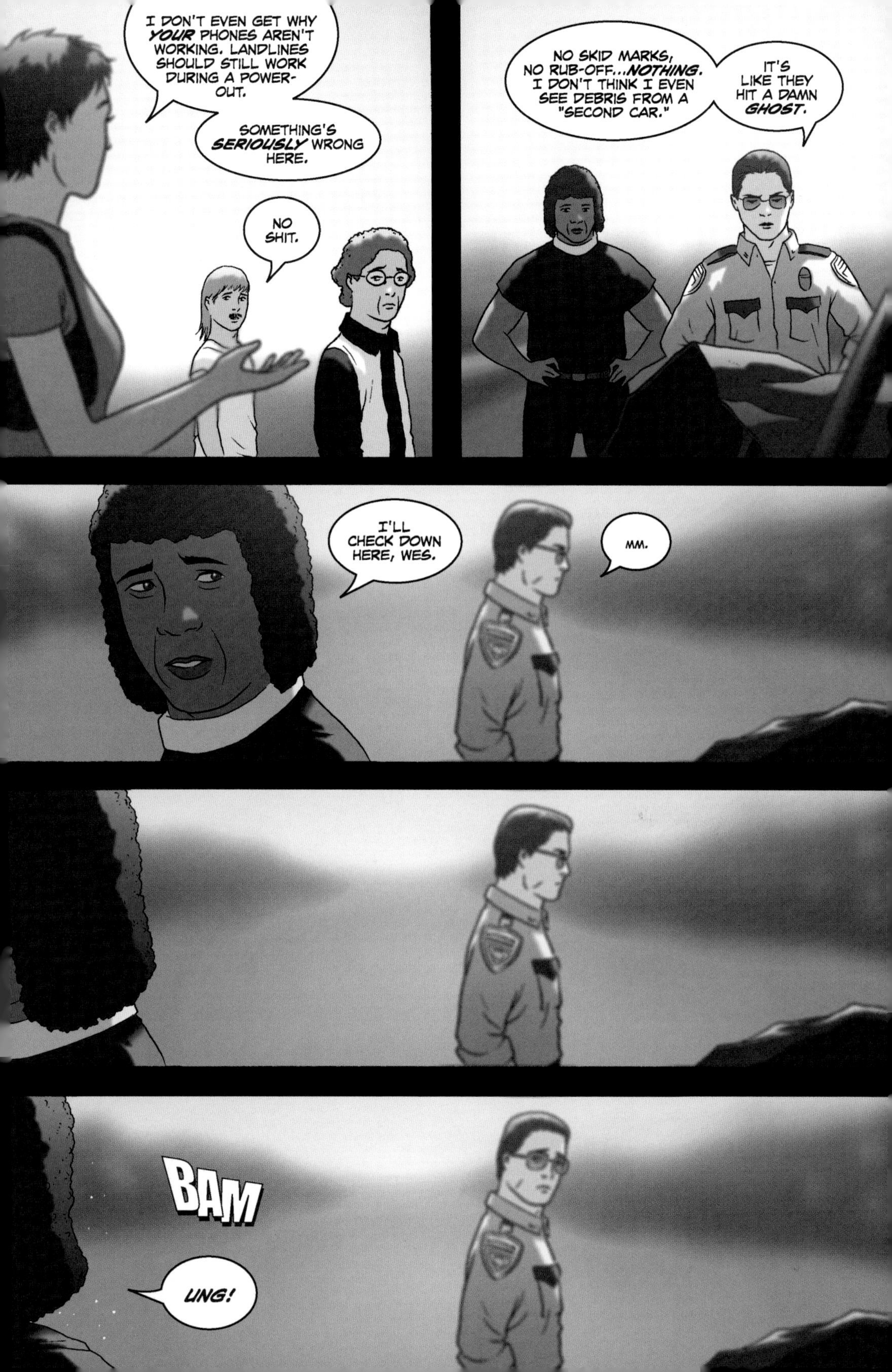
I DON'T EVEN GET WHY YOUR PHONES AREN'T WORKING. LANDLINES SHOULD STILL WORK DURING A POWER-OUT.
SOMETHING'S SERIOUSLY WRONG HERE.
NO SHIT.
NO SKID MARKS, NO RUB-OFF...NOTHING. I DON'T THINK I EVEN SEE DEBRIS FROM A "SECOND CAR."
IT'S LIKE THEY HIT A DAMN GHOST.
I'LL CHECK DOWN HERE, WES.
MM.
BAM
UNG!

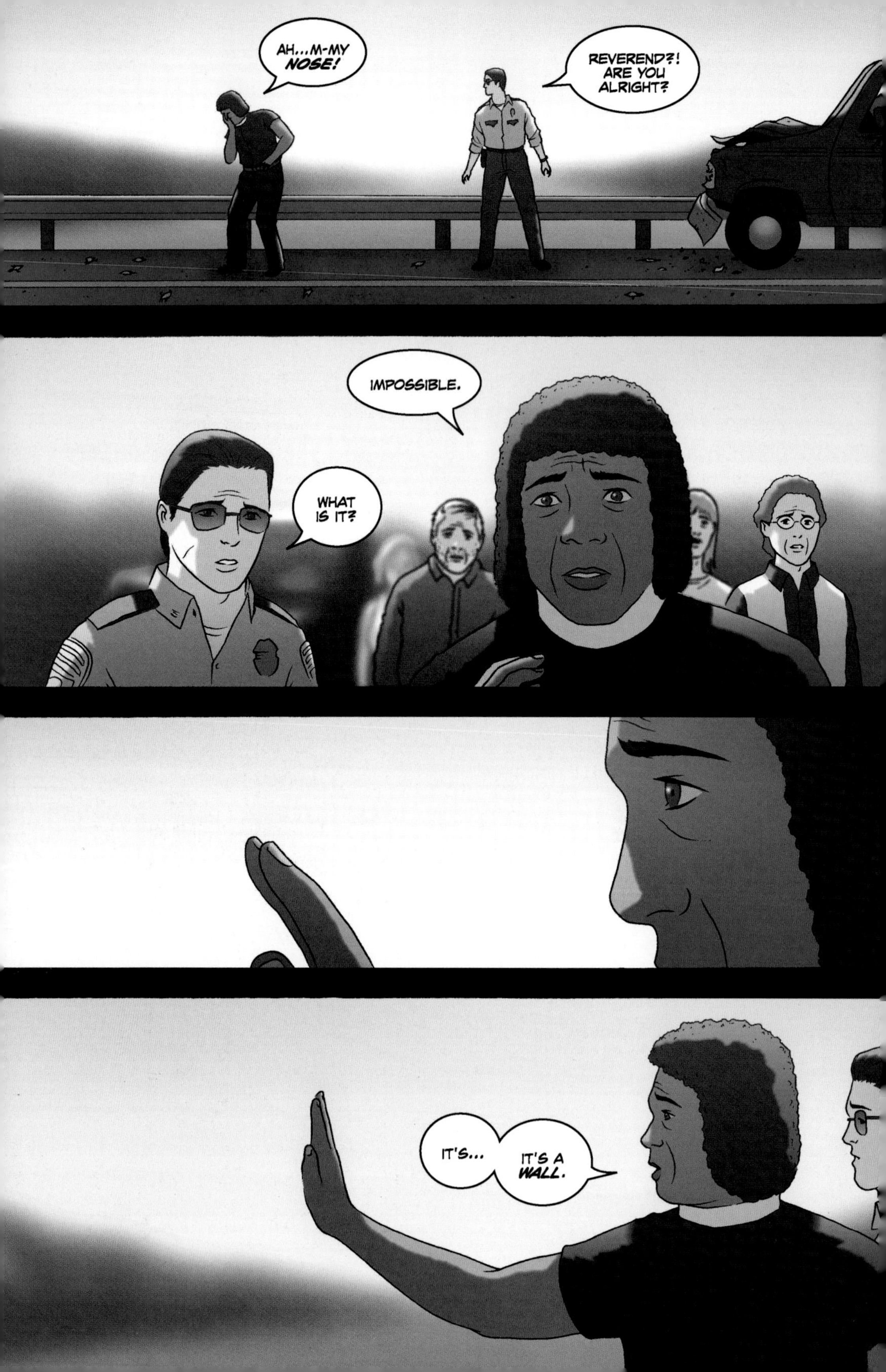
AH...M-MY *NOSE!*
REVEREND?! ARE YOU ALRIGHT?
IMPOSSIBLE.
WHAT IS IT?
IT'S...
IT'S A *WALL*.

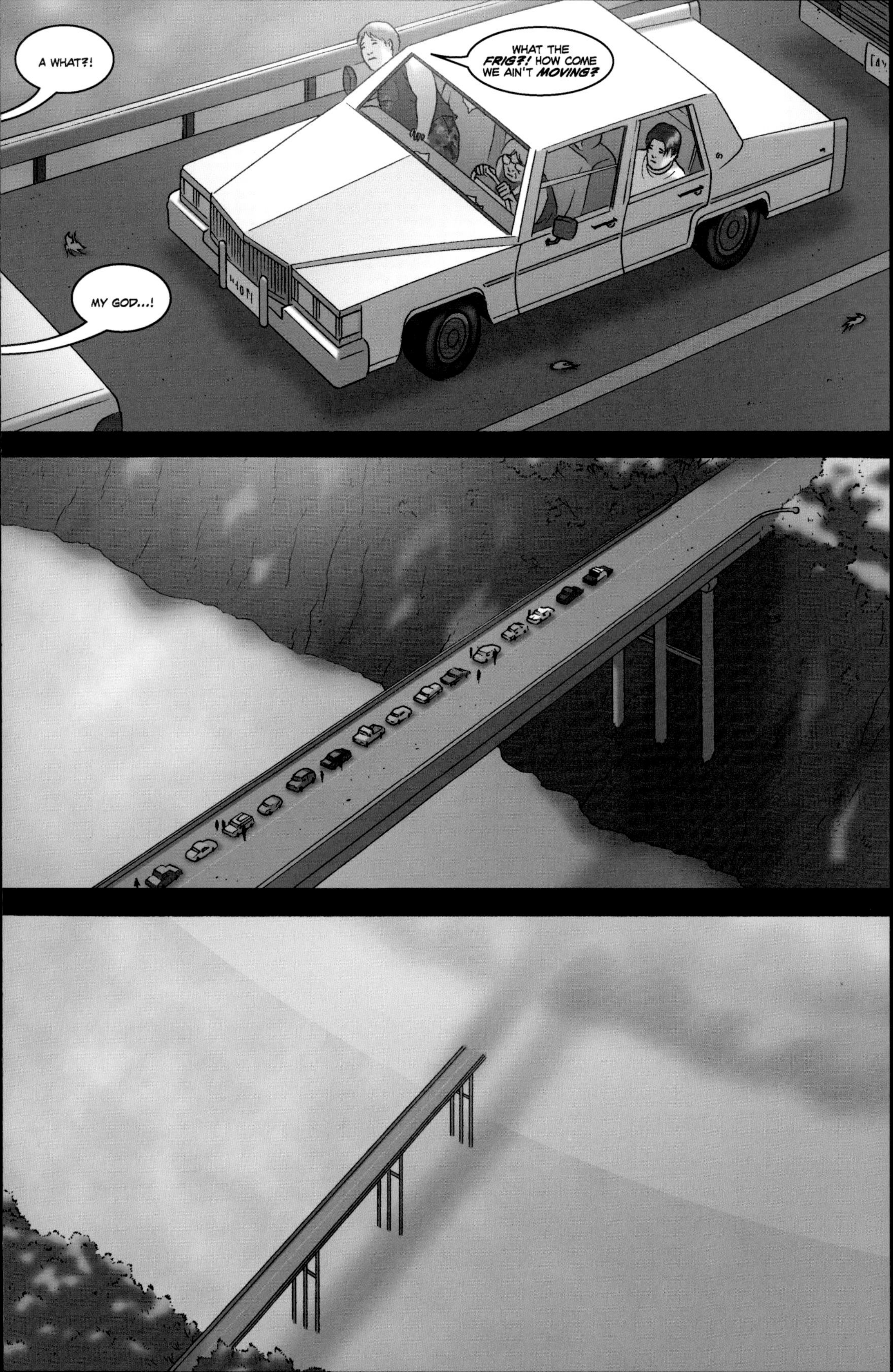
A WHAT?!
WHAT THE FRIG?! HOW COME WE AIN'T MOVING?
MY GOD...!

MORE GREAT BOOKS FROM IMAGE COMICS

For a comic shop near you carrying graphic novels from Image Comics, please call toll free: 1-888-COMIC-BOOK

40 OZ. COLLECTED TP
ISBN# 1582403298
$9.95

AGE OF BRONZE
VOL. 1: A THOUSAND SHIPS TP
issues 1-9
ISBN# 1582402000
$19.95
VOL. 2: SACRIFICE HC
issues 10-19
ISBN# 1582403600
$29.95

THE BLACK FOREST GN
ISBN# 1582403503
$9.95

CITY OF SILENCE TP
ISBN# 1582403678
$9.95

CLASSIC 40 OZ.:
TALES FROM THE BROWN BAG
TP
ISBN# 1582404380
$14.95

CREASED GN
ISBN# 1582404216
$9.95

DEEP SLEEPER TP
ISBN# 1582404933
$12.95

DIORAMAS, A LOVE STORY GN
ISBN# 1582403597
$12.95

EARTHBOY JACOBUS GN
ISBN# 1582404925
$17.95

FLIGHT, VOL. 1 GN
ISBN# 1582403816
$19.95

FLIGHT, VOL. 2 GN
ISBN# 1582404771
$24.95

FOUR-LETTER WORLDS GN
ISBN# 1582404399
$12.95

GRRL SCOUTS
VOL. 1 TP
ISBN# 1582403163
$12.95

VOL. 2: WORK SUCKS TP
ISBN# 1582403430
$12.95

HAWAIIAN DICK, VOL. 1:
BYRD OF PARADISE TP
ISBN# 1582403171
$14.95

HEAVEN, LLC. GN
ISBN# 1582403511
$12.95

KANE
VOL. 1: GREETINGS FROM NEW
EDEN TP
issues 1-4
ISBN# 1582403406
$11.95
VOL. 2: RABBIT HUNT TP
issues 5-8
ISBN# 1582403554
$12.95
VOL. 3: HISTORIES TP
issues 9-12
ISBN# 1582403821
$12.95
VOL. 4: THIRTY NINTH TP
issues 13-18
ISBN# 1582404682
$16.95

LAZARUS CHURCHYARD THE
FINAL CUT GN
ISBN# 1582401802
$14.95

LIBERTY MEADOWS
VOL. 1: EDEN LANDSCAPE ED
TP
issues 1-9
ISBN# 1582402604
$19.95
VOL. 2: CREATURE COMFORTS
HC
issues 10-18
ISBN# 1582403333
$24.95

PUTTIN' THE BACKBONE BACK
TP (MR)
ISBN# 158240402X
$9.95

PvP
THE DORK AGES TP
original miniseries 1-6
ISBN# 1582403457
$11.95

VOL.1: PVP AT LARGE TP
issues 1-6
ISBN# 1582403740
$11.95
VOL. 2: PVP RELOADED TP
issues 7-12
ISBN# 158240433X
$11.95

REX MUNDI
VOL. 1: THE GUARDIAN OF THE
TEMPLE TP
issues 0-5
ISBN# 158240268X
$14.95

VOL. 2: THE RIVER
UNDERGROUND TP
issues 6-11
ISBN# 1582404798
$14.95

SMALL GODS, VOL. 1: KILLING
GRIN TP
issues 1-4
ISBN# 1582404577
$9.95

TOMMYSAURUS REX GN
ISBN# 1582403953
$11.95

ULTRA: SEVEN DAYS TP
ISBN# 1582404836
$17.95

THE WALKING DEAD
VOL. 1: DAYS GONE BYE TP
issues 1-6
ISBN# 1582403589
$12.95
VOL. 2: MILES BEHIND US TP
issues 7-12
ISBN# 1582404135
$12.95
VOL. 3: SAFETY BEHIND BARS
TP
issues 13-18
ISBN# 1582404879
$12.95

THE WICKED WEST GN
ISBN# 1582404143
$9.95